Inner S

---

hidden patterns & secret reasons
why we act the way we do

INNER SCRIPTS

hidden patterns & secret reasons

why we act the way we do

ANGELA ARNOLD

Waterweaver Press

For Friends

First published in 1998 by
Waterweaver Press
Whistleberry Lane
Montrose DD10 0TJ
Scotland
Copyright © Angela Arnold 1998

British Library Cataloguing in
Publication Data.
A Catalogue record for this book
is available from the British Library.

ISBN 0 9525539 7 X

Typeset by XL Publishing Services, Devon
Printed and bound by Antony Rowe Ltd, Wiltshire
Printed on woodfree paper

Contents

Part Three - PEOPLE

Introduction

In an earlier book (*A Psychological Zodiac*, 1995) I introduced the concept of twelve distinct life impulses or 'motivation patterns' at the root of all our doings: the building blocks, as I called them, of our behaviour. In the present book I am addressing myself to the more general reader keen on a new angle and a deeper understanding of what lies behind our daily actions and reactions.

There are of course many theories, past and present, that attempt to explain what we are about – over and above the physical reality of our bodies, the chemistry of the brain, and so on. Their proponents have argued, hotly disputed, and all but fought over their various preferred models of personality, and of the psyche in general. Obviously, as persons we are nothing tangible, substantial. And yet we continue to speak of having a personality, or character, as if we concretely possessed it. We don't. It *happens*: we live it. We act in 'characteristic' ways, certainly, but there is nothing irredeemably fixed about them that would prevent us acting a bit differently, responding to events, growing into new roles. Or at least there shouldn't be.

We develop, we change. What we are is constantly in flux: it would be much truer to say that we 'are being' it. But most of our popular models of mind, psyche, personality, conjure up a picture of something solid, given, that sits inside us as something largely unchangeable. Layers: the subconscious tucked away out of sight below the level of the conscious mind. Container-like structures: the murky basement or dark dungeon that holds all our repressed memories and desires. Fixed, named parts-of-us that stand for different kinds of behaviour: the 'parent', 'child' or 'adult' in us, for instance, each a symbol of an entrenched role. Even when we speak in terms of drives, they have this dead flatness about them. Our supposed 'aggressive instinct' makes us, well, aggressive. Not much scope there for subtle interpretation. Are we really such leaden lumps, composed of smaller leaden lumps? Or machines, with various automatically clanking parts?

I'd suggest that the roots of our behaviour – of living, life itself

- are bound to be much more dynamic in themselves. It may be worth remembering that underlying all that is formed, material and more or less static, there is the turbulence of raw energy. Static models of what informs our behaviour no doubt have their uses, but ultimately we need a more dynamic understanding of the way we work. There aren't after all, literally, any good or bad 'parts' to us. And no conscious and unconscious ones either: all of our behaviour can become conscious or unconscious, in the course of inner changes and outward events.

Neither will it do to categorise people. No one *is* a madman or a criminal – we act and react madly; we act and react criminally. For how long? Depending on what? Are any of us claiming to be totally immune from drifting, or being driven, into such categories?

But pigeon-holing people is easy and very popular, which is why the simpler classification systems of the great psychologists have always been common currency amongst the general public of their time, much more so than the more complex theories they may also have held. Nowadays all of us are familiar with the 'introvert' and 'extravert' of Jung, for instance; far fewer with the four functions he speaks of: thinking, feeling, sensation and intuition. And fewer still know his book *Psychological Types* (1921) where he brings together the four functions with the introvert and extravert modes, to describe eight *theoretical* types.

Jung makes it quite clear that he is considering the subject from a purely theoretical angle. And when you think about it, simply dividing the population into two groups of introverts versus extraverts can't possibly do justice to the subtle mixtures we all are. What do you call the person who is painfully shy but needs outside stimulus so much she is constantly seeking out the company of others? Or the person who is cheerful and boisterous enough in any company, and yet perfectly happy to be left to his own devices, being largely self-sufficient? You don't need to be a psychologist to realise that the actual individual psyche is a complex and *composite* thing – or happening – made up of many, and often mutually contradictory, active strands. We all know it from the last time we found our various desires, habits, principles, reactions etc all at odds. We are for ever tripping ourselves up in our glorious self-contradictoriness (which, should we fail to notice it, others will gladly point out to us). Jane is stubborn and unyielding – can be ever so kind, though. John is bossy *and* terribly touchy. It's only in theory that we are at all classifiable. Life is far too lively to be tidy.

When I first came across Jung's typology I had already been working as a psychological astrologer for many years. Astropsychology, as it is also called, has only the most tenuous connection with the 'astrology' of Sun sign columns, which is designed purely for the entertainment business (and, incidentally, does the reputation of astrology proper no good at all). The reason this fake astrology has flourished, while the real thing has until recently been largely ignored, is that to set up a valid natal chart you need the precise time of day for the birth, not just the date. Not everybody has that information. No birth time – no chart – no money in it. On the other hand, there is a lot of money to be made these days in writing the let-me-predict-your-future weekly horoscopes you find in the glossies. It used to be the general office navvy who had the job of cooking them up. Now they tend to employ perfectly serious astrologers fallen on hard times. Or just liking the money.

Increasingly, though, professional psychologists/analysts are recognising the value of having their clients' birth chart to hand: not, obviously, to attempt to peer into their future, but to gain at least a measure of direct insight into inner stress patterns which the client may not be able to articulate or reveal easily.

It has to be said here that learning to interpret and work with a person's natal chart takes many years of study and practice. The chart doesn't tell you: Joe Blogs is such and such a man. There are no words, no sentences in it: only symbols. Symbols that are placed in relation to each other, together portraying a functioning whole that can be interpreted in many ways by the astrologer-psychologist. Equally, of course, it can be 'interpreted' in many ways by the person whose chart it is, who is living it – freely choosing among a large (if *essentially* limited) range of options.

So, having worked with clients' charts for years, I was well aware of both the limitations we are born with – the 'types', or rather the intricate mixtures of a few types, that we are – and this underlying freedom we have to choose to interpret our given roles in a great variety of ways, good, bad or indifferent. Certainly, Jung's eight types did make a lot of sense to me, in their theoretical sort of way. Not as a description of real-life, rounded character, but as a set of explanations that had cracked the code of the internal logic of behaviour as such. I saw his types as the basic material behind the complex and composite nature of each individual psyche. At the same time of course I was already familiar with such building blocks of personality: the constituent parts of the natal chart. The twelve life impulses symbolised by the signs of the zodiac, each with its attendant planet and its natural place ('house') within the whole, the circle. The question for me was: how did these two systems tie in?

They both spoke about the same thing. One at the entirely theoretical level, the other in more individual terms, specifically about someone born at a certain time and place. One was an eightfold system, the other twelvefold: not the easiest of numbers to combine into one unified theory! (Details of how I did it, for those who are keen, can be found in my earlier book.) The result, bringing together Jung's personal theoretical insights and the accumulated wisdom – encoded in its own system of symbols – of three thousand years of astrological practice, I called the *psychological zodiac*. It offered, for the first time, insight into the internal nature of each symbolic sign. But it also for the first time allowed astrology, through its symbolism, to contribute to the theory of psychology, rather than the other way around.

So what does this new approach to understanding ourselves do that other psychological systems don't do? Most importantly, rather than operate with hypothetical parts (Ego, Shadow, Parent, Subconscious etc) of psyche, mind, personality, it looks instead at our basic inner *dynamics*. It reveals the hidden impulses behind our actions and reactions, the root mechanisms involved. And by mechanism I don't mean something automatic and fixed. I mean a psychological process that serves a definite purpose, but which can take a broad spectrum of forms, depending on our 'interpretation': just as a basic script can be acted out on the stage in as many individual ways as there are individual actors and directors.

These given root impulses have an internal composition and logic of their own, and for this reason I prefer to call them *motivation patterns*. There are twelve of them, all of them lived by each of us every day of our lives. It strikes me as fairly essential then for us to learn to recognise them, and to consciously work with them, rather than act them out blindly.

The way I present them in this book – in fact, the way I myself find it easiest to understand them – is in personified form: as symbolic figures, with names like The Boss (in us), The Mother (in us) and so on. Half of them have to do with our *being* ourselves, the other half with *becoming* ourselves, as I shall explain.

As I mentioned earlier, we are all familiar with Jung's terms introvert and extravert (or extrovert). But if we ask twenty people to tell us what exactly they mean by that, we shouldn't be surprised if we receive twenty different answers, and all of them arguing as it were backwards from appearances – going by the impression a person's behaviour makes on us. In other words, nobody asks about the internal logic of a type of behaviour: what is it trying to do, what purpose might for instance extraverting serve? Why turn outwards rather than inwards, what for? We may be told that an extravert is someone who is loud, talkative, convivial, for instance, but never that this is someone who might *need* to be heard, noticed: someone who depends on our company in some way, let's just say. And indeed, when one thinks about it, one can imagine a person quietly desperate to be heard, and another not seeking a reaction from us at all who nevertheless blasts us with guffaws and resounding slaps on the back. As I say, either/or is far too crude a classification of real-life character. And to sort out the why's and wherefore's in all this, we need first of all to go right back to a really basic definition of the terms involved.

If you turn outwards, towards the world around you, others, then you are looking for something, seeking; you are in need, incomplete and in search of something to add to yourself, in the very widest sense. If you turn inwards, on the other hand, then you are not looking *for* but *at:* there's something in there, something you already have or are that you can turn to, fall back on, rest secure in. The first process is about newly becoming; the second about consistently being. Among our twelve symbolic internal figures we find six such seekers or 'becomers', and six 'be-ers'. In other words, we have six different ways each of becoming ourselves, of being ourselves.

Each motivation pattern, as I have said, has its own internal nature, logic, drive. Just to give a summary of this, there are basically three things to consider. One important factor in their make-up is the (conscious) function they are associated with: feeling, intuition, sensation or thought. And another is whether they are essentially of the introvert or extravert type, as defined above. But in addition to their being *essentially* either seekers or be-ers, I have found them to be also *dynamic* introverts or extraverts, depending on the direction their conscious function takes. Complex, yes; complicated, not really.

Let me give an example. The Creator in us is essentially an intro- vert, an inward be-er: that's to say he has plenty of given, existing inner material to draw on, so to speak. But dynamically speaking he is purely an extravert, for ever searching and newly becoming. Now put these two contrary pulls together and you have the story of one who finds his own rich inner self inaccessible, who is igno- rant of who or what he is, and is constantly trying to find himself... *reflected* in his environment. But in order to do that he has to 'act himself out', he has to put something of himself into the world, give of himself: this is the only way he can gain access to his inner being, truly become (conscious of) himself. It is this strange marriage of unaware inner being with aware outward becoming that constitutes the 'creative stress' at the root of our creative impulse.

Like that each motivation pattern has its own story, whether simple or more complex. Some further fine-tuning can then be provided by the inclusion of astrology's symbolic Elements (Fire, Earth, Air and Water) which add again to the individual character of these impulses – or call them drives, or dynamic archetypes, if you like. It really doesn't matter what we call them, as long as we recognise that each has its distinct function and purpose in the scheme of life. And learn enough about them to enable us to work with them in constructive ways.

In Part One of this book I simply introduce these twelve internal figures, our personified motivations: what they are like, what they need and want, the options they have of getting it, their greatest talents, as well as the multitude of crimes they are apt to commit.

Part Two then goes on to observe them in action, in a variety of situations. In the process, it considers a number of old issues in a totally new light and questions some of our traditional answers. Health, gender roles, our attitudes to wealth, food, reli- gion, politics are all examined from this angle of underlying motivation patterns and how we use them and abuse them.

Finally, Part Three weaves the strands together by looking at how all this relates to an individual's personality and behaviour. The question of cause, influence and free will is discussed. Ultimately, with the aid of this new 'motivational psychology', we arrive at a dynamic view of what we are; a view, above all, that will testify to our many possible futures.

I hope the reader will find it a liberating experience.

Part One

PATTERNS

BECOMING YOURSELF

The Hunter

The simplest of all our motivation patterns is the Hunter in us. This is the impulse that makes us go forward and reach out for new life opportunities. It presides over the most elementary level of all our becoming: our beginnings, our continued growth as such, change, renewal and regeneration. It is the psychological engine that drives us forward to our future. Personify it – impulsive, keen to get on, virile, eager to grab every chance – and you have the figure of a young man: a very Masculine, or if you like yang, type of impulse that works in all of us, male or female.

But let's take a look at the internal make-up of this figure, his own psychology, so to speak, to see what drives 'him'. First of all, we find that intuition, the quick all-over intuitive grasp of things, is the function he uses. Next, his Element nature is that of Fire: this adds a strong touch of the forward-going, the ever changing and near-unstoppable. And essentially, as well as dynamically, he is an extravert (in the sense defined in the Introduction: an active becomer rather than a settled be-er).

His story, then, is one of never-ending search, of constant progress towards the new. Unlike the Creator figure I have already briefly referred to, he doesn't start out with a state of rich inner being that by and by finds its application in the world 'out there'. Instead, he starts off being nothing defined at all. And then dynamically, too, he simply keeps moving on from one thing to the next, one person, place, life situation to the next…

There is a problem with that, of course. To become the new he first has to unbecome the previous thing he became – so what's it all in aid of anyway? A futile exercise in change for the sake of it?

What we have to realise at this point is that none of these distinct internal figures sits in total isolation from the others. (Or, to put it another way, these different strands of our psychic fabric are firmly interwoven, tied up together into a functioning whole.) They may jostle for pre-eminence all the time; be prompted to unilateral action by some strong external trigger one moment, provoked to rebellion by prolonged neglect the next, refusing to be denied their part in our life. But at the same time they also interdepend, rely on each other for their proper functioning. They have to co-operate.

The Hunter in us would indeed keep getting nowhere fast, despite constant new gains, if the Artist in us didn't prompt him when it comes to evaluating things – knowing what to rightly treasure and retain for a while, and what to reject as worthless out of hand, or to ultimately discard in favour of something better. And if the Thinker in us couldn't help him discriminate among various options on logical grounds. And, just as importantly, if the Priest in us did not show him how to be a bit more lovingly identified with the group: without that particular kind of help he would never learn to recognise others (his 'competitors' for new gain, from his point of view) as his fellows and his equals in the general rush forward to grasp opportunities.

I won't go too deeply into the internal logic of each motivation pattern here, though. Anyone interested to know more about the complex ways in which these patterns are functionally interwoven, indeed contribute to each other's completeness, I would refer to my earlier book, where I have spelled out these things in much more detail and at greater length. In this book I want to give room to considering the wider implications, the rather different take on the meaning of self and behaviour possible with a psychology based on motivation patterns. –

But back to the Hunter in us. With his archetypal go-getter approach, and if left to his own devices, he naturally stands in danger of being indiscriminately grasping, rash and rough and quite objectionably pushy, while at the same time failing to ever get his act together, staying stupidly slapdash, never learning any better. His basic impulse is to elbow his way forward, regardless, and grab – as primitive a life impulse as you can get: survival depends on it. This is his job in life, in us, on our behalf. He obviously needs educating, guiding, to develop subtler ways of gaining new life and identity for himself/for us, more considered and intelligent and certainly kinder ways that respect others' equal rights to a chance. And this is where our other motivation patterns get roped in, supplying what the Hunter in himself lacks.

Of course I'm not suggesting that we can take a hand in our most basic psychological processes, just like that: most of these transactions are unconscious anyway. But if we can't exactly control these things, then we can at least learn to recognise the signs and symptoms that tell us when the Hunter in us, for instance, is functioning to the best of his abilities and when he is out of control, doing his worst, going over the top. Once we know the full range of behaviour that goes with each motivation pattern, we soon learn to read the danger signals. And this does give us a chance to consciously rectify things, to strive to live out the better alternatives available to the Hunter, the Creator, the Mother in us – not that these are always blindingly obvious; in fact, they are rarely what we would regard as the direct *opposite*.

To make one thing quite clear: I am not talking about knowing 'your best and your worst side' as it is usually understood. I am talking about gaining detailed insight into the positive/negative manifestations of our common motivations, our underlying impulses, as such: the things that make us tick, all of us. Individuals, people, how they are composed, how they differ, how they handle themselves, all that I will be coming to in Part Three.

For now, let's just look at the Hunter impulse in us at its best. I have called him the Hunter (Hunter-and-Gatherer, if you like) to try and encapsulate in a simple image what he is about: finding sustenance, raw material for future existence. In psychological terms, this is the sort of sustenance and raw material needed to build an identity, a sense of self, a recognisable character that defines us in our own eyes and others'.

If I am using the imagery of pursuit and chase, this is not to say that the Hunter in us is essentially violent and rapacious. The impulse to gain-in-order-to-be is entirely neutral, in itself. And put into action with enough consideration, thoughtfulness, fellow-feeling for others and so on, it presents us with the archetype of the Hero.

Now the prime requirement of a hero must surely be his unwavering, incorruptible courage and, within mainstream psychological thought, I have yet to come across a convincing explanation of how courage is actually supposed to work. Why should the hero in action be immune to pain and threats of every kind, ready even to lay down his life in the course of doing what he's 'got to do'?

Looking to our Hunter for an explanation, the key word there is action. Remember the basic ingredients of the Hunter's nature: the unstoppable, forward-flowing impulse of a fiery disposition; the holistic grasp of all-as-it-hangs-together that is intuition; the doubly extravert nature, becoming followed by more becoming. There's nothing in that of staying, settling, storing something away, resting on past achievements or acquisitions. It's all about *action*, and anything gained is, so to speak, immediately reinvested. The successfully done becomes the active basis for more doing. And the future is not gained by dreaming of it, or by dwelling on the past, but by doing, *now*.

When under the auspices of the Hunter in us we actively 'become' – ie gain a (new) identity – it has to be understood that this is a fluid, provisional identity, subject to the constant changes of active self-improvement. One could say that for the Hunter being literally equals doing: characteristic, identifiable-as-himself sort of doing. Doing that has acquired distinctive qualities enough for one to put a name to it.

And there lies the secret of what we call courage. Our Hero stands his ground, he 'can do no other', because for him to act out of character would be tantamount to losing his identity. The active-self he has developed is after all the only self he possesses: not something securely had, owned, somewhere inside himself, that he can fall back on in times of stress, but rather something that is utterly exposed, for ever 'out there', employed at the leading edge all the time.

His actions are him: they are his specific individual self, they are the very essence of his life – to betray any of this, to relinquish his personal ways wholesale under pressure, would amount to a kind of suicide, when you think about it. We needn't look to acquired principles or genetically pre-programmed self-denial to explain the phenomenon of courage. It is simply part of the mechanics of our most primitive form of living/becoming, when working well.

The Hunter at his best is always a kind of hero. Constantly renewing himself, he stays ever youthful; he also stays simple, with a kind of universal appeal. Consequently, his talents find pretty much all-round application. As long as he goes about his job properly and progresses one measured, considered step at a time, learning as he goes, developing, improving, he can be entrusted with any task that involves enterprise, initiative, progress, new gain. He is the pioneer, courageous explorer, leader and generally the vicarious 'go-getter' for the benefit of others.

Selfless service in the interest of the group is indeed his hall-mark. All he needs for his own happiness, after all, is to be allowed to be himself in action – acting, in *that* sense, self-ishly. But there is nothing to stop him sharing his successes with others: substantial, concrete gains are of little interest to the kind of action man he is, so why hang on to things? And what he acquires in terms of life skills and expertise is easily shared as well, making him an ideal role model for the young.

Letting others benefit from his own gains may be easy enough for him, but any attempt to forcibly *deprive* him of what he has learned to do/be – strictly speaking, by denying him his chance to prove it and improve it in action – will be met with strenuous resistance. So in the wider view, he will not just make new gains for himself and others, but also be a staunch defender of what is rightly his and theirs. A hero in all respects, then – and yet of gratuitous bloodshed not a word.

Of course it is the Hunter in us who represents the 'aggressive' side of us, but only in the most basic interpretation of that word: going forward, tackling the next task. There is no law, of human nature, of human psychology, that decrees that the 'hunting' we do in the course of our lives should be done with a big knife, a gun, teeth bared and heart racing with murderous intent. There may be defensive situations that we would deem to justify a violent struggle. But it would be quite wrong to say that a desire for violence *as such* is unavoidably built into us.

Nevertheless, where we do go about stick in hand, eagerly baying for blood (metaphorically and otherwise), it is no doubt our Hunter motivation pattern that we are acting out of. This is the downside of the Hunter: if the Hero is the ideal, then the coarse brute, the thuggish lout type of figure is the extreme polar opposite, at the other end of the scale of choices we have within this pattern.

All our motivation patterns give us this range of interpretations to bring to the general role. Shining Hero suitably topped by halo, and Grunting Caveman swinging club above head while dragging woman by hair: these are of course extreme representations. We are hardly likely to live out either. It is still important to realise that they come from the identical stable, just differently trained. And to take on board the idea that even within the more normal middle range there will be better options available to the Hunter in us, and much less desirable ones.

When the Hunter is badly handled, allowed to 'run wild' without any help or balancing restraint from our other root impulses (usually taking place, as I have said, unconsciously), then he lacks good judgement and consideration to the point of persistent and offensive crudeness. His basic, neutral, forward drive deteriorates to something worse than a reckless rush: snatching things regardless, being rudely impatient, brutal from sheer thoughtlessness and lack of any recognition that he is part of a larger whole, a community. We are all in the same boat, all trying to gain our own individual futures, and more likely to successfully do so if we work in harmony, to each others' benefit as well, rather than in stark competitive opposition. But this he obviously does not – even unconsciously – consider. He does not 'stop and think' in any shape or form. He does first and then... does something else, and then something else again, grabbing opportunities willy-nilly, wanting it all, wanting it exclusively for himself, wanting it right now.

As a result he never learns: he fails to choose carefully what to add to his repertoire, and what small part of his identity (characteristic actions, skills, abilities) to relinquish in favour of a better, updated model. Everything is grist to his mill, anything at all will do him, but despite being feverishly active he never actually gets anywhere. He neither evaluates nor values, so he never really hangs on to anything for any period of time. He is like a man who eats and eats but somehow never puts on weight.

In terms of personal development he runs on the spot. He stays primitive and simple in the most negative sense of those words. Gaining a future for himself is what he should be about, acquiring valuable skills, know-how, making a name for himself with the things he does – so when he finds that he is patently getting nowhere at all, just starting out from scratch over and over, it only winds him up the more. He is driven, and he reacts with an aggressive form of shock-horror at any hint of being stopped in his tracks: he lashes out, he blasts everybody out of his way. Ill-considered *reaction*, rather than sensible action, is his style.

He is competitiveness let off the leash. But he stays eternally disappointed, always wanting more, never satisfied, chronically greedy – and in a sense needy. He grabs and grabs, but then of course he fails to value what he has. Knowledge, skills and such-like non-material gains would be his natural aim, something to add to his active-self. But these things he may acquire for a moment and then, uncomprehendingly, lets go of again, 'forgets'. His sole focus is on rushing forward regardless.

The only things he *can* gain and hang on to are, indeed, material *things*. But these can never be part of his active-self, he can never so to speak identify with them. He may pounce on them with the eagerness of one totally deprived, but ultimately he just ends up laying them aside, where they quietly accumulate. The picture that springs to mind is of a de facto multi-millionaire who would race a beggar to the dropped coin in the gutter. In his own eyes he *still* amounts to nothing, poor man. And so he continues to need to grasp anything and everything within his reach: yes, just as much as the most destitute.

Whether he has managed to enrich himself in all the wrong ways or not, he continues to shove and jostle, even intimidating others into letting go of what's rightfully theirs. He snatches more than his due, but he never properly 'owns' what he has. Worst of all, he treats others like dangerous competitor-enemies who would stand in the way of his becoming, his future, his proper selfhood at last attained – a selfhood that, if truth be told, is no more than a receding mirage on his own horizon. Alternatively, he treats others simply as possessions gained and stashed away but never rightly treasured in themselves... a clutch of mistresses, a bunch of servants, that sort of 'thing'.

Servants, or some kind of support structure, are pretty much a must for him, though: whatever he does, he does so crudely and badly, it soon all comes apart again. Or has some dire consequences. There are times one might think he is on the run from the effects of his own actions, but of course he isn't; the reckless forward rush is simply constitutional with him. He never notices dangers ahead, or ill-effects now, never mind the mess he has left in his wake. Needless to say, he doesn't 'own' the consequences of his actions either.

There is only a very limited use his community will have for him: general battering ram about sums it up. Where the Hunter's better side, the Hero in all of us, shows courage in the course of a measured and well thought-out pursuit of aims which benefit others as well as himself, the Hunter as Hopeless Lout is but a coarse hireling mercenary, so caught up in his mindless pursuit of anything at all that he can easily be manipulated into fighting others' dirty fights for them.

He gains nothing thereby, but then he is used to that experience. It only makes him try harder, bashing on regardless, still trying to achieve what has in effect become a futile dream of one day 'really being somebody'. We shouldn't be surprised either – much as we find him dismissive, even sheepish, about his current attainments – to hear him boasting of that future somebody he will be, should be, could be... if only.

In the end he blames his countless failures on the world around him, others. But since he has never actually managed to define himself, to make anything recognisable of himself beyond the crude level of go-getterdom, the concept of others as such remains a bit of a mystery to him too. They are only so much stuff to be kicked out of his way as an impediment, or else appropriated for a moment, then carelessly pushed aside – awkward, ultimately useless sort of stuff. Of course it's all their fault if he can't get his act together.

The Maker

The Maker resembles the Hunter in certain respects: he too has a double dose of extraversion, he too is essentially a seeker who actively goes on seeking, eternally. But for one thing the function he uses is not the Hunter's intuitive grasp, and neither is his Element Fire. Instead, the Maker in us uses his senses. And he – or she, but since this isn't a clearly Feminine archetype, let's just stick with 'he' for the moment – is basically Earth-y in character. So why, rather than dynamically go after things, does the Maker sit still, literally pottering with things in order to gain what he needs?

Our different senses are concerned with the various kinds of concrete detail in the world around us. Add to that a down-to-earth nature, and you see not only a double dose of extraversion but also a double dose of 'materialism', to borrow a word and use it in a basic, neutral sense.

Where the Hunter in us is propelled forward by his fieryness, and by the holistic nature of intuition which wants to grasp every-thing-as-it-hangs-together, the Maker's progress is for ever being arrested by each concrete detail. And what he grasps he really, physically lays hold of – and becomes: finds his identity in. Something to bear in mind next time you try to loosen a small, screaming child's grasp from some object or other, wondering to yourself what the big fuss is really about!

That is why the Maker doesn't zip through the world in the manner of the Hunter. Where the Hunter is identified with the dynamic doing he gets to do in the world, the Maker is identified with the tangible things he gets to hold and to touch, to sniff and to look at. His becoming is always a becoming concretely grounded. Unfortunately, of course, his next new-becoming will then automatically threaten him with a very concrete loss, too. He may constitutionally be very much a mover-on, but he is equally a settler: a contradiction in terms that obviously calls for something of a creative compromise.

There is a reasonably simple answer to his dilemma. It lies in him making, producing, the things he becomes – rather than chasing after, catching and appropriating 'ready-made' ones. His is a DIY sort of identity, constantly laboured over, while staying at home, as it were. First of all, he builds himself up a bit, from the simplest raw materials. And then he slowly adds to himself. He begins to make gradual, cautious changes, substitutes a bit here, lets go of a redundant bit there. Just as the Hunter modifies his way of acting, which is 'him', so the Maker varies his output, the products that mean 'I' to him.

No doubt he doodles, paints himself into the world, sings his own song to listen to and find his self in. But above all he is practical; and being down-to-earth, physically attached-to, he is also in consequence always security-minded. It is the Maker in us that has us building houses, constructing shelters of any description, and fencing in what we own/are, both to keep in and to keep out. Defensiveness is part of this particular script. But the chief problem, to put it like that, is how to keep the roving Hunter from rushing in and grabbing what the settled Maker has slowly and laboriously built up, colonising what the Maker would like to regard as exclusively his patch.

The basic weaknesses of the Maker are obvious: he is fearful, slow, clinging. He has a problem with anything new to the point of petrified inertia. By extension, he is inclined to be too literal, getting bogged down in the material detail at every turn. No irrepressible flights of fancy or inspired outbursts from him! On the plus side, he is unstoppably industrious, with an inbuilt steadfastness and dependability about him that will carry him through the long haul where others would have long given up, or died of boredom. Patience, in fact, is not so much a virtue as something he can't help having rather a lot of.

Where he works to the best of his potential – prompted by unconscious ideas, and maybe an intuitive appreciation of what a given raw material *might* be made into – he becomes a gently transformative force in the world. He always starts with the simple and as yet unformed, the sort of substance that is lacking in any character of its own and can be shaped easily. But he soon builds up confidence, grows in accumulated experience, to the point where he can be less cautious and repetitive. He branches out, he ventures further. He varies his output, reconstructs, modifies, finds new uses for. The landscape around him, literally and otherwise, takes on ever new forms – though we better picture this against a background of inherent caution: the image of a farmstead, rather than some futuristic glass and concrete tower.

None of this will keep the marauding Hunter tendency away though; if anything the opposite. Our best efforts to establish our self most concretely in the world also pose the greatest danger to our identity. The sensually grounded self is only too easily dismantled, whether by naturally occurring disasters, say, or by wilful attack. Nothing is essentially more vulnerable than the settled and solid.

And what can the Maker in us, so hesitant and slow at the best of times, do to counter these threats of being repeatedly, painfully pulled apart? Paradoxically, the best thing for him to do is to acquire a bit of 'give'. If the Hunter has to learn to feel himself to be part of the wider community, and act with others in mind, so does the Maker have to learn to share, to make for others, not just for himself. He has to learn to give bits of himself away, things he is most closely identified with, and willingly. And it isn't really as difficult for him as it might appear at first.

The crucial thing for him to realise is that he has permanently acquired the skills it takes to make good any loss, to repair any damage to himself – to his body-self, as we might call it: the Maker's equivalent of the Hunter's active-self. Once he has built up a sound 'body of experience', this spells security and a self-hood of sorts for him. Whatever might be lost to him, freely offered, or forcibly taken, he can always actively replace. Given that he tends to stick to the simplest ingredients available, as long as he has the 'recipe' to build himself up again from scratch, if need be, that is really all the security he needs. Why worry then? He can relax, possessed now of a self that is perfectly capable of transcending the level of the merely physical, at least for short periods of time.

Like that the Maker in us evolves from simply sensing his self, ie seeing himself concretely embodied in something he has produced, to also *knowing* himself: as a *potential* concrete self.

I would suggest that what we are looking at here is the first step up from the simple animal nature of the Hunter archetype: *homo faber*, man the maker, rather than just taker. Though it may be as well to bear in mind that this making is actually a more complex form of taking: taking something (simple) and transforming it (a bit).

No equivalent name for a 'heroic' Maker springs to mind, unless we call him the Master Builder maybe. We can picture his painstaking progress from a DIY builder/producer for his own needs exclusively, a self-sufficient smallholder let's say, towards being a universal supplier to demand, his door open to customers: the farm shop. Or we can visualise him as a first-rate artisan, one who knows about construction, maintenance and repair, who puts his accumulated knowledge at our disposal, reliably, his products to be trusted, his advice worth listening to, apprentices eager to learn from him. One who truly knows himself, and in consequence can share himself.

So much for the paragon that lurks inside us all. His opposite number may be more familiar to us though, if we look at the transformed landscape we inhabit, our towns, houses, and the products in our shops.

Starting out from the same position of fearful inertia, huddling in his own corner of the world and sticking to what he knows (himself to be), the Maker in us can also go downhill from there, rather than evolve.

For a start, he becomes so strictly repetitive, it reaches the point of obsessive fixity. There is neither variation nor modification to what he produces: he repeats himself *ad nauseam*, stubborn, narrow in outlook, ever suspicious of the untried. He simply churns on and on, churns out one standard-issue kind of product and that's it: that's him.

Instead of, ultimately, a 'body' of practical expertise, he acquires only a single skill (to push this to its logical limit) and a solid body only, nothing transcendent about it at all. His becoming quite lacks the newness element, the diversity and response to current conditions, never mind what others around him might want. Instead of becoming in the evolving sense, he simply *becomes bigger*. He builds up, mounts up, accumulates – spills over and pushes himself/his products all over others' territory as well. He is a one-man production line, with a one-idea product to flog to the whole world. Spreading himself far and wide is his way of newly becoming... the same thing all over again.

Inevitably, quantity takes the place of quality. Without a measure of flexibility, without adjusting what he makes to others' needs or the wider environmental context it is to sit in, what he makes can only turn out inadequate: faulty in some respect, soon outdated, and not long before it comes apart at the seams. But instead of learning to look about him, he only keeps his nose to the grindstone, obstinately, labouring mightily, honing his one skill, regardless. Instead of coming out of his corner a bit, he ensconces himself ever more firmly inside a cocoon of busyness, surrounded by a mass of stuff that is as badly made as it is uniform.

He never notices anything amiss. He has, in more than one respect, grown a thick skin. Protected by that, he can do quite without flinching what his positive alter ego would dread to even contemplate: smash and bulldoze everything in his path, in order to make room for his absurdly swollen self. If nobody stops him in his tracks, he will spread his narrow identity from one end of the world to the other. Callous and uncaring – because he knows no better – he imposes his identical-product self all over, fully convinced that it is the only option.

He remains ignorant of options, variations, diversity. He never realises his potential for future growth: in its meaningful sense, that is, growth that entails changes and adjustments, not just physical expansion. He is monoculture personified. He is mass production incarnate. He is also wasteful: lack of variety means that the by-products of his production process stay firmly unused. So for everything he makes, badly, uniformly, there is also a dump, a spoil heap. Something he strenuously ignores.

By extension, if one pictures his social relations, he will find only the narrowest spectrum of behaviour acceptable. Others better not be too terrible 'other' at all, or they will be consigned to an equivalent people dump – a parallel universe, as far as he is concerned – if he has his way. The Establishment, that's him; and if *he* flexes his muscles, others soon shift. For such a quiet chap, at the outset, he is beginning to look decidedly alarming. Ultimately, he is entirely destructive of the natural, holistic, order. He not only fails to work with it, constructively, he demolishes, breaks up and artificially divides it. And he never even becomes aware of the divisions and the damage he causes.

It is this Maker in us gone over the top who has the upper hand when we are at our most stubbornly and narrowly insistent, greedy and 'selfish' and just wanting to have things our way, yet again. But it is also he who suggests to us that strict conformity is a good thing, craven obedience with regard to the established order. Better not to make waves: one might get hurt if one got too lively. Because, for all his insensitive and insistent pushing himself forward, he is still a raw-beginner kind of coward, one who has never yet ventured to dip a toe in the real, living, *stream* of life.

The Artist

The Artist has already had a walk-on part as one of the aides of the Hunter, the one who provides him with the capacity to make value judgements. In fact, in many ways she is his Feminine opposite number. Where he is our basic urge to rush in and do, she is our opposite impulse: to stand back from, to appraise the situation, come to a balanced conclusion before we commit ourselves to action.

The psychological profile we can draw up for the Artist is really quite complex, and may at first appear strange. She is essentially an extravert, and yet dynamically she is an introvert; like the Maker, she uses her senses; but the Element associated with this motivation pattern is Air – which in turn is associated with mental processes.

The first thing we may note is a mixture of thought and sensation: intelligent sensing, directed inward. But inward at what? To put it rather crassly, there is after all nothing there. As, essentially, an extravert she is inwardly empty, not yet a be-er, but only a seeker. Always bearing in mind that these are personified strands of human behaviour we are talking about – not people – let me put it this way: what the Artist is thoughtfully looking at, inwardly, is nothing *personal* to her. She is aware of images on the inner plane, but these are and will ever stay 'beyond' her. She is a seeker for self in the out-there; but she is also in possession of an inner knowledge that will inevitably inform her particular ways of seeking.

We will see a lot more of this inner landscape, especially when we come to the doubly introvert impulses, so let me explain. In the Hunter and the Maker we have met two double extraverts: totally outward-directed, both continually finding their new or renewed identities in the physically happening world of time/space and matter around them. The double introverts whom we will meet later – the Eternal Child and the Revolutionary – have both their being and their new becoming inwardly: they take what they need for their inward becoming from their *inner* surroundings, beyond the personal inner self. This, to give the thing a name, I call the Inner Plane. Unlike the outward environment, it is timeless, insubstantial, 'ideal', perfect.

Going back to the Artist then, we can say that before she ever turns to the imperfect world out there to find her identity in, she has an inner vision of how things could be - should be, even - and this she considers thoughtfully. She has prior expectations. Standards. Basically, she is a perfectionist. In her 'imagination' she finds a host of wonderful worlds, but they are no good to her at all, personally. Essentially, she has to turn outward in order to become. But needless to say, the world out there bears scant relation to either the beauty or the meaningfulness of the inner vision.

The first thing she does is swither, recoil, feel affronted, withdraw, complain. She's good at that, in fact she's good at not much else, by herself. Call this impulse our innate aesthetic sensibilities, if you like; our inner sense of rightness, fairness and justice too; our instinctive knowledge of what a perfect life would look like - if there could be such a thing, in the material world. But like all our motivation patterns this one too needs the co-operation of the others: if the Artist helped the Hunter find the patience to pause and consider, for instance, now the Hunter can prod the Artist into action. Any action has got to be better than being stuck in a limbo of endless hesitation, born of disappointed expectations, while there is actually an existential need to get out there, get involved, find oneself in the process.

And so the Artist in us stops passively finding fault, and gets actively involved in finding *the* fault - and then doing something about it. She puts things right, she sorts things out. She rearranges what doesn't sit the way it should, takes out what doesn't fit in, finds the right place for it, adds some little thing that was crucially missing, unites what belongs together - and equally separates what doesn't - introduces the magic ingredient that makes the whole gel... and the reason she can do these things so well is because she always keeps that bit of a critical distance.

It doesn't matter how engrossed she may momentarily become in her work, sooner or later the transcendent images that continue to stand vividly before her inner eye pull her in the opposite direction again, back from too deep an entanglement with things material and worldly. In fact, as the strange hybrid she is (an '*introverting* extravert', technically speaking), she is constantly struggling to maintain active contact with the world out there – it doesn't come naturally at all. She has to work at it. The net effect is one of being committed, yes; but never so far as to miss the wood for the trees. She *will* be critical and 'nag' away at the wrongs she so clearly perceives when comparing the (perfectly valid and real) inner vision with the flesh-and-blood reality under her nose. And having that sort of 'distance' to proceedings, she is especially good at catching the whole picture.

Within the whole, things sit in relation, hang together. This she can see clearly. I have called her the Artist because careful composition and evaluation of overall effect are so clearly exemplified in the artist's work. It is far less obvious to us just how much of this is needed in ordinary daily life. Likewise, without critical appraisal there can be no judicious action at all. Without doing, saying, giving the right thing *within the context* our various relationships would surely founder. Without taking into consideration all the contributing factors, there can be no true justice. So the Artist in us, at her best, is essentially about relating: standing oneself in proper relation to, standing one thing in meaningful relation to another.

Using our innate inner vision, our inborn sense of right and wrong, in the wider meaning of these words, we are called to work at improving the world around us, and to do this in the course of becoming ourselves: we too benefit from an environment that is harmonious and fair, where needs or burdens are noticed and dealt with early, where excesses are checked promptly, where mediation begins long before actual fights have broken out – a balanced environment, one might say. And the crucial point to note here is that balance isn't something that sits there, just nicely – it takes constant critical vigilance and hard work. If we do that work, then we are rewarded with a better environment to take our sense of self from, as the constantly 'becoming' extraverts that we all also are.

Incidentally, this is the sort of basic give-and-take situation to be found in all our motivation patterns. For the most part, we do not act selflessly, in that sense. But then if only we would act 'selfishly' in the best possible ways open to us, then there should be no need at all for anyone to act selflessly, so-called.

As Hunters we *do*, in order to find ourselves; as Artists we *re-do,* rectify, embellish, counteract, also in order to find ourselves. When the Artist in us is working to her best potential, she will soon pick up the mistakes the Hunter in us may have hastily made, and unpick the Maker's misconstructions as well, while she's at it. One could say she re-establishes the natural order of things, relatively speaking, within the parameters of the possible.

The word relative really is crucial to understanding what the Artist is about. Her 'prior' inner knowledge, this gift of a vision of things on the Inner Plane, refers of course to something absolute – an Underlying Order, an Ideal World in its own abstract dimension. But as the Artist's basic constitution (ie introverting *extravert*) shows us quite clearly, this has to constantly apply itself to an already existing world out there. Art purely for art's sake is clearly not the idea. Relative adjustment is the keynote of this script, application together with compromise and balance. Above all the Artist has to learn to balance the conflicting pulls on her: the commanding inner vision on the one hand, and her personal need for active involvement in the world on the other. If the former predominates, she will find no identity, have no life of her own. But if the latter is ever allowed to win the upper hand and our paragon of an Artist 'falls for the world' altogether, then the picture may still look pretty, on the surface, but underneath it there will be rot and corruption.

Realising that the Hunter or even the Maker are not making a job of things is not particularly difficult, but the downside of the Artist in us is rarely recognised as such – not so surprising maybe when you consider that she represents an important part of our self-critical faculties! When, as I have put it, she falls for the world, she literally loses her critical distance: she no longer finds (the) fault, she simply drags her all-perfect expectations with her when she begins to participate in life; she imposes them. She *super*imposes her inner vision on outward reality.

I have dubbed this kind of deliberate self-delusion wearing a pair of 'expectacles'. These are in no way different from rose-tinted glasses, but I think putting it like that explains rather better what is involved.

Too wilful in all respects, the Artist at her worst insists on grabbing a life/identity for herself come what may, and without wanting to relinquish one jot of the beautiful Ideal either. Just as 'gifted' as her diligent sister, she squanders her insights, her imagination and innate high standards by simply throwing them at the world as a demand: please please me, and be 'good'. The way she insists on looking at it, everything has just *got* to be wonderful the way it is. Problems, well, what problems? That anything might be amiss becomes inconceivable. As an attitude – we could call it a determinedly passivist stance – it certainly saves a lot of work and bother.

The pity of it is that, essentially, she is right: every thing is beautiful – in the right setting or context; every person is *potentially* good. But all this positive potential needs actively liberating, through right relating and constant adjustments and readjustments. This she is not prepared to do; literally, no longer in a position to do. It isn't that she has simply become lazy, preferring to sit back from things, but rather that she has become so heavily involved and deeply embroiled in all around her as to have lost her capacity for judgement-at-a-distance. Her excessive appetite for life has cost her her objectivity, and now all she can do is put a subjective gloss on everything.

She is good at ignoring what wouldn't please her if she really allowed herself to notice it. Things are a tasteless, imbalanced, unfair, worrying mess, but with her expectacles firmly in place, she sees only what she wants to. She is also an expert at making everybody feel churlish if they don't live up to her impossible, unrealistic expectations. She tells everyone how adorable they are – and they aren't likely to disagree – so they start pretending to her face, and cheating behind her back. In short, where she has her way, life is made to be superficially pleasant: whitewash and hypocrisy become the norm, the culture of the relentless smile. Problems, ills and injustices are simply denied, never tackled. Anything ugly, mean and threatening is ignored, active 'evil' quickly banished to corners... where of course it only thrives, unseen. The rot has truly set in, underneath the skin-deep prettiness.

She is incapable of saying no, having lost her natural reservations or reserve. And she has an air of all-acceptance, a deliberately maintained false naivety, that sets her up just nicely for all kinds of exploitation and nasty shocks. The awful truth can't be dismissed for ever. When it finally catches up with her, her screams of horror could almost move one to pity – if she hadn't brought it on herself with her greed for an all-perfect life, presented to her on a plate.

But she soon recovers. Whatever it may have been, it is dismissed again: it was a one-off, it wasn't quite real, it wasn't normal, it isn't what she 'would like to think' people are *really* like. Then again, she'll have us lock up the more unignorable perpetrators, throw away the key, forget about them: that's all there is to justice, where she is concerned.

Where her saintly sister works hard to make the world as a whole a better place, by standing everything and everyone in the most beneficial relation, the Artist as mere Prettyfier in effect cuts the world in half: good half, bad half; consume the one, throw away the other. Except that you can't throw it away.

Curiously, this theme of division is quite prevalent among the downsides of our various motivation patterns: they tend to either develop an internal split, or else divide the world around them. Thus the Hunter in negative mode sees competitive opponents, enemies, everywhere. And the Maker is prone to shove out of his way, out of his sight, anything and anyone who doesn't conform to his narrow norm.

The Artist in us, wilfully expecting only the best, can end up passively encouraging all the worst to flourish unattended – and then reject it out of hand as being no fit part of her kind of world. Ultimately, her false peace shattered, she will be seen to have 'created' quite as many enemies as the Hunter. But does she ever get the blame she deserves?

The Destroyer

Closely related to the Artist, while in many ways her polar opposite, is the Destroyer in us. I make no apologies for the daunting
name which means exactly what it so bluntly says: this is the
impulse that has us demolishing for good, getting rid of without
compromise.

If this sounds irredeemably negative, you have only to think of
surgery: removal of a cancerous growth, say, or a gangrenous
limb; think of a badly damaged building threatening to collapse;
picture festering rubbish piled by the side of the road, a danger
to public health. No point pussyfooting around in these
situations: drastic action is called for. From somewhere in us
we have to be able to muster the requisite uncompromising
attitude that wipes the slate clean and allows us to make a new
start. When you think about it, our very doing, making and
improving talents need an 'undoing talent' beside them if they are
to operate at all.

The Destroyer, like the Artist, is an introverting extravert –
another one with prior expectations of the world in which he has
to find himself. The crucial differences lie in the nature of the
function he uses, which is holistic intuition, and the Element
involved, which is Water – itself traditionally associated with
emotion. Where the Artist thoughtfully observes 'inner pictures'
and coolly compares them with her environment, keeping her
famous critical distance throughout, the Destroyer has no such
detailed reservations. Approaching the world intuitively and
emotionally is pretty much an all-or-nothing affair. We may think
about the detail, analyse; we certainly see, hear, finger the details
as such. But the moment we feel or intuit, we are trying to be in
touch with the whole, as a whole.

As a result, instead of standing back from the world and finding
it wanting, the Destroyer is drawn right into the life around him
– and *then* finds that nothing meets his expectations. He doesn't
hold back, hover and dither endlessly critical on the threshold of
involvement, needing a lot of persuading. Instead, he rushes in
and, finding life a severe disappointment, he then as it were crit-

icises the world from the inside: we can imagine him rudely
flinging things out of his way, discarding everything in sight in
search of the 'promised' perfection. Instead of clinical detach-
ment and a penchant for well-judged compromise, the Destroyer
has this instantly active not-good-enough approach: 'Complete
rubbish! Throw it out!' No half-measures, that's him.

Or her. He/she is such a strange and unique mixture of the
Masculine (Fire/intuition) and the Feminine (Water/emotion),
one can only describe the Destroyer as being strongly both. The
combination of fire and water yields steam of course, and this
seems an entirely appropriate association with an impulse so
forceful, so no-nonsense direct. Despite the 'mixed gender' I still
think he will be most easily memorised as the Artist's big brother:
he who steps into the breach when the last compromise has
failed, when no attempt to improve, this way or that, will make
enough of a difference, when no amount of well-meant effort can
mend the unmendable or restore the injured to health. This is
when our straightforward impulse to simply get rid of comes into
its own – else we might cling to and tinker with for ever.

It needs tempering of course, if it is to be of use. The Thinker
in us, for instance, will have something to say about taking a good
logical look at the situation first, and about taking account of the
finer detail, rather than condemning the whole lot out of hand.
And as ever it will need a sense of connectedness, feeling himself
to be part of the larger group, before the Destroyer can play a
beneficial role in our lives.

Basically, it is all or nothing with him, but he soon learns to
stand his absolutist attitudes aside for a moment: the whole might
not please him, but amongst the constituent parts something of
genuine value might just be found, if he looks closely enough.
The Artist, starting out with the details as viewed from a distance,
comes to integrate things into a harmonious whole. But the
Destroyer, starting out with the whole as experienced close up,
in the end comes to scrutinise the detail, *the intimate and
internal detail*.

So he is not just demolition squad and amputating surgeon, he
is also psychoanalyst, detective, investigator of obscure facts. He
goes deep: he tries to understand the world from the inside, and
relate to it that way. He burrows under the surface of things like
a miner in search of treasure (still always trying to find something

acceptable to add to his own becoming) and he has a most disconcerting habit of laying bare everyone's best-hidden secrets. Above
all, he needs to listen to the Priest in us, to humble and gentle
him sufficiently, before one would want to let him loose at all.

The superficial never satisfies the Destroyer. He develops a
knack of homing in on the essentials straight away. It is the
obvious thing to do for him, really: not only are essentials
contained within, or tucked away underneath the surface, but
they also represent whatever is best – and it is only the best he
is interested in, after all. We will have to picture him dismantling,
with all due care, to find something inside that can be salvaged.
Gently stripping away the useless wrapping, to get at the worthwhile contents. And asking, respectfully, to be taken into
another's confidence, so that ultimately he can share in what is
'real' about them, behind the public façade.

Just as relating is a keyword to bear in mind where the Artist
in us is concerned, so sharing is an important word to associate
with the Destroyer in us. That sounds strange, of course. But the
thing to remember is that he destroys only what needs to be: the
harmful, or even just useless. What after all can we genuinely
share with others? The rubbish in our lives? Or the shallow veneer
and the unreal gloss we put on things? These obviously stand in
the way to true sharing, so they need to be ruthlessly discarded
fist. Considered like that, it stands to reason that the most talented
getter-rid-of is also the best sharer, if by sharing we mean something truly intimate and for real. There are of course also our very
real hidden miseries and painful secrets – they too are there for
the sharing. But again these need unearthing first. And in the last
analysis it is another of those give and take situations: others learn
to give up and let go, while *he* learns to accept his share of the
less than perfect, to put it like that.

Giving up, letting go of, getting rid of, throwing out without
qualms, making a clean break, radical upheavals, drastic termina-
tions. It sounds like nothing but loss, even supposing it is the
'positive loss' of something detrimental – a kind of necessary evil.
What few of us ever realise, at the time, is that there are actual
positive gains involved when we part with what isn't worth
having. A totally different outlook. Being able to newly treasure
what we are left with. A useful reappraisal of our situation.
Transformed attitudes. Space. A fresh start – with much better

expectations.

There is no doubt that the Destroyer is simply utterly demanding. The Artist diplomatically suggests changes, at a polite distance, as it were. Not so the Destroyer. He doesn't relate-to-at-a-distance; he needs to deeply and closely share in others' lives. And he brings the whole baggage of prior expectations right into this attempted symbiosis. But the insightful demands he foists on everyone should actually serve as a kind of inspiration to them. His intuitive inner knowledge, his feel for things that are intrinsically valid and valuable, means that the empty spaces he leaves – the empty spaces he *creates* – are always suggestive of something far better. In effect, he drives everyone on to more considered efforts, more heedful of what should be, of what we could do, if we really tried to do our best.

He is a hard taskmaster, not to be fooled by appearances. Glib tales won't stop him poking around, finding out, holding up any deficiencies to the cruel light of truthful evaluation. But without him, the Destroyer in us, we would be incapable of making genuinely new starts. We would be hopeless when it comes to rigorously testing what we are about to acquire/become for its true worth first. We would not know how to purge our lives of the useless accumulations of years, clutter that holds us fast and impedes our future. We would be ignorant of the magnificent benefits of 'nothing'. To wit, the personal integrity and higher standards that come with refusing to believe that something, anything, has got to be better than nothing. And the ability to forgo cheap gratification or dodgy gain because, somehow, 'deep down, we know better'.

For all the intensity that goes with this impulse, it also represents our potential for rightful abstinence: an innate requirement that would have us do things properly-or-not-at-all.

As can be imagined, the picture is drastically different when it comes to the downside of this motivation pattern. Disappointed expectations easily lead to intense resentment. Feeling cheated, in ways he cannot specify or explain, the Destroyer constantly claims to deserve better. He complains loudly, endlessly. He comes to view the world with a mixture of deep suspicion and unmitigated contempt. His attitude is 'Well of course it's all rubbish anyway', but that doesn't stop him partaking of it. One can picture him stuffing himself with a complete lack of relish, shovelling it in with a look of disgust, downing another drink with a shudder, and never a hint of true enjoyment. It is a moot point whether he is only pretending. The fact of the matter is that he comes to enjoy rubbish.

He too learns to analyse the situation, but only in the crudest and hence the most brutal way: he smashes, he cracks open, he violates everyone's integrity – no wonder that at the end of it he finds nothing worthwhile. By the time he gets to the bottom of things, he's already spoilt them, more often than not.

In a world where nothing of value (in his view) can be found, he has to make do with the shoddy, the broken, the useless, the contemptible. Of these he acquires and consumes considerable quantities, just slurping it down, just kicking it around some more, perpetually disgruntled. He no longer has idealistic expectations; instead he has come to anticipate the worst, and in a perverse sort of way this is the only positive pleasure life offers him: to find his *negative* expectations mostly justified. His sarcasm bites deep. He gloats and belittles, he drags all and everything through the mud. He makes a point of deliberately setting out to prove one wrong, show one up. His cynicism hurts, and is meant to hurt: he enjoys hurt.

What one has to remember is that, as an extravert, what he contacts he also becomes. If he avidly seeks out the worst, the broken and the hurting, then he too will be trash, broken, hurt. As he does to others, so he does to himself, automatically. He rapes and corrupts his own prospects in life. He tortures himself when he flays his victims – quite literally, perhaps. Dismantling the world around him without a hope of some beneficial outcome at the end of it, he destroys himself on a daily basis. A fully paid-up nihilist, he expects nothing of or for himself either, holding himself in utter contempt. He has a greed for punishment that simply defies one's normal logic, feelings and assumptions (for normal read positive, or healthy, if you like), but it has to be admitted that his behaviour does make an awful kind of sense, within its own context.

But what of those things even he can't inadvertently or deliberately spoil? Take the few things that don't corrode, rot, cave in, prove fickle – gold and diamonds, if nothing else springs to mind: something even he can't make a mess-to-relish of. If he does happen to discover genuine treasure hidden somewhere, what on earth can he do with it? It defies his perversely negative expectations. It proves him wrong, for once. It stands in total contradistinction to what he has found the world to be, what he has indeed helped make of it. At this point it becomes clear that what he has actually achieved with his crudely destructive trying and testing is to actively divide the world in two: absolutes of trash and treasure. And by extension: 'black' and 'white', heroes and villains, absolute good and bad.

Of course he does not know how to integrate these two opposites, stand them in some unifying relation. Even at his best this has never been the Destroyer's job; he has never had the requisite 'distance' for it. And so best and worst, rare gems and total junk, stay categorically unmixed – in himself just as much as in his environment. But that gives him, personally, two options. Either he keeps the best of himself out of the public eye, hidden away in some obscure corner of his life, while openly displaying only his shabbiest qualities. Or else he walks about positively gilded: displays his true riches, all of them... but behind the promising surface appearance (a rather thin veneer, inevitably) one then invariably finds very bad surprises. Two figures of modern myth spring to mind in this connection: the proverbial tart with a golden heart; and the gangster in his immaculate suit, a fat gold ring glittering on every finger.

Whichever way he wants to play it, he has lost his integrity. He is not what he seems, on the surface. And one can never be sure what side of him one will encounter next: he might do any number of sudden about-flips. One might coax out the best in him, or trigger off the worst. Funny enough, as a bit of a baddie oneself, one would be more likely to catch a glimpse of his better side. Clean-nosed goody-goodies are only too apt to 'provoke' that part of him that wants to mercilessly smash them, rip them open, prove their inherent worthlessness or ultimate corruptibility. He *will* test to destruction all he can.

Let us compare this with the Artist-gone-wrong. She of course takes the greatest care to become/identify with 'only the best', evades unpleasantness, pushes 'nasty' things promptly away out of sight. She too ends up dividing the world into halves, the good and the bad, but she manages to cut herself off from the bad half in the process. (Or so she fondly imagines, anyway. Every time something less than entrancing suddenly emerges from the woodwork, she gets a terrible shock.) Not so the Destroyer: sharing intimately in all that goes on in the world, he splits *himself* in two. He becomes a double-headed creature, one face smiling, quite for real, and the other snarling, just as really him. His abrupt changes and unpredictable 'outbursts' shock those around him again and again, and never to any useful purpose.

It would be easy to look only at the most actively sadistic expression of this motivation pattern and dismiss it: 'Not me!'. The point is, we all have the Destroyer impulse, we all use it. And none of us are perfect. The most well-behaved and ordinary life will display some of the symptoms of the Destroyer getting out of hand. Sado-masochism, coprophilia, rape, murder and the loving dismemberment of corpses: these are the extremes. But even just cackling with *schadenfreude* is obviously part of this pattern misused. We need to learn to look closely indeed: there is all the world of difference, for instance, between someone not hesitating to identify the rot and the pretence – and someone being a lipsmackingly avid debunker.

The Thinker

I will have to introduce the 'Thinker' with a word of caution. Obviously the names I have chosen for them can never sum up, in one word, what the whole pattern is about: impossible, given the wide range of potential interpretations, implications, the different facets, uses and abuses that each pattern holds. I could have called the Artist in us the Judge instead, but then that might have sounded rather too harshly censorious... it would be hard to justify each name.

The Thinker certainly did not get her name because she is the only one among these symbolic figures to be associated with our rational function. The Boss in us too is a thinker and we will meet her later, among the introverts, the inward be-ers. Here we are still considering the various ways in which we newly become ourselves; and with the use of our Thinker impulse we do our becoming thoughtfully.

If the Artist in us is constantly critical, the Thinker is positively nit-picky. The Artist of course has her given inner guidelines to go by: her natural gift of discrimination. The Thinker has no such starting stock of insight. Neither will any amount of thoughtfulness tell her what is best, in the sense of absolutely best. But then trying to 'live up to an ideal' is not her job. Her job, basically, is to make up her mind what to be. She *chooses* what to become. I could have called her the Self-Stylist, if that didn't sound so obscure. This is precisely what she does, though: take a good close look at what's on offer, finger the material, analyse and compare and from *that* background criticise, and then pick the garment she will put on, figuratively speaking.

But to start with her basic make-up. She is of course essentially an extravert, like all the other 'becomers'. Her Element is Earth, associated with the use of our physical senses, and this chimes well with the structured nature of thought: she is a practical, down-to-earth thinker who will nose about among the nitty-gritty detail before making her choice. Dynamically – and here the picture gets complex – she is both an extravert *and* an introvert. In other words, she can apply thought to the world out there, but also to the world in here, to what she is inside herself. She can turn her mental searchlight in either direction.

Let's take this step by step. First of all the Thinker has to become whatever she thinks fit to become. This is thought directed outward. But since thought in her also 'wants to be' applied in the inward direction, we have to see her as having a sort of empty inner space waiting to be filled. Once she has acquired something to fill it with, she *introjects* this: carries it inward, embeds what she has become deep inside her and establishes it there. Thus she goes from outward becoming to inner being: the Thinker is a sort of self-made introvert, to all intents and purposes.

It is difficult for us, complete human beings with all our diverse psychological strands present at the same time so to speak, to pick these strands apart and look at how they function in their different ways. It is especially difficult to imagine an 'outside self' and an 'inside self'. So far we have only been considering our outside selves: the way our identity is derived from and wrapped up in our environment. The Hunter in us, whose most developed essence still always lies with action *out there*. Likewise the Maker. The Artist, whose inner vision is nothing personal to her, nothing she *is*, only a gift to be used in the course of her work/life out there. Neither does the Destroyer have a personal inner life – not even when, in negative mode, he splits into (say) a flawless surface and the murk that lies concealed underneath: this 'underneath' does not amount to a state of innerness. The rigorously separate sides he divides himself into are still all out there: part of his doing, his active becoming. Inner being is not something he does.

It is only with these last two symbolic figures among the extraverts, the Thinker and the Priest, that our 'superficial' becoming evolves into something we can begin to call inner being. Being inside ourselves what we have become, after actively working on ourselves, so to speak. This is not the same as simply, naturally, being what we innately are; it is more of a journey inward. We venture into a new and in that sense un-natural dimension. We make a further effort, in order to steadfastly *be* what we have (in the case of the Thinker) thoughtfully become.

Which is where the Thinker's story continues. Once she has firmly established what she is, inside herself, she keeps thinking of herself as being just that, she continues to be inwardly self-aware: this is still thought directed inward. But the moment she turns thoughtfully outward again, in search of new things to become, her position is suddenly very different. Now she actually experiences the world around her as being truly 'out there'. She understands her inner self as being *separate* from her environment. And with that, something of a gulf has opened up between her inner being and her outward doing, a rift that needs constant mending.

Becoming, changing, simply living, all become much more tortuous and complex. Outward changes have to lead on to inner changes as well; meantime established inner being makes subsequent outward change so much more difficult to negotiate. In short, where the other 'becomers' just get on with it, the Thinker makes a whole complicated procedure of it.

Nothing is easy for the Thinker. The world is a somewhat threatening, suspect place to her – not surprisingly, since she is only partly identified with it. This makes her more than just choosy: cautious, fussy, meticulous, having to scrutinise everything minutely. Her newly acquired inner guidelines too stand in the way of her accepting anything easily, or doing anything at all in a hurry. When she acts, she now *acts out of* what she is, thoughtfully, inside herself. She has developed a sort of conscience: laid down thought patterns that tell her how to act. Though it has to be said that this DIY conscience of hers is a thing always in flux, ready to change in accordance with her more outward changes. Then again, with all these criticisms and scruples she has, she might well grind to a halt altogether unless she can get the positive co-operation of other, less pernickety impulses.

Once we can get her to be more acceptingly and givingly involved, her talents are many. Her careful choosing and attention to finicky detail make her good at things like designing, styling, lay-out, organising, ordering and generally tidying things up, each job undertaken with something like analytical precision. Honing and 'polishing' things to a fine finish come naturally to her. That inner base she acts out of – her current intellectual self-image, her ideas of what she should be, the conscience she has adopted – makes her methodical, conscientious, responsible in everything she does. And she is nothing if not thorough.

Thoroughness is one of the big themes in her script: becoming turning inward, growing into something so deep it leaves the superficial life behind.

If all this makes her sound boring, like a work-horse who never sets a foot wrong, there is also another aspect to her nature. She is a self-styler, freely (if thoughtfully and pragmatically) choosing what to be. She develops, in outward matters as well as inwardly, along whatever lines *she* sees fit. In the last analysis, there is something of the eccentric in her. She thinks nothing of improving on nature; experiments and innovations are all in a day's work for her.

These two aspects, the thorough and methodical and the off-beat and innovative, are not in any way antagonistic. They are both part of her ongoing story of outer/inner development: tayloring her actions to what she is inside herself... adjusting her inner being in response to what she has learned in the course of her work 'out there'... and so on, in an endless round of (self)improvement and (self)adaptation. This makes her good at such diverse jobs as checking the minutiae of something, making sure they are correct and conform to reasonable expectations – and on the other hand, say, making wholesale modifications to things, converting them for some totally novel kind of use.

With so many 'styles' to her, it was indeed difficult to decide what to call her. The Improver? Alright, as far it goes, but then it never even hints at the most crucial thing about her: the inner self-awareness she develops.

The Thinker, as I have said, comes to see her inner self as separate from the world around her. Or to be precise, being transitional between a pure extravert and a genuine introvert, she has both an inner and an outer self. And she needs to constantly update the one to go with the other: repeated internal and external adjustments are needed, to keep herself intact and all of a piece. Nothing wrong with that, as long as this doesn't develop into an outright split, but remains only a sort of mental distancing. It gives her, on the one hand, a sober and workman-like attitude to what she is, inside herself: aware introspection, ready to find fault. But of course she can also view her own worldly activities from a not totally involved position, making possible more self-criticism.

This then is the crux of the whole complicated story: with this motivation pattern we become at the same time self-aware, in a no longer only material, physical sense, and we become capable of self-criticism and all that goes with it, like deliberate attempts to improve on what we (naturally) are.

One more set of talents can be added to the Thinker's already long list: being not just analytical but 'understanding' with all that that implies. And recognising what's involved when it comes to intactness, wholeness, health.

So she represents what makes us want to double-check the spelling, certainly; but equally it is her that has us inventing new words, phrases, a new language (why not?), just because it seems a good idea. And in addition, she has us nursing the sick, counselling the insecure, reassuring the threatened – knowing from personal experience how, if we want to 'hang together', we have to work at it, outwardly as well as inside ourselves.

It should be obvious that things can go wrong very easily here. A mishandled Thinker impulse does indeed not hang together properly. Those useful mental reservations vis-à-vis the world can easily turn to loathing. That productive mental distance to one's own doings can become an ugly schism instead, a split between two irreconcilable halves.

This is what happens if the Thinker in us is left to pursue her own agenda unaided by our other impulses. With much painstaking fussing and picking she at last makes up her mind what to be – and promptly becomes so utterly convinced that she has got it right, she comes to guard her established inner self like some fragile treasure inside an impregnable fortress.

She no longer cares to respond to life with changes of her own. She regards her self as quite good enough: has she not given it a huge amount of thought, after all? So why upset her self, inside herself, with inner changes? Self-improvement is unnecessary, in her opinion. And the world out there, in her increasingly insular view, is a dangerous place that only threatens to unmake her, should she set foot in it. So she doesn't.

From now on she simply keeps her inner self out of the world, keeps it safe in a 'higher' dimension of its own. At the same time, she comes to regard the world as not just out there but *down* there: pickiness turns to disdain, even disgust, and ultimately complete intolerance. And distrust grows into fear, a horror of having her nice above-it-all self polluted by lesser things. The picture that emerges is of someone terribly proper, snooty, stuck up, prim, prude and awfully smug. Someone with a downright phobia regarding all 'lowly' things, creepy-crawlies, dirt of any description... but it is a general fear of life, really.

Life, however, changing and becoming, has to go on. While the inner self huddles 'up there', the Thinker's active-self (her extraverting half, now neatly split off from the introverting part of her) is busy in the world, one might say despite herself: despite her inner self that only wants to stay out of things. And since personal development has become a complete no-no for her, any becoming she actively brings about has to be not her own, but the world's.

This is another instance of fake becoming. We have already seen how the Maker at his worst becomes the same over and over again, firmly stuck in his established groove. The Thinker, for her part, when split in two and with one half stuck up there, does her becoming at on remove: by doing everyone else's becoming for them.

From her elevated position she wants to change the world. She has developed a deeply entrenched better-than-thou attitude, and now she conducts nothing short of a crusade. The narrowness of her unchanging inner convictions beggars belief, but it is more than made up for by the breath-taking scope of her desire to cure the whole wide world of its imperfections. She wants nothing more than to cleanse it, rid it of all its horrible dirt and filth, not to mention evils of a higher order. Nothing escapes her compulsive scrubbing and pedantic ordering; nobody can avoid her intrusive scrutiny, which truly knows no bounds: she pries and snoops and spies to hunt out the least little outward blemish or dark inner secret. Thorough to a fault, she is never content to deal only with the surface of things. Instead, she has to 'convert' everyone, inside and out, to her particular system of being-oneself, properly. No use arguing with her either. Her mind is closed – sealed off in its own little enclave, untouchable.

This is her absurd life situation: an inner and an outer self ('mind' and action; her private, personal identity, and her official working self) which have become two scrupulously separate parts that go in opposite directions, desire totally different things. 'Head' wanting to guard its purity, while 'hands' poke about in the obscurest corners, *hoping* to find some more dirt. Actively hunting for sleaze; and being, in herself, shocked at such things. Studiously averting her gaze from impropriety, in one sense. And in another sense, in *practice*, enthusiastically seeking it out. To say she is a hypocrite is one way of looking at it.

The strength of her perverse desire for what she so categorically disapproves of actually represents her terrible need for life, as such, ever since she stopped becoming, inside herself. Fear of life, to the point of complete touch-me-not rejection. And thirst for life, to the point of wallowing in it – let's just say with rubber gloves and apron on, to make sure nothing will infect or pollute her, but wallowing nonetheless. She thinks all too highly of herself. And at the same time she thinks nothing of debasing herself, stooping to the level of the gutter to feed a perverse appetite for the worst she can find, while 'in herself' staying as pure as the driven snow.

Because she has slammed the doors shut on any ideas of personal development or improvement, now she has to take the world's for her own instead. But the more she improves the world (though with her narrowness of outlook and unresponsiveness to others, and situations, it can hardly be called improvement), the lower she will have to sink in search of something or somebody she deems in need of her ministrations.

Ultimately, when all has been scoured and scourged, down to the last petty detail, and there is nothing and nobody left to convert, there is really just one way forward for this professional Shudderer at the Unthinkable. She has to make a complete, painful U-turn: turn her herself upside down and inside out, convert herself. Practice what formerly she only preached, and preach what formerly she only practised.

We have to bear in mind that her outlook is not just fussily detailed, but quite detrimentally narrow: a kind of tunnel vision. There is no end, then, to how often she can betray a former position, adopt a brand-new conscience, be the archetypal turncoat. At her simplest and mildest we may just see her adopting ever new mix-and-match styles and fashions, one after the other, each trumpeted as 'it', exclusively... until the next complete makeover. At a more serious level, monomanias come and go;

new neurotic rituals spring up overnight. Meantime her hypochondria leapfrogs from one favoured ailment to the next, while her many allergies to life as such go through a puzzling series of permutations. (And all the while she will be lecturing the whole world on their proper diet, reductionist as ever but, reliably, moralising while she is at it.) At the far end of the scale, though, we find her active as a serious indoctrinator, a brain-washer of no mean talent.

The absurd thing is that this most fastidious chooser, so endlessly fussy about mentally sniffing things over before committing herself a million per cent – for how ever long it may last – is actually quite easily brainwashed herself. Freely, even wilfully, choosing what to be is all very well; but she is only selecting from among the options presented to her by her environment. Give her a choice of dark, medium and light blue 'during her formative period' and she will be not just blue but pinpoint-specifically so, and with a strength of inner conviction that says: I have freely thought this through and chosen it! And so she has of course.

The point is that without any insight into perfection as such, lacking access to the wider inner landscape where such a thing can be known – and without for instance some sound advice from the Artist and the Destroyer in us, who do have such insight – the Thinker in us stands in danger of simply taking the options this imperfect world offers for good enough to select and cobble together a perfect self from. But no amount of 'superficial thinking', no matter how nicely internalised or abstracted, will make up for this essential ignorance.

Her perfectionism is just that: an ism, arid and sterile. And her fixity of outlook does not amount to inner integrity or conscience; neither do her endless twists and turns and pointless revolutions amount to something one could call development. Finding both these contradictory traits improbably combined under the same heading just shows how easy it is to 'crack', or become a fanatical crackpot, once the Thinker in us is allowed to run wild.

The Priest

With the Priest we come to the last pattern in this section on becoming ourselves. As I have already mentioned, this figure too is transitional, starting with outward becoming and progressing towards inner states of being: another essential extravert who is dynamically both (first) outward-directed and (then) inward-turned. Another one with an empty inner space waiting to be filled.

The function the Priest in us directs both outward and inward is the very opposite of the one the Thinker uses: feeling rather than thought. Feeling which, like intuition, is basically holistic – thought and sensation being the functions that enable us to approach and understand the world piecemeal, in detail, while intuition and emotion let us grasp things more as a whole.

The Element associated with the figure of the Priest is Water, denoting emotion again: she is purely emotional, and yes, she is very much a Feminine archetype – even more so than the Thinker. But let's follow her story from the beginning.

There is nothing picky and choosy about the way the Priest goes about acquiring an identity: she never divides the world into sensual or logical units first, and so has no way of making comparisons. Instead, feeling simply flows outward from her in search of something to 'identify with'. She is quite content to settle for anything; whoever happens to be around, for instance, can be assured of her 'sympathy'. The word No certainly does not feature in her vocabulary.

She might go on like this for ever, emotionally identified with all and sundry in turn, if she did not also have to introject what she has so lightly, almost automatically (indeed 'superficially') become. But the moment she starts internalising acquired attributes, it soon becomes apparent what an ill-chosen ragbag it all is. Add them up together in one place, as it were, and nothing chimes with anything else. A chaotic emotional state of simply going-with-the-flow is one thing, inner emotional disharmony quite another.

With the Thinker pattern, we stand in danger of excessive discrimination, and of getting stuck with being something untouchable and unchangeable inside ourselves. Quite the reverse with the Priest in us: here the danger is of excessive acceptance, followed by the repeated loss of an untenable inner state of being. We might liken it to a process of uncontrolled eating that ends in our inevitably being sick, disgorging what we have gobbled up without discernment, various substances clashing horribly in our stomachs. A hasty becoming that is not really fit to lead to depth and permanence. And an equally hasty un-becoming, from out of our failed depths. If still stuck for a mental picture of this process, just think of a toddler's tearful, screeching tantrums when faced with something that goes against the (emotional) grain of his current situation.

It needs a touch of the Artist's eye for what goes with what; a dose of critical appraisal from the Thinker; a good measure of the Destroyer's understanding that 'less is more': input like that from the other motivation patterns, just as they benefit from the Priest's ready talent to feel at one with all the world.

Being more careful, and keeping it simple – that is to say, not attempting to take on board too much – are absolutely crucial. Given these precautions, there is no reason why the Priest in us should not successfully establish an inner self that is emotionally all of a piece, harmonious, enabling her to live at peace with herself, inside herself, at last.

But as with the Thinker, this is only half the story. Becoming, the search for personal development, has to go on. The Thinker of course can always hold the world out there at a safe mental distance first, coolly analysing how it might fit in with her established thought patterns, before getting too closely involved with anything that might be totally unsuitable. But the Priest, being all-emotional, is only too easily caught up and entangled, deceived, misled, in up to her neck before she knows what she has let herself in for: this is our Achilles' heel, the really vulnerable part of our psychological functioning, when our feelings extravert.

Feeling flows out *into:* thus we get to know this piecemeal, structured world we live in *from the inside*, as it were. We are emotionally shaped, moulded, by what we contact. Or to put it another way, if we extend feeling towards others, we have identified with them before we know it – or them – properly. Viewed purely by itself (as part of an isolated motivation pattern), this is a very risky business indeed. For the Priest in us, the world out there is a terribly dangerous place to try and find her inner renewal in, ultimately.

There is however another environment she can turn to in her predicament. I have already referred to the Inner Plane that both Artist and Destroyer take their inspiration from. When I come to discuss the Creator in us, I will be calling it our Creative Base. Inner Reality may be an acceptable blanket term and, as we will see, all the essential introverts are closely in touch with it. As for the Priest, essential extravert that she is, her identity is such a fragile, vulnerable construct that sooner or later she will have to go further inward than the Thinker in us would ever think of going: if she is to do her job reliably, she will have to turn to Inner Reality for her becoming, her inner growth. Breaking with tradition, as it were, she will have to become a proper introvert now.

This has far-reaching implications. For a start, she no longer needs the world around her, relying on her inner environment instead. In effect, she has made contact with timeless perfection: all it takes to feed an eternity of totally safe inner becoming, or simply being. She has reached her nirvana, would be one way of putting it; or come to rest securely in the all-emotional-needs-providing Love of God; or become as one with a higher Self. I am not sure that there is a phrasing I could offer the spiritually disinclined that would really capture the essence of it. Suffice to say that the moment she no longer emotionally *needs* the world, it is quite safe for her to return to it.

And return to it she must. Her story doesn't simply stop there, with her finding all she requires in the inward direction, her development now a purely inner one. But when she comes to direct emotion outward again, towards the 'real' world of flesh and blood and threat and doubt, she can now do so truly selflessly.

She literally leaves her self out of it. What in the Thinker threatens to become an inappropriate split, if it goes too far, in the Priest becomes an instance of perfectly healthy transcendence. She stands herself aside from the world – she no longer 'takes it personally' – while being self-lessly active in it. Fearlessly as well now... another species of Hero, if you like. To borrow a well-known phrase, she is in the world but not, self-seekingly, of it. This is of course why I have called her the Priest. Because she is in touch with the Inner-Plane All, and now acts out of that, rather than acting out of the little bit of a personal identity she has managed to gain, the humble bit of a self she can call her own. One could say that rather than act out of her inner self, she comes to *channel* what lies beyond it.

She channels, acts as mouthpiece, serves, mediates something, adopts the role of. What the Priest in us does, when well handled, allows us to go much further than the Thinker's intellectual introspection and her understanding of others' inner struggles. We are looking at a true transcendence of the self-ish state. One result of that is a great feeling of being essentially at one with others, all others, easily, naturally, with no personal hang-ups to get in the way: a genuine fellowship that we can only gain once we no longer depend on others for anything, having discovered 'higher' or 'deeper' things to depend on.

Obviously, there is a religious interpretation in all this. But purely as a process, and in the wider view, we can equally see this at work in children grown up (grown more inward, too), away from their dependence on the parent, finding their emotional sustenance in other directions: it is only now they can begin to give true affection, freely, to the person who cared for them in their emotional infancy. Or we could think in terms of a trained singer 'serving' her music, or the composer of it, by becoming a note- and word-perfect mouthpiece. Again, we could consider the figure of an archetypal Mother Teresa, living in personal poverty but also, in Christian parlance, 'living in Christ': selflessly caring for complete strangers; strangely unmoved, in herself, by what goes on around her. Less emotionally mature, most of us would constantly burst into tears at the sight of so much misery and death – automatically making another's misery our own, that is. When you look at it like that, it takes more than a glance to distinguish crass heartlessness from selflessness of the highest order!

What can we say about the nature and activities of the Priest, specifically? She much resembles the Hunter, that most energetically 'self-seeking' of archetypes, in being ready for action in almost any capacity. Both are simple to the point of being primitive. But with the motivation pattern of the Priest we have reached a form of simplicity that is, paradoxically, quite complex and especially hard to achieve. And the crux of it is what we might term the universal priesthood of all: having discovered our inward source of renewal, we are obliged to carry this 'emotional insight' forward into action – free of charge. Lovingly, that is.

The touchiest, most vulnerable, instantly malleable, the most easily captivated and exploited of our impulses, the Priest in us is for ever being thrown off course by the most basic vicissitudes of life and fails only too readily. Let me say here that of course I don't mean to imply that we live out these root impulses *either* in their full glory *or* in the most negative manifestation or inter-pretation possible. We probably play out the whole spectrum repeatedly in the course of one day, though we may leave more or less untouched the furthest extremes: what you might call our divinity and our devilry.

Looking now at the downside of the Priest in us, we find that it can actually take two different forms: one more passive, the other decidedly active. Though both contrive to look harmless, at least at first sight. And both involve huge doses of make-believe. In the first instance, we simply fail to introject properly and may end up with a fake-inner self. The other form is much more sinister, behind the surface appeal: it shows how we may attempt to smooth out, level and artificially 'harmonise' the whole world first, in an effort to make it safe to be emotionally identified with.

To start with the passive form. She may keep trying hard, but somewhere the Priest in us goes wrong in the long process of emotionally growing up/inward. If the Thinker fails to help for instance, she won't manage to be circumspect enough. She will only go on importing disharmony into her inner space, repeat-edly, endlessly – and blaming herself, feeling guilty and worthless every time it happens. Or she may fail to grow far enough inward, abandon the road to real profundity, too easily persuaded to return again and again to superficial things for her emotional development. Either way, her depth of feeling never amounts to much. She stays emotionally shallow, and fickle with it.

Anything will set her off laughing or crying, all commiseration one moment, and everything 'forgotten' the next. And yet the strength and speed of her emotional reactions is such, it may quite easily be mistaken for depth of feeling. Her repeated 'outbursts' add to that impression: she loses hold of her barely introjected feelings the moment something else comes along – whether better or worse makes no difference at all, so long as it differs irreconcilably. She utters screams of not-really horror, or screams of facile delight, at every change of tune.

Emotionally, she is incontinent. She quite fails to be reserved (fails to reserve anything inside her, for long) with the result that her feelings wash into and all over any situation without let or hindrance. In effect, instead of going deep, her feelings tower sky-high. She is 'over-emotional'. She 'takes things personally' to an absurd degree: literally, she takes the surrounding ambience of the moment to be her very own condition.

If she can manage to be just a little bit more circumspect, then she may try to establish a false sort of 'innerness', a fake that mimics the real thing. She may immerse herself in a sheltered environment that, if not necessarily pleasant, is at least all of a piece and in that sense harmonious, monochrome, polarised along whatever lines. It may sound absurd, but one could see her being quite happy inside a prison or a hospital ward, say: anywhere tightly regimented where her feelings won't be pulled about in opposite directions constitutes a desirable environment. Religious sects and communes are of course very good hiding places for her. Even the unreal world of TV soaps and pulp fiction is an area she can establish her pretend-deep emotional identity in, just so long as it is all quite predictable, and hence ultimately safe.

In each case, she wears her fake inner self wrapped around her like a protective bubble. She lives cocooned in unreality. Institutionalised living, dogma, escapist dreams and various drugs may all play their part in keeping the painful turbulence of the wider world at arm's length.

But bubbles are apt to burst, sooner or later. The time will come when she finds herself as nakedly homeless as a snail minus its shell: a complete novice seeker yet again – with, it has to be said, a by now strongly established taste for spurious emotional heights or depths.

And so it turns out that neither her inner space nor any number of contrived cocoons prove to be safe for her to settle in, emotionally. She will have to be an eternal drifter then. Instead of delving into her own inner depths, and learning to transcend all the superficial moods of the world, she will have to beg and borrow and steal what she can of others' achievements in that direction – or what, in her ignorance of such matters, she takes for such.

Her life now becomes entirely vicarious. She peers into people's 'depths' with the avid need of the true voyeur. She lusts after their deepest secrets, whines for their presumed-deep sympathy... and at a pinch will make do with the contents of their pockets. By the same token, she will make anyone's high worldly standing or achievements her own, simply by a process of emotional identification: she is a hero-worshipper, a groupie, an obsessive royalty watcher. An emotional diet of royal scandal, nicely combining height and depth, is entirely acceptable to her. Then again, someone's deepest rage bursting out of its usual concealment is, perversely, just as acceptable. She soon learns how to provoke it.

The Priest as Vicarious Leech takes all the innermost bits others have to offer, practically borrows their 'soul' for her own, and never has anything to give in return. She is poor in all respects, she is empty, emotionally hollow, and more than that, she is insatiable: a bottomless hole where receiving charity is concerned. No matter how much one gives her, none of it seems to stick to her, it is all just so much through-put. Compare that to the true (rather than literal) selflessness the Priest is capable of at her best. Not to mention the channelling of genuinely higher things. And while the true Priest will lovingly 'do anything' for whoever asks her, this fake article will zombie-like do anything a zealous reformer may push on her – though only for as long as it takes for someone else to come along and dress her up in different clothes. She herself of course couldn't care less. She will lend herself to anything, sell herself at any price, just so long as we share our 'innerness' with her: all those hidden, inner, treasured, secret bits she no longer even dreams of having, in herself.

If the above pattern is more about passively courting harm than actively doing it, the same can certainly not be said of the one that follows. This is the other option, if one can call it that: here the Priest in us stops trying to introject anything at all, for the time being. She keeps it all out, emotionally at arm's length. No inner disharmony, no 'outbursts', no painful failure. Instead (and in a weirdly remote, *impersonal* way) she starts making active changes to the world around her in order to render it safe for her to 'identify deeply with' at some later date.

This is make-believe of an aggressive order, fed not so much by failure and non-cooperation from other impulses as by much wrong-headed help from an obsessively fussy Thinker, a sadistic Destroyer, a pie-in-the-sky Artist etc. (One could conjecture that one rotten apple in the barrel will inevitably have a knock-on effect on the functioning of a number of other impulses. The more so if these are basically labile and impressionable, rather than proactive, like the Hunter, for instance.)

But a Priest who must convert the whole world first, in order to gain her own soul? A World Improver – purely for her own benefit? An Idealistic Seeker whose idealism is no more than an unavoidable prelude to self-seeking? As we shall see, we are entering the emotional realms of a Hitler, a Stalin, and a host of lesser emotionally seductive Leaders.

When the Priest makes it clear that she disapproves of the world as it stands, it isn't the bad and the horrible that really bothers her. It is simply the lack of smoothness, evenness, harmony: the differences, the inequalities, the disconcerting lumps and bumps of life that, if she took them all personally, would make her hurt, inside herself, and then destroy her, as a secure identity. The most important thing for her then is to find guaranteed unity in her environment: whether obedient bland sameness, or state-regulated flamboyance. Anything will do, just so long as it gels (and remains that way, stability being sameness spread over time).

A vision of universal peace and harmony is easy enough to sell, of course, and adherents will not be hard to find. Equality is a different proposition, though, and strict toeing of the existing line never popular for long either. The Priest in the guise of Glorious Leader may be seductive first and foremost, but she soon finds her emotionally brainwashed cohorts a handy force to implement her rule of law. Non-compliers will immediately find themselves purged. Whole swathes of dissenters and misfits are disappeared. Even those who quite inadvertently fall short of the mass ideal have to be got rid of: failures and the obviously crippling she can well do without.

The suffering of those around her simply leaves her cold. She is emotionally dead to the world, completely switched off – as well as staying emotionally empty, chronically undeveloped in that respect.

Orchestrating such mass murder and destruction (or the silencing and suppression of others' true identity, at any rate), the Priest more than rivals the Destroyer in us, in terms of destructive potential. Which is surely ironic, given her basic sensitivity, her touchiness, her desperate need for a sheltered environment, and so on. But engineering for herself just such a guaranteed safe haven – by 'infecting' others with her limitless perfectionism, before the world can get a chance to infect *her* with anything hurtful – is unfortunately one of the possible answers the Priest in us finds in her script.

It should be obvious that her totalitarian attempt to be the founder/finder of complete and everlasting harmony in the world isn't going to get her anywhere. The utopia she expects to reach in the material world lies of course in the inward direction, on the Inner Plane alone. Her unrealistic plan to gain a ready-made inner peace and stability from out of her environment will never come to anything. And so her centre remains ever empty. And where there should have been inner growth of the highest order, there is only the appearance of worldly megalomania. Meantime her distant machinations, conducted without any emotional involvement on her part at all, are not only meaningless but truly heartless.

BEING YOURSELF

The Creator

We now come to the six motivation patterns concerned with being ourselves – actively being in the world what we inherently are – rather than gaining our selfhood or identity from out of our environment. That isn't to say that the figures we meet here are in any way designed to be immune to change: as we shall see, if they want to apply to the outside world what they are inside themselves, then they have to give a bit, learn a lot – that's if they are going to do the job properly.

We start with the Creator in us. I might even say the Creator-in-us, because here we are looking at our personal creative potential *as well as* the Creative Base as such: the Inner Reality that inspires both our Artist and Destroyer impulses, the Inner Plane that is the appropriate 'environment' for the Priest in us. Here, in the Creator archetype, we see personal inner-being and Inner Reality coinciding: if we like, we could say that it represents our 'divine spark' in its neatest form.

As I have already outlined earlier: the Creator is essentially an introvert, but dynamically – with his conscious function, intuition, directed exclusively outward – he is purely an extravert, one who ever seeks to become. What *he* seeks to become, though, is aware. Aware, rather paradoxically, of what he is inside himself. His inner self is a mystery to him and the only way he can gain conscious access to it is to give out of himself, to actively put something of himself into the world, and thus find himself as it were reflected there. He finds himself via other.

Fire, itself associated with intuition, is the Creator's Element. This makes of his instinctive search for himself a no-holds-barred holistic and strongly impulsive affair. Consider a young child seriously at play. I say seriously because there is nothing really playful about it, in the sense of relaxed 'playing around'. The younger we are, the less chance we have had to discover ourselves, and the harder we still have to work at stamping our recognisable image on the world: footprints in the sand, pictures to be pinned to walls, noises that elicit the response 'I see you' (or even a shout of annoyance that mentions our name and thus tells us we are who we are, that we exist at all). This being a decidedly Masculine archetype, we should not be surprised to find men more especially carrying this kind of behaviour pattern forward neat and undiluted into adult life, purely by way of trying to be themselves, awarely. If we say 'Relax, it's only a game' or announce that building model airplanes is fit only for kids, we are definitely missing the point somewhere. Creativity, a measure of applause, some kind of public recognition, these are all entirely essential to that part of our psychological make-up that is forever actively in search of itself.

Ultimately, for the Creator in us to produce something beneficial out of himself – especially since it is all done so unself-awarely, full recognition dawning only after the event, so to speak – it needs a lot of restraint, patient application, and above all loving response to others' needs. (The other introvert impulses, like the Mother, and the Boss, have to guide the Creator there.) So despite the omnipotent sounding name, he has to take his cue from others: give, rather than impose; respond appropriately, sensitively, to given conditions, rather than go off at a tangent of his own that will add nothing desirable to the situation as he finds it.

Thus the Creator at his best is a fulfiller of needs and wishes: from his point of view it really doesn't matter at all what exactly he 'creates', produces, brings about, what life role he enacts for the benefit of others. He can pull anything at all out of his vast inner store, his inherent potential. Anything that suits others, will automatically suit him as well – as long as there is plenty of variety, that is. Variety is not just the spice of life, but life itself for him: it is his becoming, in ever new ways (his becoming self-aware from all sorts of newly visible angles, that is). It is his gradual unfolding out of his own dark, hidden depths: a purely inner life taking on concrete form, an entirely transcending reality pushed into the light and time/space of what we call 'real' life.

So he is a giver, a provider, a generous patron, and so on. And obviously a sociable sort as well, whether host or life and soul of the party, or family man, or public entertainer... in each instance getting the kind of feed-back from others that allows him to get in touch with himself – to simply 'feel himself' at all. But there are wider implications that tie in with this pattern.

Variety, to put it like that, is the way he moves forward from one bit of self-realisation to another. He gets to know himself piecemeal, over time; something his fiery nature does tend to chafe at, rather. But if this is not to be a series of sudden and insensitive *impositions* on his part, then he needs to learn to transform his environment gradually, work respectfully within his given parameters. Transform, rather than sweep away and replace; change gently, rather than transform abruptly; and always bear others' needs in mind.

Also, he may be a transformer, but at the same time he is an establisher and unifier by nature. For one thing, his holistic nature demands it. And, in the long view, it is standing completely revealed (to himself) in the world that is the aim – even if gradually, piecemeal, is the only way of achieving it: ongoing becoming, life. Those bits and pieces after all add up, hang together, inside himself. And so they must hang together for him where he can see them as well. Consequently, he works hard to ensure that none of his contributions should be found wanting, be easily abandoned or forgotten again by anyone: he needs to be universally appreciated, widely loved, and memorable. By logical extension, supposing he throws a party, it would hurt him to see his guests fall out, or to find some of them go away hungry while others have been able to overindulge. In short, any situation of his making should be evidence of his integrity, reflect his inner wholeness.

It is tempting, initially, to see him just as a kind of sugar daddy who simply gives whatever one may demand of him. But it soon becomes obvious that some basic rules have to be respected if one wants to keep him happy and handing it out. He will insist on fairness, tolerance and peace, for example. He will ask of the totally catholic mix of people he attracts and surrounds himself with (variety!) that they treat each other respectfully, as equals. Anything else would only present him with a painful picture of himself, a splintered mirror image. Those who want to profit from his gifts, his limitless generosity, have to learn to live up to his expectations of harmonious wholeness. No archetypal sugar daddy then, but more of a Beneficial Ruler figure whose laws are well worth obeying.

If one looks at the whole pattern in some more depth though, one can see the falling apart of a basic unity, followed by a different kind of coming together again. A giving up of the simple integrity that prevails within (eternally, as it were), in order to find piecemeal self-realisation in time/space and matter. So we find the intriguing image here of a self-sacrificing Creator who rends himself asunder so that (his) life might come about. And the whole point of the splintering, many-creating process is that the One should know himself – through his becoming aware of a multitude of others. Not, ultimately, 'obedient' others, but others whom he has to serve, respect, take into account, love – not unilaterally dictate to. The Creator as Cosmic Servant. Something to ponder, maybe, in connection with this particular pattern; though, as I say, they can all be taken as symbols of (our) divinity, each a different aspect.

If we were to say, simply, that the Creator impulse is about 'finding yourself', this would probably give the wrong impression. It suggests an entirely individualistic, self-indulgent activity that could easily direct one's attention away from others altogether. Quite the contrary applies, as we have seen. At its best, getting in touch with our inner self means developing a creative generosity that recognises others' requirements and puts them above our own momentary urge to 'realise' ourselves in any particular way. And hand in hand with this we develop the moral authority to promote a general spirit of fairness and justice in the world. To 'recognise' others, as such, as our fellows and equals, simply goes with properly, awarely, being ourselves: it's the way we are designed, it's inscribed in us.

The worst scenario (and every possibility in between) is of course also given – in that each inner script is set only in so far as the basic task itself is concerned: the scene is thoroughly set, and what we can most positively and most negatively make of it follows logically, really. What we do in effect make of it, and all the myriad of subtle interpretations we bring to it, is down to a mixture of free choice and environmental pressures, as I will discuss later in this book.

Without the right support from other motivational strands, the Creator in us can of course never find the kind of self-control and loving responsiveness, never mind attention to detail and concentration on the job in hand, that are all part and parcel of the creative process. Instead, there is only a passive expectation to see it all happen, to have his identity dished up to him visibly on a plate.

He can recognise himself in any passing stranger, knowing no better. Any show one might put on for him will momentarily satisfy his hunger for identity: the shining hero on the screen is he. - But the other one, the professional baddie antagonist too, is he. Sooner or later, incapable of introspection though he may be, the very fracturedness of such random mirror images will tell him that something must be wrong. He expects to find, not just identity, but integrity with it. He objects to being plucked apart.

Uncontrolled, insensitive, slapdash attempts on his part to replace this unsatisfactory feedback, to paint a truer portrait of himself in the world, don't get him anywhere either, except in a rage. He ends up throwing the paint pot and blaming others. It has to be said that others, to him, are only the raw material that should yield up the sense of self that is his by birthright: and some dreadfully stubborn stuff it is too. He is soon complaining bitterly. His querulous tantrums bring everyone running.

He becomes convinced that if he persists long enough in shouting for it loudly enough, then the world will give him at last what it owes him. Impotent in himself, not even trying in fact, he simply becomes one monstrous demand. Issuer of commands is the only role he is fit to play, while those around him have to take on all the roles he fails to take up actively. One gives to him and does for him, and he promptly looks for more, naturally. One gives him more, and he objects that it's the same thing again: he wants something *different*. Of course he does; variety is his life blood. So one gives him something totally different... and now he moans because one has fallen foul of his expectations of seamless integrity. Whatever one does for him is always insufficient, boring, and somehow deeply threatening - possibly all at the same time.

A ceaselessly howling infant may, rightly, spring to mind. But there are plenty of adult versions to draw on, and since variety is the name of the game, we can recognise the dark side of the Creator in many guises. There is the helpless exhibitionist, and the for ever puzzled voyeur as well. And the vain show-off strutting around in his borrowed plumage, obviously unaware that the grand identity he trumpets is strictly a second-hand (a mediated) affair. Look at me! is a perfectly reasonable request, if only he would work for all the attention he gets. Meantime the autocratic megalomaniac who parades about town clothed in nothing more than admiration and applause is not just absurd, but dangerous.

At his worst the Creator quite fails to put anything (new) into the world and instead commandeers, appropriates, uses, consumes endlessly. Which is bad enough, but the matter hardly stops there. He is also a prime instance of the naked will to power: wanting, in effect, to be the only one in the world; wanting, in effect, to be accorded that position without having to lift a finger. One might just ignore him. But though he may not learn how to give of himself properly, he works out soon enough how to misuse his unique talent for giving – and in the process he tears the unity of the world apart: he literally divides and rules.

To get others to serve him, to make and build and fetch and re-do, and generally transform the face of the earth in his name, he has to pay them, bribe them, feed them vain promises if nothing else, fuel the process somehow. But of course his rules keep changing, and so does his workforce, the puppets who dance his life for him. He bestows favours here one moment, and there the next. Consequently quarrels, intrigues and plots how to get into his good books soon abound. And while his current favourites grow fat, others have to go without altogether.

Instead of giving himself into life, piecemeal over time – as mere momentary aspects of himself, that is – he passively demands to be given himself, and in one big lump sum at that (mass demonstrations, thousands chanting his name, will do nicely). And he further demands to be a hundred per cent reliably received wherever he goes (forgetting his name is unforgivable, turning one's back on him an unpardonable crime). Yet at the same time he insists on being presented with ever new aspects of himself (his nearest and dearest scurry to put on increasingly weird fashion shows for him; they might consider the odd nose job as well). Humility is obviously not for him, so to be merely first among equals is clearly not an option. But his endlessly self-contradictory commands are the worst part of it: they create a climate of fear and constant behind-the-scenes battles, with an ever-changing cast of rising stars and wretches newly fallen from grace. Variety of sorts there may be, after all. But unity and integrity are shattered, any kindness and fairness forgotten, inequalities become rife. This is the effect he has on others, just being himself.

And all the while he can't help getting increasingly paranoid. He is forever suspecting that something is being withheld from him. Of course it is: that's life. But he doesn't understand the bittiness of life-in-time, and that he has to restrain his urge to live up to his fullest potential, all of it, *now*, not just for others' sake, but for his own. After all, if he holds nothing back, what future does he have? But, big baby that he is, others have to keep him in check all the time, for his own good – not that they reap any thanks. His grasp of 'others' remains just as non-existent as his understanding of the most fundamental life processes. He may have momentary favourites to admire his own self-image in, but as they come and go at every erratic unself-controlled whim of his, really 'they' are all the same to him: just an anonymous matrix for him to foist his name on. Anyone sticking out in the mass, individualists who make a bid for personhood in their own right, are perceived not so much as rivals (ie on an equal footing with him) but as some utterly incomprehensible threat to him, his life, the very depths of his being.

He never does gain any proper self-knowledge. Self, other, and the mutual dependence between the two, it all stays a mystery to him. No wonder then that he is so easy to take advantage of, hoodwinked and milked for what he is worth, in his ignorance and total dependence. Many will be tempted, but they are playing with fire.

Ultimately, he does not flinch from murder. Let no one try and claim the right to be themselves – there is only one self to be in the whole world: his. Consequently, anyone trying to steal it from him should not be surprised to find themselves liquidated on the spot. And, sadly, the same goes for any who assault him once too often simply with personal failure. Failure, that is, to show him an acceptable face: making him look shabby in his own eyes, when what he is used to by now is feed-back that looks gratify-ingly and dependably impressive, at a mere snap of his fingers.

Someone's poverty of 'performance' may be his fault entirely, due to his uneven distribution of goods and favours, his neglect to provide and care for all impartially. The unfair culture of haves and have-nots he has created may even be brewing up a civil war. But blame is not something he can own, any more than he has truly got in touch with his inner being. A stranger to himself, he simply cannot cope with any uncalled-for otherness in others. They are not so much enemies to him as monsters, unreal, aliens in his universe, and deeply frightening to the absurd tyrant he has become. They have to be destroyed.

This is the ultimate irony: the Creator in us turned destroyer – setting up a mad, repetitive cycle of creation/destruction, in fact – and all from fear of 'others'. Others who, ultimately and if we would but understand them in that light, just show us other aspects of our own limitless possibilities of being self in the world.

The Healer

When it came to naming this pattern, it took me a long time to decide. So many things suggested themselves: the Mender, for instance, the Bridge-builder and Mediator, Communicator, Messenger. He can also be teacher, trader, craftsman, organiser... to mention just some of his jobs in life. He is a veritable Everyman, and pinning him down to any particular role isn't easy. In the end, Healer seemed to me to encapsulate the essence of what he is about: assembling disjointed parts together, making whole (again).

In the last chapter we had a look at the relationship between the One and the many, our integral inner potential and the multiplicity of practical expressions it can take in the world. That was one aspect of this relationship, the Creator's side of the story. With the Healer we take a look at it from a different angle.

As the reader will by now have noticed, our motivation patterns come in twos. A common basic theme or task, with two often very dissimilar ways of handling it. Two extraverting extraverts: Hunter and Maker, simple and straightforward seekers of an identity to call their own. The Artist/Destroyer pair, both introverting extraverts, both 'inspired' seekers with a 'background talent' of dynamic insight. Thinker and Priest: two seekers who eventually introject their gains, who introvert and in some degree come to resemble inward be-ers.

And now, among the true inward be-ers, we have this pair of extraverting introverts, Creator and Healer: both ignorant of their already given identity, having to actively seek for its reflection in their environment. But again, there are crucial differences in their basic make-up and hence in the way they function, the role they have to play.

The Creator is all Fire and holistic intuition; he looks to find the whole of himself reflected in the mirror of the world, in one grand go, if possible. The Healer, for his part, uses his various senses – he quite literally sees, and hears, smells, feels, tastes himself reflected in his current environment. And his Element is Air, indicative of thoughtful analysis.

Where the Creator automatically tries to hang together, is reluctant to find himself pulled apart, and has to learn to give of himself/find himself only piecemeal, there the Healer has no problem at all with 'coming apart'. *His* identity automatically scatters itself into small pieces, ends up strewn all over the place. Because he looks for it, at it, in a different way: in sensual and analytical detail. So many details, his inner integrity is quite lost to him. Fitting himself, and with it the world, together again is his task, his function in life. He is a jigsaw kind of puzzle to himself. He is the Wounded Healer of legend, eternally mending the broken limbs that constitute his own torn and scattered condition.

If I use words like torn, broken and wounded, I don't mean to imply sickness and pain, specifically, though that may be part of it. Primarily, what we are looking at is simply a state of disjointedness which asks to be mended, because *essentially* things do hang together. Bittiness, variety, and with it divergence, is the way of the world, the way life takes place, in effect. But at bottom, really, it all comes out of the same pot. In the transcending Reality, it hangs together, meaningfully. That is the story behind our Healer impulse, looking at it from a more philosophical angle, if you like.

Obviously, synthesis is the keyword here. Equally obviously, this can take a million and one forms. Hence the figure of Everyman is apt. Each man and woman in the street tries to 'get it together', somehow. All of us try to re-member our inner wholeness: the only way we'll ever make *sense* of our individual selfhood. 'Becoming centred' is another way of putting it. And this particular circuitous route to getting in touch with the inner centre – the Healer's way – is via collecting, and then connecting, all the odds and loose ends we find in the world, then pasting all those scraps into one unifying book.

For the Healer in us to work well it needs a bit of thoughtful concentration as well as an intuitive grasp of how things might fit together, and the wish to be actually helpful, rather than just tinker with things haphazardly – all these to be supplied by the other introvert impulses. Ideally then, the Healer in us stops going in all directions at once like an untrained child, but sits down at his desk and learns the basics, focuses on his central task of setting in context, 'adding up', making sense, making whole.

Versatility begins to take the place of scatteredness. And more sophisticated forms of connection-making gradually take over from simply stringing letters together to make cats sit on mats. He builds roads, designs bridges, engineers reunions, plays matchmaker. He talks and writes, broadcasts, teaches, researches, informs, all with a view to enabling others/himself to get a glimpse of the larger picture and begin to make sense of things. He reconciles sworn enemies; he glues the shards; mops up the spillage; devises the schedule for a public event; stitches that cut lip; finds the lost toy; negotiates another export order. The list of examples one could enumerate is literally endless.

Once he has learned how to join all the right dots, he automatically transcends the superficial level. He goes at a task with more than a fair idea of what the whole will look like (in a sense already looks like, in the dimension of potential and meaning). He is ready to recognise that he himself innately transcends the bittiness of his current life situations as they come and go. Comings and goings at first did disturb him rather – representing sporadic losses of self – but by now he knows from experience that the missing will always be found, in some form, and that new things inevitably find a meaningful place in the existing order, sooner or later, somewhere. This is the nearest he will get to knowing himself as a unity. It is enough for him though to rest assured, relax: the invisible centre *will* hold. And practising his unique craft, he can reassure others, too: he not only doctors the superficial ills, but in a sense delivers a practical message of something inner-dimensional, transcendent.

When he works to his best potential, his doings cease to be haphazard and accidental and become meaningful, purposive. Thus he transcends the 'accident', the wreckage and spillage of his own coming to life. Things literally come together for him, and ultimately they make for something of a different, higher order. When he looks in his world mirror he sees himself as an endless number of disparate *facts*, things that exist, and situations in which he finds himself playing a multitude of roles, bit parts. But together it all hints at the underlying *truth* about him. Just like the dots that are really, already, a complete picture. He'll never be able to hold this world picture at enough of a distance, so to speak, to save himself the work of actually, laboriously drawing those lines in between – but that is as it should be. Else we would have no (re)connection-making function. And no universal Healer in us to embrace all others as brothers: everyone an equally valid dot on the page, and every page an inalienable part of the reflection of the Whole.

Complex character that he is, like the Priest the Healer has two downsides to him, best understood as active and passive. In both instances his basic outward disunity never does find its own cure: inconsistent, unpredictable, erratic, fickle – his life is a long tattered list of broken promises, forgotten bits, chronic disorder, chaos. There is quite a difference though whether he just allows this to happen, or cleverly brings it about by design. Let's have look at him in passive mode first.

A sense of his inner unity is really what he needs to find, and in order to find it, to engineer. But he is far too wrong-headedly wilful about it: he brings no patient application to the job, or any of the other psychological tools he would need. Instead, he simply takes – grabs, pounces on – every single life situation as a reflection of the whole of him. Utter acceptance and contentment reign... till something disappears from view, crumbles, melts, fades out; or else breaks in on the situation, appears as from nowhere, illogically adds itself to the 'whole' of him that he thought he was grasping so securely. At which point his passive illusion is shattered, of course.

He does his best, in his unfocused, 'shortsighted' and generally discombobulated way, to guard against such horrors. He encapsulates himself, as far as possible. He sits in his blanket-curtained cardboard box, clutching one sturdy toy, playing the same game over and over. Let no one intrude, even to offer him food: it is no kindness to offer him anything. It only tells him that he hasn't got it all, hasn't seen it all and done it all, doesn't know it all. He protests most strongly against such assertions. He treasures his monotony. He loves being stuck in his narrow groove. Repeating himself is all he ever wants to do. If people won't stop springing horrible surprises on him, then he'll talk to dead things instead: much safer.

His wilfully limited outlook and stubborn insistence don't get him anywhere, of course. His life would literally grind to a halt if others did not drag him out of his box, jolt him out of his groove, get him to sing a different tune. The funny thing is, once his cherished status quo has been disturbed, he really couldn't care less what he settles for next. He will accept any substitute or alternative activity: one thing has always been as good as the next to him. He is as ready as ever to recognise 'his like' in anyone at all, so he is perfectly pleased to keep company with whoever might chance along, once his initial reluctance has been swept aside. Push a sweetie under his nose forcefully enough and he will come along *whole-heartedly*.

His concentration on the (short) moment, his focus on the (tiny) detail, prevent him from ever taking stock of the wider world. He saves himself the bother of having to 'add up', make mental or indeed any other connections. Instead he clings to something small and simple as if it were all there was – and, forcefully disabused of his current illusion, quickly adopts another one. Thus he finds himself exchanging one 'life box' for another, and the whole never comes together for him. He forgets. He does not plan ahead. He is constitutionally untidy: leaves things lying, never turns back. Past and future are insufferable intrusions on the all-important now. He fails to learn. He fails to make any kind of smooth progress, moving unaccountably from one craze, obsession, style or persuasion to another, all punctuated by frequent crises. He lives his life in a string of such boxes, each as different from the last as could be. He sees no problem with that, no inconsistence. One remonstrates with him to no good effect. He is good at not listening to what doesn't fit his current idea of self. And what he did yesterday, well, that can't – no really, honestly! – have been him. To say he lies never captures the flavour of it.

He is a picture of self-contradiction if ever there was one. An expert on minutiae; a complete idiot. Trusting and all-accepting in his ignorance; yet regarding as taboo anything that goes against his current grain. Obsessively clinging to the well-worn and established, repetitive and apparently impervious to change; and totally disloyal, fickle and unpredictable. He seizes up, and then it is all rush. His progress through life is a series of involuntary jerks. Short-lived phases and fashions. Unexpected conversions. Sudden thoughtless enthusiasms, at someone else's behest. It is all puzzling skips and hops with him.

He means no harm. He will be popular with some: a bit like a superior wind-up toy; crank hard and you can get him to do anything you like. His thoughtless mimicry, simply *being* some other person, to the exclusion of all else, is also appreciated. Indeed he is funny in all sorts of respects – till one becomes a victim of his untrustworthiness, realises just how amoral he is, lacking in depth and trueness to self. He is a parasite, staying a dependent child all his years, getting others to manoeuvre him with much pushing and shoving through his own life.

Don't recognise yourself in that at all? Next time you find yourself refuting an argument with 'Oh well, *that's* totally different', dismissing it, discounting it... have another read of how the Healer in us is so easily tempted to take shortcuts to making sense of world and self.

Where the Healer is concerned, there is simply no curtailing the endless labours of productive all-acceptance: weaving each new thing that appears on the horizon into the one fabric of life. Only that way can he/we truly, wholly, come in touch with the inner self. Cheating, leaving all sorts of bits out, just means we will come unravelled, sooner or later. The one thing we can say with certainty about this pattern.

Coming to the active type, the story takes a different twist again. He, too, happily recognises his given inner potential in all and everything that goes on round about him. He, too, needs to actively work out how it/he hangs together: in space, slotting things into meaningful places; in time, getting to grips with the consecutive nature of life, things following on from, things going in cyclical rounds, disappearing, reappearing. Subjective wholeness meeting its objective counterpart through a smooth flow of meaningful reactions: functioning in a way that makes overall sense.

We have seen how the above character failed in this task. All those irrational lumps and bumps and hops and jumps, and only reinforcing the disunity of the world by establishing categorically separate closed compartments. But his equally no-good sibling here makes a very different mess of things. His attempts at world-uniting take the form of a ceaseless, hectic, indiscriminate mixing:

stirring it and stirring it, allowing nothing to settle, making sure nothing ever gets a chance to take on a definite shape that might stick out from the mass. Any separateness, distinctness and distinctiveness, is simply anathema to him.

He will not be found huddling in corners, refusing to look at the new and the different. On the contrary, keeping him still for a moment is a struggle, keeping him from sticking his nose in everything quite impossible. He would instantly seize it all as his: his business to know, his place to make himself at home in, his things and people to keep in touch with. Everything-all-in-one-go is what he wants to grasp hold of, grasp objectively – not understanding of course that the lump sum of his wholeness lies in the subjective dimension, not out there; not all at the same time, anyway. Determined to find it there though, he chases from one place to another, needing to hear, see, lay his hands on the lot: wait! that's me! that's mine!

He takes what doesn't belong to him. He feels quite justified in being a thief, though he'd hardly be able to explain himself. Less concretely, he snoops, eavesdrops, spies, intrudes shamelessly. Closed doors are an affront to him, the very concept of privacy is a pain. He makes it his business to unlock, prise open, winkle out every secret.

His manic rush to contact everything at once has him constantly dashing hither and thither without apparent good cause. Frenetic, hyperactive, inclined to run off altogether – just to make sure nothing is escaping him there, on the horizon – erratic, chaotic, slapdash: no wonder he frequently trips himself up in his careless haste, has accidents at every turn.

But can they really be called accidents? His inconsistency is far from being a matter of passive helplessness, of accepting whatever might happen to him, the way his 'brother' does. As a matter of fact, he is working hard at being inconsistent. The reason is simple, and so fiendishly clever as to be totally daft. He wants to recognise (preferably at one easy glance) his 'oneness', his inner unity, when he looks at his mirror-image environment. In short, he wants the world to be one single, amorphous mass, with not a single thing separate or noticeable in itself. Hence he drops large things, so they all break into a mess of littler pieces; knocks things down; scatters every orderly pile; dismantles and leaves the fragments nicely strewn about. He deconstructs the world. He also redistributes it – steals here, only to 'generously' give there – not so much in the name of equality as we would positively understand it, as a moral principle, but simply for the sake of the sameness he desires so much. And with all this shuffling and shifting he is, actually, 'shifty', his quite deliberate clumsiness 'crafty'. There's a lot more to him than surface appearance tells us – or him. He is certainly deceitful, but since self-deception is part and parcel of the situation, it is not at all easy to decide whether to judge him innocent or guilty!

One can see him as an amusing scallywag, with a kind of Robin Hood appeal thrown in for good measure. But the more sides of him one gets to know, the more worrying the picture becomes. He is the harmless nosey parker, certainly; and the newshound who quite legitimately trades in people's secrets; but also the eternally subversive double agent; the trickster, the conman with no regard at all for individuals (*what* individuality?!); the scandalmonger and blackmailer who engineers the downfall of prominent personalities, and the insidious tempter who would corrupt and drag down any who dare occupy the moral high ground... Levelling out, creating a homogenous mass, a faceless crowd, subject to the rule of a non-negotiable common denominator, this is the aim. Helping the lowly-placed to rise in the world is, with him, not a matter of recognising the essentially equal worth of all, as separate parts of the one life fabric, but simply one aspect of his clever, foolish, calculating ploy.

With his constant, inconstant, manipulations, he has become a sly and secretive creature, full of pretence, false promises and deceptive appearances. He will hardly know himself who or what he is from one moment to the next. Even his lies don't hang together. They are just words he grabs in passing, to plug an unhandy gap with. He is only fooling himself if he thinks running just that little bit faster and pulling off just one more trick will get him there: as a whole, he constantly undermines himself, trips himself up, does himself in, his one given identity subsumed in a multitude of 'faces', his integrity gone.

So he throws an endless number of spanners in his own ceaseless works, and then complains that life is beastly to him. He feels hard done by, pained by life's horrible habits: growth (pull it down!), birth and death (trickery! theft!). But all it proves is that he has failed to grow up, or 'grow in': to realise, in all respects, the nature of his unique, integral inner-self. As it is, he scattered himself to the four winds in the beginning, and now, with all the frantic string-pulling in the world, he is still his own undoing. Only more so.

The Boss

With the Boss we move on to another pair of motivation patterns: Boss and Mother, essential introverts both, though dynamically as much outward- as inward-directed. Where Thinker and Priest had to find their way inwards, these two have to see their way to 'coming out of themselves'.

So let's start with the Boss in us – not the most Feminine of our impulses by any means, but since it has if anything less of a Masculine feel to it, I shall refer to it here as 'she'. Her function is thought; her Element Earth; and she is an introverting/extraverting introvert. Translating this, the picture we get is of a constitutionally deep thinker, one who is thoughtfully, and awarely, in touch with her inner being. For her, there is no mystery attached to who she might be, no circuitous route to self-knowledge via other. Consciously inward-turning, she makes sense to herself, inside herself.

What's more, as the 'introverting introvert' she (partly) is, she is quite capable of transcending her personal inner self: having an inner life, that is changing inside herself – as even settled be-ers must, if they are to be alive inside themselves. Inner Reality, our Creative Base, to her is simply her own inner environment, where she can find all she needs for her own future becoming, after her own fashion. Even to start with, she is nothing if not a purely 'ideas person'. She is all abstract, all underlying and surpassing logic, a pretty fleshless thought-construct of a being... never mind then constantly dipping into some far out Ideas Realm (as it will appear to her) for her personal progress and develop-ment. In short, content and lacking for nothing in her inner world, she would remove herself even further from life in the flesh.

But there is also the 'extraverting introvert' part of her make-up: her ability to direct thought outwards, in search of a future for herself *there*. This too, simply by virtue of existing, demands to be lived out. And there lies the crunch of course. How does such a fine and tidy abstraction as she is apply herself to 'real' life in all its messiness? Disorder everywhere, stupid actions and senseless constructions, a meaningless coming and going of stray bits and pieces: no obvious plan or coherent structure to any of it. And in this she must take part, find her rightful place in, find her concrete future?

The first thought that occurs to her (after the initial sniff of contempt) is that this is some kind of test: her ideas will have to be put into real-life action now. Her otherworldly kind of understanding, pure reason and pristine principles, all have to prove themselves in the flesh-and-blood application. A whole wrong-headed world is asking to be sorted out, put to rights. She, all-knowing, has the job, single-handed, to tell others how to do things properly: it would appear to be her duty.

The more she ponders it, comparing perfect Theory with prevailing practice, the more she dreads such a seemingly impossible task. As a thinker, she is no stranger to self-examination; and noticing the huge disparity between her and others' understanding of things, she can't avoid a measure of self-doubt, when it comes to the crunch. It doesn't help either that her share of the world's work is not exactly given an enthusiastic welcome. She is hardly fun to have around: being hyper-logical is one thing – but principled to the point of complete inflexibility, invariably strict, over-conscientious, judgmental, for ever banging on about the right and wrong ordering of all things... who wants to hear it? Worst of all, she has a point every time, if one cares to think about it deeply enough (of course she does, with her concepts all drawn from the Creative Base in its rational aspect: a sort of limitless fund of Faultless Ideas). But her intellectually pure, or purely intellectual, approach is not really all that helpful, as it stands.

Above all, she needs lightening and loosening up. The Healer's talents are needed here: a bit of flexible accommodation to things as they happen to be would make all the difference, help to leaven that dreary ponderousness. And she has to learn – same old lesson – to truly give her gifts, not impose them in an exercise of compulsive self-will. She will also do well to take on board the idea that others have a role to play in her life story: accepting her, validating her ideas, and thus making it possible for her to actively be all she is meant to be. This last would be the Creator's contribution, something that would serve to both give her the courage of her convictions *and* knock some of that arrogance of the intellectually self-sufficient out of her.

Humility. Sensitivity to need. A measure of flexibility. We can now imagine her more successfully going about her business: ordering, structuring, injecting both method and ethics where they have been lacking; guiding, counselling, teaching and generally 'bossing' people – but without causing offence or alienating others with too rigid a code of conduct. Maybe even managing not to get bogged down in excessively deep thought processes when all that's needed, really, is a bit of tinkering with minor details.

What she needs to work towards is that others should *accept* her as an authority figure: as one who 'knows better', but who also knows how to share her knowledge in a caring way, respecting others' feelings, their illogical habits, their idiosyncratic ways that don't always tie in with what's best. She does have to work hard, in all sorts of ways, to prove her abstract self in action, as it were. But in the last resort it is only her respecting others' integrity that will earn her, in turn, their respect. Regard and esteem, rather than cowed, browbeaten obedience; and enough of it to allow her to do her job as properly as an imperfect world will allow.

Parent might have been another apt name for her; Guide might have served too. She is obviously designed to keep us on the right track, and the proverbial straight and narrow one at that. A comparison with the Thinker pattern may be helpful here. The Thinker, too, applies much intellectual rigour, builds up a fund of knowledge, eventually has the basis of an inner-guide or conscience to work from. But as a thoughtful extravert she chooses her knowledge from out of the imperfect world out there. Hers is a partial knowledge, at best; while her conscience is very much a DIY affair. Interesting, helpful, challenging – but hardly what you could call authoritative.

The Boss in us, at her best, manages to be truly authoritative because she continues to look inward for guidance. Deeply inward, way beyond whatever personal thoughts or ideas she is currently identified with, towards new inspiration from out of that matrix of underlying Thought Patterns and First Principles, to put it another way again. It is, by the way, up to the reader how literally they want to take this Inner Reality, as such: there are many ways of interpreting it, as we will see later. But for the purpose of understanding why our individual motivation patterns take the form, or actions, they do it is vital simply to take it as read, for the time being. –

It is entirely necessary that the Boss in us should continue to grow (and hence change) in inner understanding, at the same time as she also grows into an understanding of the uncertain ways of the material world. That inward growth gives her added flexibility: a wider range of ideas to offer, and a better grasp that there may be more than one point of view that makes sense. In the end, while she may be a dab hand at laying down the law, it isn't just one lumpish, ever-same law. Things are allowed to depend a bit, she can be reasoned and argued with... as long as one speaks truthfully to her, that is.

A Boss figure who is perfectly amenable and caring one can live with, welcome even. But the only way for her to achieve that kind of standing in the world is to maintain a healthy balance between an active inner life – where she can be as bossily sure of herself as she likes, to put it like that – and (a restrained, limited) involvement in the life around her. It is only that kind of self-discipline that gives any legitimacy to her role as disciplinarian, moral and general authority figure.

But we can extend this picture further and, strangely, in two diametrically opposed directions. On the one hand we can see her, not just as literally the boss who calls the shots, but also as the reliable employee: with her own, private, inner life, but also a parallel life where she has to fit in with – obey – the rules of material existence. That is one role she plays, that of obedient servant knuckling under, listening to the demands of a 'lesser', physical world.

But only up to a point. Her inner life, where it transcends her personal self and allows her a glimpse of Truth, ultimately takes precedence over the uncertain facts and figures, not to mention the dubious expediency, of life in the flesh. There are the seeds here of dissent. She is quite capable of disobedience, making a stand against the prevailing, less than *truly* sensible ways of the world, the non-sense of greed, cruelty, corruption and the like. Which brings us back to the (moral) authority figure. And how, from that position, does she deal with others when they quite refuse to 'behave themselves'?

Respecting others, as we have seen, is the key to her personal success, her self-completion (as being both thoughtfully inward-turned, abstract, and ever outward-turning, Earth-ily). Overpowering others, pulling rank as one who inherently 'knows better', is not an option, then. But the only other way to stop them committing crassly foolish acts is the way of the wise parent: to sneak the dangerous toy out by the back door unseen. This is the subversive side of the Boss. Scrupulously obedient to inner Law, when it comes to having to obey the laws of material necessity as well, the choices she has to make are hard ones.

Ultimately, she is responsible to both the worlds she inhabits, inner and outer. No matter how sure of all the right answers she is inside herself, and how well versed in the ways of the physical world, she continues to have to think hard and long how to apply pure Idea to living practice, transcendent self to life with others.

By now, I suppose, the reader will have no great difficulty imagining this pattern in its negative manifestation. It is nevertheless worth looking at it in detail, to examine some of the less obvious implications.

The first thing that goes out the window is her initial hesitancy, her natural self-doubt when faced with such an alien world and the task of making a valid contribution to it. Full of a sense of her own superior knowledge, she declares the world a complete shambles and everyone in it a total idiot... she'll soon sort them all out! Her inner certainty is ready to be translated into unrestrained action. With the arrogance of the all-knowing, she approaches life clutching a whole long codex entitled Rules of Life. And she means to apply it, neat, without hesitation, humility or kindness.

What happens, of course, is that everyone tries to give her the slip. She'll have to work harder than that: at the end of the day she still needs everyone's co-operation, acceptance of some sort. A dictator without dictatees, after all, would add up to something of a non-event.

If she can't – won't – adapt surpassing knowledge to fit the circumstances a bit, to suit the individuals she is dealing with, and thus make it a genuine gift (without, obviously, abandoning the broad principle altogether), then the least she needs to do now to earn some acceptance is *to be obviously clever*. There's nothing succeeds like success. Showing herself to be usefully knowledgeable, having all the answers that earn real material benefits, is the carrot she soon learns to dangle. Acquiescence, obedience, slavish observance of umpteen rules and regulations is a price worth paying, it would appear, when there are substantial gains to be made.

Ruler was the first name for her that sprang to mind, but I soon abandoned it as too suggestive of a flamboyant, crown-wearing sort of figure. Flamboyant this particular despot is certainly not. The image of a dreary, greyly repetitive bureaucrat churning out a mass of forbidding forms is far more apt. Both ponderous and relentlessly finicky. Rationalistic to the point of absurdity. For ever issuing instructions, with copious footnotes, that leave no room whatsoever for creative interpretation. Dogmatic, strictly moralistic, endlessly 'lecturing' and finger-wagging. Uncompromising, rigid, predictable. Her thought-patterns are set, her mind made up. She is of course intolerant of others' opinions. Convinced that she knows It All, as such, 'objectively', she holds any dissenting voices to be no more than expressions of individual stupidity... and above all 'merely subjective'.

In other words, she takes herself to be personally identified with that realm of supreme knowledge she used to dip into for her personal, inner growth. In fact, with all that striving for mundane acceptance, she has quite lost touch with it. She never even finds time for inner being, never mind inward becoming, she is so busy pursuing worldly gain, public standing and sanction and validation. All her becoming now is a becoming more concrete: increasingly, she works herself into the established structure of the world, the accepted form, the orthodox practice.

Her sole aim, in a sense, has been to be have her ruthlessly imposed 'gifts' taken off her hands. And in the struggle to somehow make the unwelcome palatable she never flinched from prostituting her deep, insightful knowledge, debasing it, making it serve as superficial cleverness, for superficial gain. She has become a slave to outward success. And this is precisely the practical example and moral tone she sets for others to follow: simply, mindlessly, obey. Give up any ideas of being someone separate, subjectively, inside yourself. Forget about 'higher' considerations as well, having principles, following your conscience – just follow the rules.

Whether the Boss in us gets a chance to act as slave driver, or urges us on to be willing slaves and abject conformists ourselves, the motivation, the mentality, is entirely the same.

It is a hollow success, of course, nothing truly worthwhile or lasting. She is the archetypal materialistic reductionist: for her there is nothing beyond the bottom line, the cash reward, obvious expediency and apparent progress – nothing beyond the physical level of being and becoming at all. Just an endless round of dreary striving for more and more 'success'; and not for the pleasures it offers, ultimately, sitting back and enjoying the fruits, but success purely for its own sake. She is a manic kind of boss; a hopeless workaholic; a busy puppet of prevailing 'form'.

She has failed to develop the self-restraint that would have enabled her to maintain a balance between inner and outward life. Arrogant and undisciplined, she has thrown her all into extraverting, 'forgotten about' the introvert she essentially is, and in the process not just debased but truly denatured herself. She has long stopped obeying inner laws and rules of conduct: watered down, twisted, sold off her conscience bit by bit in a relentless bid for 'acceptability' – and while initially she thought she could just please herself, she has actually ended up, cravenly, pleasing the world. No longer thoughtfully in touch with a self-transcending inner dimension, she has long stopped learning anything new. Her much advertised understanding is after all only limited, faulty. Not a living lesson of superlative ideas to be drawn on, but only a sterile, set text.

That is why, in the last analysis, her gains prove to be ephemeral, spurious, only 'apparent' ones. *Appearances* – like her own compulsive, exclusive, immersion in the material sphere – is all her life boils down to. A meagre harvest that can only, sooner or later, lead to real hardship.

The Mother

Most of what I have said about the basic nature of the Boss goes
for the Mother in us as well. But the function employed is feeling
rather than thought; the Element is Water, not Earth: this is a
pattern that operates entirely at the emotional level.

Feeling, as we have seen, is not only holistic but pours-out-into,
fills the forms around it and gets to know them from the inside,
so to speak. This makes the Mother's story a very different one
from that of the Boss, despite the fact that they are both intro-
verting/extraverting introverts. Let's look at the inner being and
becoming part of it first. Where the Boss knows herself in rational-
analytical detail, the Mother understands herself primarily as a
whole. She experiences herself as emotionally intact, you might
say, inside herself. Likewise, where the Boss makes contact with
a self-transcending Source of ideas, the Mother – in touch with
the same Inner Reality – *feels* herself to be part of a larger Whole
that nourishes her personal inner growth.

The difference really becomes apparent the moment these two
begin to extravert. The Boss, all logical scrutiny and practical
considerations, hovers and dithers and has her doubts. Not so the
Mother: it is a case of (emotional-holistic) all or nothing with her.
She will throw herself in at the deep end with never a question
in her mind. Something like trust in essential, underlying wholesomeness is built into her at the outset. She never suspects the
emotional shock and pain that await her. But simply pouring all
her feelings indiscriminately outward – into the diverse, scattered
and utterly contradictory parts of the world around her – she only
comes to feel indescribably stressed, broken even.

And another thing: if any aspect of her isn't given a positive
reception, she will interpret that as a complete rejection. Aspects,
parts, of herself are not within her inner line of experience. As
far as she is concerned, if you don't love all of her, you don't love
her at all. Result: she goes off in a huff, withdraws inward to nurse
a mighty hurt... only to re-emerge later, emotionally restored, yet
again nothing daunted.

To a purely rational observer, her outward behaviour makes no sense at all; but then the outward behaviour tells only part of the story. Hers is an emotional knowing, understanding with the aid of feeling, and her blowing hot and cold, being distant now, then being all too close, do make emotional sense. But such 'moodiness' is hardly useful, or particularly welcome. Becoming an active part of the life around her is written into her script, though, and without it she isn't really complete in herself. One way or the other, she will have to learn to 'fit in', acceptably, do her bit, constructively.

A large dose of the other essential introverts' skills is needed to guide her. For instance the keen attention to detail the Healer is so good at. But maybe above all an inkling that (whole) things are susceptible to rational analysis: that both abstractly and concretely they come in distinct bits, if one wants to play it that way. There is no real need for her to pour out *all* her feelings in one go; or indeed to apply them to all and sundry and everything in sight.

She begins to assess the details of the situation, to bear in mind the company she is in, rather than emoting wildly all over the place. She learns to treat her essentially whole-and-intact inner fund of feelings more as a source of separate emotional strands, to be produced and withdrawn as common sense and others' needs might demand of her. In short, she learns about emotional self-control.

The Creator creates like that: not imposing his all in one crushing go, but supplying this now, that later, in living response. The Boss, while adhering to absolute Principles, in practice implements sensitively modified rules, people-friendly regulations. The Mother, too, has to learn the lesson of 'staying inside herself' for much of the time. She can enjoy a sublime and all-surpassing Wholeness in there to her heart's content, but when it comes to doing her job in the world, then a bit of sensible, practical whole-making is all that will be required.

Being a promoter of growth-to-wholeness comes naturally to her: fulfilling the role of nourisher and educator, receiving small things into her care to nurture to full development. Likewise with the sick and the injured, the deficient, the lost: she picks up and mends; adopts; nurses back to health. These are jobs she does with sensitivity, not least because she knows from personal experience what it is like to hurt, to have lost one's intactness, to feel lost and painfully scattered, broken, in too big and uncaring a world.

Where the extravert Priest's empathy is simply a measure of her ready identification-with, the introvert Mother's sympathetic understanding is based on a whole complex 'history'. It is all about perfection needing to find its application in a less than perfect world. Grown-upness needing to respond to primitive demands. Established inner contentment *of necessity* finding itself for ever disturbed, yet also serving as inspiration, as a broad life guide. Whichever way you want to put it.

It is her own experience of feeling a bit destroyed, distraught, shocked, under attack, rejected or at least unwelcome in the world that gives the Mother in us the sympathy – the emotional understanding – that allows her to contribute a welcome and much needed service. It also teaches her early on to restrict herself. Not just to retain some of her feelings inside her, but to guard herself in more outward ways as well. Self-control as such means again and again having to decide when and where, how and how much: a constant wariness and caution. But she can make life a lot easier for herself if she learns to restrict her range of operation as well. This means in effect creating a safe haven, a sanctuary, a more private place set apart for her work. And not only does this fit in much better with her holistic nature – to have a smaller but more whole sphere of influence, as it were – it also tends to benefit the young, small, sick or unfit things and creatures in her care.

'Motherly' places may spring to mind first of all. The shelter of a womb, a nursery, a home as such; or the sick-room, hospital ward, playground, classroom. But we might just as well picture a commercial-size greenhouse for the raising of half-hardy bedding plants; or a busy retailer's remote back room, specially equipped for the repair of things; or a counsellor's consulting room, a safe enclave for the broken to pour out their grief.

But we mustn't be beguiled by all this talk of needing/giving shelter, of hurtness and the job of mending, to think of her exclusively as a giver. Restricting herself is not just a trick to avoid hassle. Paradoxically, it is actually part of her own self-completion, as an also-extraverting introvert. But at the same time it also proves to be part and parcel of the job of fostering wholeness, wholesomeness, in others. To see her purely as mother who lovingly darns socks, bakes cakes, hugs and kisses things well, would be an absurdly incomplete conception of her. She is just as much of a no-sayer, an energetic sweeper away of rubbish and nonsense alike, a defender of what should not be spoilt, a determined withholder of things liable to be harmful, a confiscator not to be bargained with. Maybe this is in fact her primary role, making sure things stay well, won't require patching up later.

Her story has something of the balance sheet about it. She adds: nurturing, restoring, teaching; she removes: burdens, dangers; she maintains: a stable, sheltered environment where her emotion-led contribution to life can be made and received in the relative peace best suited to the job. She is good at balancing things so that there is neither too little nor too much. She has learnt to do this with regard to her own emotional involvement in the world, so she is well qualified to teach such things: self-restraint; and how to find one's own particular place or niche in life; and self-assertion. All it needs if one is to successfully adapt to life, while still maintaining one's feeling of inner integrity.

So much for the sunny side of this archetype: the Good Mother. The Bad Mother is of course just as likely to emerge from the same abstract root. The crucial point in the story, where things can go drastically wrong, is the moment she starts investing her up till then purely inner feelings in entirely outward givens.

In the worst scenario, we are looking at a case of entirely compulsive, headstrong, no-holds-barred emotional investment. She totally disregards the particular circumstances of the situation, never mind the needs of the other players on the stage. She does not even ask whether she is welcome. The Bad Mother, in her excessive urge *to actively live* what she innately is, simply imposes herself, emotionally. But since her feelings are quite fragile and easily hurt things, forcing them on others means somehow forcing others to accept them willingly – or at least, outwardly willingly. And the only way to accomplish that is through a mixture of emotional blackmail (the stick) and a great show of giving (the carrot).

But let us take this step by step. Giving of herself, in its true sense, is something she only does once, once and for all that is, at the beginning: without hesitation or consideration, she throws herself into life. That is to say, she pours her feelings into whatever current forms, patterns and formats of living she finds herself surrounded by – to become inextricably emotionally identified with them. Thus she becomes an ardent supporter of the 'establishment'. Yes, it is initially quite painful for her to 'fit in', but it quickly becomes bearable... provided that nothing ever changes much.

If one visualises things being gradually squeezed, pushed and pulled out of shape – old shapes into newer shapes, the normal course of life – and then imagines what happens to the feelings she has allowed to take up permanent residence in these things, forms and processes, one gets an idea of the strange and inexplicable pains life is liable to cause her. No wonder then that she becomes attached not only to the prevailing fashion of the day, but ultimately and most strongly and securely to the most traditional, rigid, never-changing structures and procedures, the set, the expected, the long-accepted, the utterly safe and mercifully dull. All else she will treat with the greatest suspicion.

The only way to really protect herself from life's unbearable assaults is to box herself into a smallish corner, no bigger an area than she can personally control, and make sure the door is always safely locked. If life is to visit, it will have to ring the bell, be peered at cautiously, vetted, wipe its feet. The moment anything nastily unprecedented manages to sneak past her defences, there is immediately a drama of shocked, pained reaction. Others soon learn to behave themselves, not to spring surprises, not to answer back or anything untoward like that, for fear of setting her off. This is the blackmail part of the arrangement: the bit about how one not only causes her indescribable pain, but makes her feel positively ill, will be the end of her one of these days, if one isn't more careful. So why does anyone bother with her, or indeed she with them?

Let's have a careful look at what she has actually done. Turning her back on her inner life, she has rejected inner forms of being and becoming in favour of purely outward ones. She has inextricably tied in all she is with established form – but then proceeded to narrow down her range, restrict and confine and ultimately marginalise herself. For one thing, becoming, self-renewal, is now quite out of the question. But there is much more she has lost in the process. She has literally cut herself off from the more painful aspects of herself/her life. Any of her initially so eagerly and automatically 'embodied' feelings that chanced to end up in areas too controversial, people too unreliable, forms too inconstant etc, she has simply jettisoned, disowned, rather than suffer endlessly with them. Cinderella's sisters spring to mind, dramatically cutting off a toe or two instead of, sensibly, withdrawing the ill-fitting foot from the shoe!

She has diminished herself. Become emotionally impoverished, limited in the kind of feelings she will allow herself access to, in her embattled corner of the world. What kind of *life* is that? Now she desperately needs others, with all their potentially unsafe, hurtful ways: she needs some of their liveliness for her own. And she needs to be needed.

Such an unattractive controller, forbidder, denier. So dried up in her herself and incredibly boring in her repetitive outward ways. What would anybody want with her, much less need her for? She pays dearly for the wilful way in which she has grasped hold of life: now she has to be the skivvy, doing all the jobs everybody else hates, down to the most elementary and unpleasant. That is the bribe, the enticement, that makes others stay with her and willingly submit to her emotional rein of terror. At least she feeds them, keeps them clean, warm and (it has to be admitted) protected in her barred and bolted corner of the world.

She has done some very peculiar things: emotionally 'prolapsed'; voluntarily 'gone to pieces'; denatured her feelings, allowing them to become no better than rigid things. Above all, she has split off large areas of herself that she no longer 'owns' but, literally, locks the door against. Her emotional life has become shrivelled and set; but each time her defences give and something long disowned forces itself back into her life, she has a major outburst of uncharacteristic and highly emotional behaviour. Things are yelled that are not at all nice. There are gales of coarse laughter and floods of tears entirely inappropriate to the situation. Though to be correct, one had probably better call these 'inbursts', rather than outbursts. She herself, no longer recognising parts of herself for what they are – or not caring to, anyway – will maintain that something came over her, took hold of her, possessed her. Something uncanny, something invisible, some alien force or other.

She is the weirdest mixture. Unrelentingly strict, controlling, overpowering, making those around her toe the accepted rules from morning till night: no give to her, no heart to her.

And yet she wears herself out day after day, working to supply one's essential needs – though she will hardly ask what *exactly* might be needed; and certainly not what one might actually want, or how much of it. The plate is filled to overflowing. 'Eat!' is her command... few manage to demur.

And then again the littlest unscheduled thing has her in a complete flap, hysterics shading into histrionics, pitiful wailing, or maybe an uproar of fury, cursing like a trooper: you can never be sure what to expect. Lacking inner control, she veers unpredictably from excessive controllingness to moments of total loss of control. Without personal equilibrium or integrity – inner and outward emotional life hanging meaningfully together – she has become emotionally imbalanced, split, fractured and even lost to herself, in parts.

The Bad Mother's gifts are truly more like burdens, and her carrying others' burdens is more of a calculated trick than a gift. She does not teach and train others to become whole, healthy and adjusted. Instead, she fosters a sick dependency in them, restricts their outlook, frightens them off life beyond the closed door altogether. She does not promote growth to self-sufficiency and then 'let go' – invest emotionally somewhere else, at some other point in time. Instead, needing to cling on herself, she promotes nothing but prolonged inadequacy.

The weak are obviously at her mercy. The young will grow only in the physical sense, while staying in all other respects stunted. Even the grown and able, tempted with titbits, are easily caught up in her web of emotional string-pulling, threatened and bribed in turn, their (moral) integrity soon eroded by these underhand tactics.

Letting the Mother in us get out of control (indeed take control of us) is obviously a very bad idea. Life soon becomes a contradiction in terms. On the one hand all this compulsive clinging and meddling, the total inability to stay out of any of it; on the other a permanent unease, a million unreasonable fears about life's unseen threats, a wholesale rejection, even, of perfectly harmless aspects of it. We hardly dare move. What is more, we expect life to stand still for us; not bend us, reshape us, painfully. And yet there has to be some 'life' in such a life too – but where is it to come from?

To crown all her other perverse doings, the Bad Mother in us becomes a studious quarreller, a fighter so skilful no one ever stands a chance against her: whenever she feels in need of something *happening* in her severely limited life, she simply provokes those around her to be just that little bit 'naughty'. She nags, nettles and needles them, till they can't help but get a touch controversial, defy her, contradict her. Only to be promptly slapped down, of course.

Thus she manages to squeeze liveliness, life, out of others in strictly regulated measures, to deal with as she feels able and sees fit. That is the manner of her becoming now: becoming master of life, again, and again – till, yet again, her absurd system of control breaks down altogether, spectacularly, as ever. She should know full well, from experience, that she juggles around with life at her own peril, but can she stop herself? That would require self-control, something she has never yet learnt.

The Revolutionary

We now come to the most inward-looking impulses of them all: the introverting introverts among our cast of psychological archetypes. Needless to say, they too have to show their face and participate in life somehow. They have their own particular role to play, gifts to contribute, like the rest of them. But initially at least, they are quite difficult to put into a mundane gear. And once persuaded into action, they are then particularly susceptible to what in the last chapter I called a prolapse. So the balance between inner and outer life is more important than ever; the wisdom to stay inside oneself for long stretches of time, stay connected to inner, non-material, 'otherworldly' experience, really becomes the crux of the matter.

The Revolutionary looks at Inner Reality not with the surpassing abstract logic of the Boss, nor the deep emotional understanding of the Mother. He looks at it with the eyes of one whose function is sensation: like the Artist in us he sees inner pictures. And, also like the Artist, he senses in Air-y, that is thoughtful, ways: the pictures he sees (to put it like that) hang together for him in a logically meaningful way.

To him, as an essential introvert, these inner visions have of course a very different personal significance. To the extravert Artist they are never more than 'impersonal' inspirations which she uses to keep changing the world for the better, even while struggling to find her identity in it. The Revolutionary, for his part, has his existing inner identity constantly, and pretty much effortlessly, updated from out of this fund of self-surpassing vision or inspiration.

His function is inward-turned only. There is nothing in his script about living 'out there'. He exists inside himself truly self-sufficiently. He becomes, changes, renews himself quite spontaneously and abruptly with each new inner image he sees – impossible is not a word in his vocabulary. Unhampered by material considerations, he can respond easily and instantly to what he senses on the Inner Plane, become whatever might offer itself as the next option.

Anything this pattern has to offer us will be in the nature of a free gift, not something offered in the course of searching for self-completion, self-validation, self-realisation in the world. These are truly selfless contributions we are looking at, and we need to ask for them, so to speak – the Revolutionary's gifts, talents, are not as widely used as they might be: we need to coax them to the surface, encourage them to stay, handle them with great care.

Now picture this self-sufficient figure casting his eye over another world, right on his doorstep and yet entirely alien to him. What he sees will make no kind of sense to him. He is used to images of perfection – but out there it's a chaos of incompleteness, defects, failings, the weak, the broken, the gone-wrong, all held together with poor excuses. He is used to smooth, rapid, hitchless transitions from one state of inner being to another. But for others, out there, becoming would appear to be a lengthy and painful procedure, strangely fraught with danger. What reaction can one expect from him but incredulity, and a measure of contempt.

Not unnaturally, he is regarded with suspicion. He is seen as strangely aloof, arrogant, full himself: obviously convinced that others have nothing to offer him. Worse, he appears to be totally eccentric (and unpredictable to boot), with not a shred of patience, civility or respect. And whenever he does reluctantly get dragged into involving himself, he just ends up upsetting apple carts all over the place. His visionary brilliance may have its uses, but really a small dose of him is more than enough.

To make a good and useful Revolutionary of him we need, in turn, to inspire him with the best the Mother in us has to offer, or the Boss: whatever it may take to evoke in him sufficient sympathy and self-control to apply himself carefully to some particular job that needs doing, while leaving all else well alone. To lend us his talents – and then to go away again, back into his head, as it were.

He finds it difficult to understand that the world does not need half an eternity's worth of good 'new ideas' flung at it, all in one glorious go. Or that instant transformation of everything in sight, even for the better, simply translates as havoc. His own inner history contradicts that. Loss and upset mean nothing to him, personally, because on the Inner Plane all is good, all is potential gain. In other words, his inner becoming is invariably painless and without disappointment. He can simply abandon himself to change and change again, secure in the expectation that all will be well with him. Now, looking more thoughtfully and in detail at the material world around him, he can see only too clearly what's wrong with it – and also visualise immediately how to sort things out: leave it to him, he'll have the job done in no time at all! Others keep looking doubtful, wary.

In short, he is extremely useful, in a salt and spice sort of way. But he does need to acquire the ability to limit his involvement to where and when he is genuinely wanted or needed. His self-sufficiency, the fact that he really doesn't need anything (back) from others, is important in that respect, because it literally leaves him free to 'come and go'. Meaning, if nothing else, that the world gets time to recover from the upheavals in his wake.

Like the Destroyer, the Revolutionary is hard to appreciate properly (and a difficult impulse to live out well). No matter how patiently and caringly he goes about his business, something always has to give, to go, to be replaced or utterly turned round. He will never be an Artist in approach: tentatively searching to transform the world, hovering between a transcending vision and the need to make do with what the world has to offer. The Revolutionary has no material needs; he is himself the vision, he is the transcender; we can take him or leave him, but he can do no more than tread a bit softly.

He is of course a non-conformist by nature, an iconoclast, the archetypal rebel. Not, though, because he has something against, an axe to grind. He goes against the grain only because he has a billion and one better ideas, a whole raft of much improved models of life that he can see quite clearly, looking inward. They are his special gifts to the world, free of charge.

At his best, he stands for (humane) reform and (practicable) innovation, for progress (one step at a time), for utopian visions of the future (to be, inevitably, cut down to size); also for personal freedom, originality, autonomy (within the limits dictated by the well-being of others). And another thing he stands for: equality.

Equality, because, to put it like that, he is such a practised chameleon inside himself. Distinct inner visions come and go, and his personal response to them is to change his identity like light-ning – one could say randomly, though never meaninglessly. That is the way of his inner life and development. As a result, his underlying attitude is that one self, one person, is as good as the next. And – another important point – that essentially all these different selves or persons are intimately connected, hang meaningfully together, can even be viewed as the constituent parts of a larger Self which can painlessly accommodate them all within the flow of its own, transcendent life. Viewed from that perspective, we are all closely related. Brothers under the skin.

In the last resort, when he looks at it in that light, the Revolutionary cannot really claim to be personally unconnected to the world. He may not need anything from it, but that it needs him is only too plain to see. So in the end he does overcome his initial reluctance, and his subsequent impatience: learns to bite back his too many clever suggestions, learns to go easy on his giving, but freely takes on the responsibility of keeping an eye on what is happening out there on his doorstep.

If one cares to look at them, his suggestions – insightful, meaningful, but also quite detailed – save much time and effort. Instead of endless trial and error there's a ready-made blueprint to go by. It still doesn't mean one could wave a fairy's wand: zap the old, instantly substitute the new. It still means patiently applying oneself to the job of dismantling first, then building up anew, with due consideration and sensitivity throughout. All the same, we are looking at something like *quantum leaps*, rather than plodding, linear, small step by small step sort of progress. We are dealing with unpredictable lateral thinking, flashes of sudden illumination, the totally unexpected.

Not all the world is pleased at having their routine thus disturbed, of course, finding their expectations thwarted and their lives transformed. If there is too much grumbling, he will obviously have to lay off and 'go away again'. Not that he minds, having no personal investment in worldly things. But he is not all tangible work, zany inventions, technology so new it still defies ordinary understanding. He also has a message to deliver, an example to set. And in that respect he will not so easily be told to go away. He does, after all, see himself as meaningfully connected to those strangers out there, and consequently he holds himself to be responsible for their welfare. So when it comes to the crunch, he *will* interfere.

For all his non-conformist behaviour he does, inside himself, recognise an underlying coherence, order, lawfulness. He may be ready to break worldly laws, but only because he knows of better ones, of a higher order, or more deeply truthful.

His message, ultimately, is demonstrated by his own life, inside himself and in relation to others. It speaks of our individual freedom, of diversity, pluralism. And of our inherent relatedness, in a profound sense even interchangeability, and hence equality. Of personal autonomy and at the same time responsibility. Of obedience to an ideal Law, even while breaking the rules of the day. Of independence and interdependence all in one breath. Of caring about others no matter how different or distant, strange or deficient they may appear, even without having a personal, 'selfish' interest in them at all.

A mixed and complex message on the face of it, hard to attune to at first, maybe because he is in the fullest sense an idealist – a passing visitor from another, ideal world: disturbing, automatically demanding, rattling the status quo with every well-meant but unexpected word or deed.

In his negative manifestation he is of course nothing but Trouble writ large. He goes from aloof disdain to destructive interfering in one compulsive bound. Unrestrained by such virtues as patience or sympathetic consideration of others' particular needs, he meets any request for his participation with an all-out attempt to impose his superior vision, his better model, his lofty ideal, instantly, totally, exactly.

Of course it doesn't work like that. Frustration, annoyance, outrage. Before he knows it, he has become fanatically obsessed with *making* it work. He loses his grip on inner life, ongoing insight, personal growth independent of what is happening on the material plane: all he wants now is to change the world, 'show it', master it.

Not for him the time-consuming work of dismantling the old, laboriously constructing the alternative; and no half measures, no adjustments, no tinkering with the Grand Plan to cut it down to more human(e) dimensions. His blazing promises of a new dawn – tomorrow, if not sooner – have a magnificent ring to them, even if they do seem a trifle obscure. No doubt he appals some, but he definitely intrigues many. Condemning the world order as it stands, ridiculing the establishment, belittling current practices and achievements as poor efforts, it is no wonder he finds the disaffected flocking to him. Soon the disadvantaged, the poor and badly treated all unreservedly put their faith in him. The bored, for their part, just think he makes a fine change. Unsuitably inspired, they all set to: what stands must fall; in fact, none of it is any good, so away with the lot!

We can follow this pattern right through, starting at the level of the street corner hooligan. Lacking a history of personal invest-ment; dreaming of something better; obsessively destroying everything in sight that does not match their impossibly high expectations. If it gets any worse, we soon see some serious fomentors of civil unrest. And only a bit further, we meet The Glorious Leader himself, at the head of a great crowd of zealous followers all ready to smash the existing order: *he* may envisage a new order to take its place, but much as with the basic street hooligan, the desired is never attained, the dream stays a dream, utopia is never reached, while the process of destruction goes on and on.

The reason for this is simple: what the bad Revolutionary, the Troublemaker, is trying to do is to instantly substitute one complex thing for another, rather than transform what's there one step at a time – and to substitute an abstract ideal for a mate-rial given, at that, without modification. It can't be done. The dream reality can only become material reality if one works on, and with, the given. The future won't magically appear unless something is done with the present. There are no 'empty spaces' in the world where a vision could simply suddenly materialise. Neither does a heap of rubble constitute a sufficiently empty space, *tabula rasa*. As long as the senseless smashing up goes on, and on, the magnificent dream just hangs suspended in mid-air, as it were.

The situation is most peculiar. Abandoning inner life, the Revolutionary has transferred all his dynamic *becoming* into the world out there – but in terms of *being* he is still personally iden-tified with the 'dream', the ideal self. In effect, he has split himself in two: abstract being and practical doing. Or to be precise: all-perfect being, and totally destructive doing. Fine vision and foul deed are totally at odds. He does not hang together any more, has lost his integrity, and makes no sense either. Nor will the self he is ever fit into the world. It isn't designed to 'fit in': he is a natural misfit, so to speak, an eternal 'outsider', and shouldn't try to personally impose himself, beyond lending himself as occasional inspiration, when and where required.

He suffers from that common condition that afflicts introverts: he has prolapsed. Except in his case, not actually fitting in, he has got stuck somewhere mid-way! Square peg into round hole won't go, however much he tries. So now he hangs suspended in a strange kind of existential limbo, an unreality hard to imagine; a mixed-up and totally out-of-it sort of state that is neither proper inner-being nor real material existence either.

He flails and lashes out madly, punishing the world endlessly for not accepting his superiority, for not accepting him at all. Most absurdly of all, he accuses others – those wicked, crazy, alien others he has nothing in common with – of having robbed him of the self he himself has 'mislaid'. And they have stolen his proper, rightful future too: what he meant to become... in this impossible world, where he is constantly thwarted... by some mysterious means. He is truly lost to himself.

Much of course will depend on the exact details with this pattern. How 'different' did he chance to be when he first launched himself into action with such unrestrained world-reforming ambition? We may only be dealing with a harmless fanatic obsessing endlessly about a trifle, a single point of contention. Or he could turn out to be a bit of a zealot, a minor subversive who peddles some patently impossible ideal to a few oddballs with nothing better to do. Then again, at the far end of the scale, we may me looking at a successful inciter to all-out internecine war, his followers increasingly divided amongst themselves (each feeling free to take the law into their own hands) and within themselves (all 'really' being and intending one thing, while actually doing the opposite).

That is the natural direction the Revolutionary in us takes, if misdirected and badly used: brother fights brother, as anarchy becomes complete. Past and present go up in smoke, and an unrealistic future stays firmly unimplemented. The grand Cause causes nothing resembling itself. Meantime the actual shape of any future to come would seem to be abandoned to chance. And still the initial Great Vision will be the same: that is the one thing that doesn't change. Unhitched from the inner source of continuing revelation, all of the Revolutionary's message has become reduced to one obsessively tendered 'good idea for change', unchanging in itself, fixed, inflexible. It is no fit contribution to make to life. And so, in effect, life struggles and fights to keep it out; as he struggles and fights – against himself, *in effect*.

The Eternal Child

If the Revolutionary in us is about individual uniqueness, about otherness as such, and at the same time the deeper relatedness of all, the Eternal Child in us stands for an altogether simpler theme: our indestructible wholeness.

Again, we are dealing with an introverting introvert, self-sufficient in his inner life, wanting nothing from others. The difference is that this one is purely intuitive, by function as well as Element nature (Fire), and hence takes a holistic approach. His inner life is nothing as complicated as the Revolutionary's, no multitude of interchangeable pictures stand before his inner eye. Neither can he thoughtfully (ie critically) compare inner vision with what meets his eye in the material world around him, once his attention has been attracted.

Rather like the Mother in us, he enjoys a state of inner wholeness within a larger Wholeness, but without her personal need to find herself a role in material life. Hence anything he has to give to the world will be free of charge, no strings attached. First though, one has to get him to take an interest at all, to come out of himself. As I have already said, he is not in a position to make critical comparisons. He may appear distant, wrapped up in himself, but never contemptuous, dismissive and full of 'better ideas', in the manner of the Revolutionary. He starts out simply happy and fulfilled inside himself: living in a world of his own where he is never hampered or disappointed in his fiery-intuitive progress, his personal development at the purely inner-life level. The other, to him, is the Perfect All that cradles him in his own faultless paradise, his own timeless Golden Age. – But when it comes to tackling 'real life' he is truly clueless: invite him to take part in something and he will rush in with a breathtaking naivety, expecting everything to be just fine, hang together, be whole and healthy and lacking in nothing. Problems are an alien concept to him.

He finds material existence a sore disappointment, a complete let-down after what he is used to. Knowing only complete 'freedom of movement', he falls over every obstacle available.

Never having encountered hitches, glitches, hold-ups, break-downs, he is left speechless and simply helpless. He is a complete stranger to misery and disaster. He just can't cope. Fortunately, he has his inner world to return to.

Others see him as a figure of fun, foolishly innocent, unbe-lievably clumsy and rudely contravening every rule in the book, from sheer ignorance. He is a nuisance. And he's a quitter. But at the same time he does convey this desirable quality: an endearing optimism that appears to be part of his essential nature. He seems constitutionally incapable of foreseeing anything negative. Even if thwarted and annoyed, ridiculed and berated for getting it all wrong, hurt and stopped right in his tracks, he still, at the end of it, has this puzzling capacity to regain his ever-hopeful outlook.

As for him, once his horizon has been stretched to encompass material life, in all its sometimes mystifying awfulness, he can't very well deny it a place in his intuitive-holistic view of things. He can't exclude it, can't exclude himself from it, altogether (though always retaining his essential independence from it, of course). Like his twin all-out introvert the Revolutionary, he will have to 'come and go': be no more than an inspiring visitor, a messenger from another, higher/inner (and better) world.

It goes without saying that he needs much support from other members of our internal cast before he can usefully take on such a role. Boss and Healer especially can help tone him down a bit. He begins to expect less in the way of ease and perfection, to accept things more as they come, ie imperfectly and painfully slowly. Above all, he learns to connect with the details of a situ-ation rather than dash around in fiery pursuit of *everything* – the material equivalent of inner integrity to him.

He soon realises that being unequivocally whole, in touch with the greater Whole, is something to be done purely inside himself. That if he is to venture into the hazardous area of a substantial, objective life then he must stay well anchored in his inner reality. For one thing, in order not to be lost and broken in a world of endless limitations and harsh demands, he needs to hang on to the subjective factor, life 'inside his head', where all is possible to him. At the same time, and if he is to have a worthwhile message at all, he needs to stay in contact with that wider Inner Reality which is not only his own source of renewal but everyone's Source, from his point of view, which is both holistic and transcendent.

He is a Teacher of insight. A Guide to higher things. A Philosopher concerned with the underlying Reality, a Preacher of truth with a capital T, and in his own, different way another Priestly figure. And yet I call him the Eternal Child, because in his transcendent simplicity he not only marks our true origin but stays faithful to it no matter what material life may throw at him. A novice and fool in the ways of the world, he is nevertheless deeply insightful from the beginning – one could say he is a practised Wise Old Man even in his infancy.

It is precisely this underlying capacity for intuitive inner-knowing that he is ultimately to demonstrate, teach, awaken in others. But more immediately, his message to the world is much more down to earth: he stands for hope. Hope pure and simple, and hope with all its wider implications.

At the crudest level, he is extremely good at hunches: he is a very useful chap to have around when it comes to finding the way, the best moment or place, or something that's been lost. We can visualise him as closing his eyes, withdrawing inwards, divining the meaningful connection of all things there... and ending up with a pretty good idea where to look when he opens his eyes again. He knows something of the future too. Whether he considers it wise to always impart that knowledge is a different matter.

Acting as some kind of guide to shepherd and pilot the lost, and serve as occasional oracle, is hardly the extent of his job in life. But even at that humble level he manages to convey an inkling of the benefits of inner life. He is used to enjoying only the best; and seeing all of life as a whole, he is happy to freely share that with others. But as he realises, the best is not the concretely biggest and most expensive, the glitzy and superficially most impressive. The best *for all* can only be found in such 'things' as peace, freedom, sufficiency, ease.

At the most basic level, then, he is the holiday guide who leads one away from all daily cares, out into the wilds, to contemplate nature. To stare at rock faces, ice fields, massed greenery, a horizonful of water: none of it the least bit meaningful in a worldly sense, all of it quite useless to plumbers and accountants alike. And yet it leaves them happy, relaxed, feeling more at peace with the world. They have been led to leave their worries behind. Not by a matter of miles, but out there in the material life: they have been shown how to distance themselves from it. They have been guided inwards.

Something similar happens when he foretells a positive outcome to some bleak-looking situation, or finds an object that was given up for lost. He shares his insight – into an underlying Reality where, simply, all *is* well. More immediately, the hope he induces in us is definitely an inner state. The hopeful future, at that point, is after all a non-place, in an unreal time: only to be found inside our heads.

Slowly, he may be able to wean his audience on to less basic fare, teaching more overtly about the usefulness of having an inner-life anchorage to hold fast to: keeping one foot in another world, to counterbalance the ills of this one. We are not speaking about escapism here. Rather the realisation that only inner freedom and contentment will help us through our momentary disasters, carry us through long periods of facing difficulties and want, loss and repeated disappointment. Only the discovery of 'innerness' allows us this measure of disinterested distance, the philosophical stance, which puts things in their proper perspective.

All very serious stuff. Philosophical overview born of profound insight; transcendence of the merely mundane. We can just see him there, in the lecture theatre: impossibly enthusiastic, if entirely abstruse, and wearing odd socks. But beside the bespectacled prof there is another equally valid view of him.

He is also the giggly child in us, the one who will play superbly silly-pointless games all day, if left to it. Much of this is his inner freedom and carefreeness simply and literally aimlessly acted out, but there is also his unique sense of humour to consider. Humour, like optimism, derives from being able to hold the world at arm's length – in a relaxed sort of way, that is. And there is none more relaxed than the Eternal Child in us. Others may find him absurd at times, but he finds them and all their works a far greater source of amusement than they will ever realise. And he's not above poking fun, playing tricks on people, having a laugh at how terribly seriously they take themselves. (That, too, is a lesson, if not often consciously received as such.)

Fun, laughter, inner joy spilling over into impulsive singing and dancing: he finds it decidedly odd if others, sour-faced, disapprove of such useless cavorting, refuse to join in his celebration of the riches, the sheer goodness, of inner-life. That they may not (realise that they) have one, will always remain something of a mystery to him.

By now it may seem as if all he can contribute to life is levity and, even at his most serious, a shrugging off and belittling of life's very real difficulties. But there are more far-reaching implications. I already hinted at this when I referred to the best he innately knows – the absolute best – having to translate, concretely, into the best *for all*. And how else could there be anything like peace and freedom from the worst stresses of life, unless there was also justice, fairness to all, and so forth? His seeming foolishness is deceptive: a closer look will reveal that he stands for another kind of inner conscience, another Law above everyday rules. This is the all-in Truth that puts mere scattered facts in their place; the meaningful wholeness, indissoluble oneness or integrity, of all things on the inner plane of life. That is to say his – our – own innate integrity.

Anyone who doubts this I would advise to look into the faces of young children. It may be only sporadically visible (remember: the Eternal Child in us is only a come-and-go visitor) but it is all there: the strangely old wisdom, the basic trust, the uncompli-cated faith in a universal goodness, the sky-high expectations – of fair play all round; generosity informing daily life; everything ultimately making sense – the sheer incredulity if they catch us telling lies or treating anyone badly.

Our children's faces tell us only too clearly how to handle the Eternal Child within ourselves: to stay true to that in us, draw inspiration from it for our actions in the world around us. Participation may not be actually demanded of us, free spirits that we are inside ourselves. But the boundless enthusiasm of this motivation pattern would be hard to keep from spilling over into the so-called real world. And when we do get involved – and find ourselves automatically having social and moral obligations – we can only regard ourselves, not as burdened, but as gifted.

Spilling over into the 'real' world altogether, to the point of no return, is what happens in the worst possible scenario. The inner anchorage is lost – the famous prolapse again – and immediately living wisdom and inspiration become a matter of the past. A fortunate and privileged past, but now spent, squandered, gone: nothing to pride oneself on.

Thus is paradise lost. The Eternal Child in us is only too easily persuaded to throw himself wholeheartedly into the fray, with a boundless appetite for life's free and easy pleasures. When disappointment and hurt begin to set in, he refuses to delve back into his more abstract depths and look for some useful inspiration there; it seems much more attractive to him to stay where he is and simply yell for help.

He can be a thoroughly Spoilt Child: proclaiming himself needy and helpless at every turn, constantly asking to be indulged, protected, humoured, above all expecting others to give, give and give to him. He looks so genuinely innocent and lost, so bottomlessly unhappy the moment things fail to go his way, he has no problem at all latching on to willing benefactors.

Conversely, he is just as good at sitting on a high horse: he's not any old chap, you know, who could be treated like other people. He really is *somebody*. He can boast an illustrious past. He is actually a higher sort of being – ah yes, and a more profound sort as well. He soon becomes a dab hand at giving himself aristocratic airs, impressing the 'lower orders' with no end of outlandish claims. Ordering others around, with the aim of making life easy for himself, soon becomes the norm. He is an accomplished windbag full of bluff and bluster, a top-notch humbug, an impostor of the finest order.

Being intellectually and spiritually (or what passes for something like that) condescending is another turn he does rather well. But if he starts off by dispensing genuine pearls of wisdom, it doesn't take long before they become worn-out mantras, a case of empty sermonising and false prophecies: he can't find anything new, true or appropriate to say, having abandoned insight in favour of ogling material goods. He becomes the figure of the Fat Priest, always the first at the trough, muttering abstruse blessings and waving a lazy hand in so-called benediction.

Arrogant snob or greedy child-man (in fact, managing quite well to combine both these roles), he refuses to recognise limits, he will accept no personal restrictions, shoulder no responsibilities. Social obligations have been replaced by social pretensions.

Also, he has no inner riches left at all for his own enjoyment, never mind sharing them, so now he relies exclusively on others to supply him with all that his heart desires. And *his* heart desires nothing short *everything*. He takes it for entirely granted that the world should be his oyster.

His appetite is gargantuan, his search for satisfaction manic. If true quality, his ill-remembered birthright, can't be found, then quantity will have to do. He is a coarse and vulgar glutton, disgustingly unrestrained in his personal habits. He is irretrievably addicted to the pleasures of the flesh and nothing is ever quite enough for him: no music loud enough, no car fast enough, or big enough, or shiny (with gold knobs on) enough, no mass orgy riotous enough, no plate – symbolically and otherwise – piled high enough. Symbolism, hinting at abstract values, is not what he is into; it is all earthbound second and third helpings with him.

This boisterous back-slapper with his exaggerated cravings is truly the Hooray Henry of our internal cast; but behind the endless jollifications, the conspicuous consumption, the wall-to-wall fun dished up at a leisurely wave of his hand, there is a hidden sadness. No amount of worldly riches and instant gratification will make up for what he has lost. There is no real, reliable happiness to be found in the material world. Even having to demand things, whine for more, is hard and unpleasant work for him. And then there are the snags. The brick walls he keeps running into. Sooner or later, his manic drive gives way to an all-enveloping depression. Whatever has he done?

There is no hope for him at all: as long as he stays addicted to flesh-and-blood enjoyment, there is no returning to the deep joy and inner peace he once knew. Self-sufficiency has given way to complete dependence. Relaxed humour to a desperate jokiness. Simple games to lose oneself in (actually: to find one's, inner, self in) and so offset the stresses of life, have turned into a serious pursuit of something called self-fulfilment. He will never be full. The truth of it is: he is empty inside. Nothing but a hollow sham.

Obviously he is a pain in the neck, a fraud and a scrounger. Still, he seems harmless enough. But is he? Others have to feed this parasite; house and protect him; put up with the dreadful liberties he takes, and the categorical inequality he saddles them with – and all that it entails. They have to do his work for him too, and for a mere pittance, if that. Essentially he is a poor stranded exile, or maybe more of a prodigal son, now down on his uppers. One can't realistically expect anything from him in return. But one could do without being treated like a lesser being who owes him a living, a good fat living, with no more than empty promises or the sight of his splendour for one's wages. In the end he will have to find some spare scraps to throw to his slaves. To them they are riches, of course, so then he can pride himself on how generous he is!

Unchecked, he exploits the whole world: people, natural resources, the environment. Constitutionally invasive, he will go to any lengths. He is amoral, irresponsible: nothing is safe from him. The damage in his wake is incredible. It isn't just that he is unstoppable, throwing things away half-eaten and compulsively grabbing the next – though he does use up resources at a fast rate, wasting them, looking for ever greater heights of luxury – but he also needs, quite simply, something to look forward to. That's to say something new, unheard of, never before seen or done. Somehow or other, he has to keep his hopes up: life, never *really* satisfying, might improve yet.

He is an inveterate risk-taker and gambler. Losses as such may not particularly hurt him (easy come, easy go), but not actually winning is much harder to bear. His overriding need now is for hope. And where there is some kind of chance, there is at least that, guaranteed. He better quickly forget about all his previous losses, then.

When he is not being profligate with what he has to all intents and purposes stolen from others, he may be seen cutting an absurd figure half-way up the highest mountain, crossing the remotest desert, or some god-forsaken bog. Others will be carrying his voluminous baggage, pushing him to victory and pulling him to safety, risking their own lives in the process, just so he can pursue his typically over the top aspirations.

And none of it is necessary. He doesn't truly need any of this. If he hadn't thrown away his spiritual 'inheritance', he would not be so needy now, stuck with this insatiable greed for concrete things, material gain, purely physical aims. If he hadn't turned his back on his true inner nature, then he would not be sitting atop his latest conquered mountain now, forlornly looking about him and wondering: what next?

Table of Summaries

These easy-reference summaries are intended purely to jog the reader's memory. They are not an attempt to capture, in a few words, the essence of each motivation pattern.

Hunter (extraverting extravert)
> finds an ever developing identity-in-action, is what he 'characteristically' does

Maker (extraverting extravert)
> identifies with his 'DIY' products – and, eventually, his acquired skills as such

Artist (introverting extravert)
> has inner visions, expectations: puts these into practice, evaluating and improving

Destroyer (introverting extravert)
> introduces insight into situations: abolishes, abstains from, shares... as appropriate

Thinker (extra-/introverting extravert)
> chooses what to become; introjects it; then acts out of her inner convictions, plans

Priest (extra-/introverting extravert)
> her fragile self finds inner refuge; inner growth; renewed, inspired, 'selfless' action

---

Creator (extraverting introvert)
> in search of his 'hidden' inner self: gives of himself, and consequently finds himself reflected, in a variety of ways

Healer (extraverting introvert)
> in search of his underlying integrity: finds it through various connecting, mending, whole-making activities

Boss (intro-/extraverting introvert)
> comes from a position of inner knowing; has to apply/prove these ideas, principles etc in practice; guides, advises and corrects

Mother (intro-/extraverting introvert)
> comes from a position of inner emotional integrity; has to

find her place/role in life; promotes growth to 'integrity' and self-integration in others

Revolutionary (introverting introvert)

inhabits an inner world of ever-changing visionary insight; can contribute new ideas, inventions and the impetus for (social) change

Eternal Child (introverting introvert)

in constant touch with the eternal verities; can teach the 'philosophical approach' to life, including a willing acceptance of (social) obligations

Part Two

THEMES

'You're Just Being Greedy!'

We have now examined twelve distinct motivation patterns, their basic aims, the complex actions and reactions they may result in – a great variety of them: from the inspiring to the downright frightening, and from the simply straightforward to the most twisting, turning, circuitous routes to the desired goal. But despite this diversity of purpose and action, the reader will have noticed similarities, echoes, overlaps of form or meaning. Identical looking symptoms, so to speak, that clearly sprang from quite different basic conditions. There is certainly potential here for muddle, confusion, 'misdiagnosis'. Are we for instance looking at a brave bit of Hunter-type pioneering – or is that the Eternally Spoilt Child going too far again, never getting enough?

Something else we are up against in our struggle to understand what drives us, is the sheer inadequacy of everyday psychological language, the bendy-stretchy words we quite happily employ to describe behaviour. 'You're just being greedy!' we exclaim, no matter whether the culprit was just predictably refilling her plate; or maybe sneakily taking what wasn't legitimately due to her at all; or obstinately refusing to relinquish something; or indeed roughly elbowing past to snatch something right from under one's nose... as if all these instances of 'greed' were merely variants of the same affliction, the same crime in different guises.

We carelessly apply these blanket terms to all forms of behaviour that have some superficial resemblance, or that happen to have a roughly identical effect on us. This actively prevents us ever enquiring too deeply what it is that motivates the 'greedy' one, to use that example. Is it really the Hunter impulse at its rawest: fighting to gain an identity for us with every thing successfully seized? Or is it after all the compensatory gluttony of an Eternal Child long stranded in a world of exclusively physical gratification? Or should we blame the Artist-manqué in us: determinedly picking the raisins out of life, quite unable to resist choice titbits? Then again, maybe the woman shovelling petits fours into a doggy bag is obeying her piqued Healer's voice:

affronted to see such a large pile of goodies, needing to redis-
tribute them elsewhere. Who knows? There will be no point in
jumping to rash conclusions. We need to observe closely, over a
period of time, try to determine the root of the illness, as it were,
not just study isolated symptoms.

And another thing: before you can pass judgement on
someone's behaviour you need to ask yourself first, what position
are you (currently) looking from? To a healthy Destroyer –
eschewing quantity in favour of things of real value – even a mild
case of Maker, clinging to what little he senses himself to be, can
look suspiciously 'greedy'. And speaking of clinging, do we not
need to recognise yet another form of 'greed' when faced with
someone's Mother who *forces* us to accept her, totally and intimately: forces us to accept into ourselves, eat up, what she so
overwhelmingly dishes up?

Words are not so much misleading, as leading us nowhere in
particular at all. The Hunter in us can reasonably be termed 'ambi-
tious'. But then the same could also be said of the Maker, the
Creator, the Boss, the Eternal Child at his most rampantly worldly,
even the Priest in us actively seeking to bring about a grandly
unified, loveable world for herself. But if we don't know one form
of so-called greed or ambition from the other, then how can we
hope to find adequate responses to such behaviour – or control
it in ourselves? And how do we cure the wholly or partially self-
destructive perversities of Thinker, Destroyer, Priest, Mother or
Healer in us if all we have to go by are words: simple, superficial
labels?

We desperately need to learn to look deeper; forget about the
words, study the hidden subtleties of underlying motivation, the
'stories' that attach to them. We need to get a feel for these inner
dynamics of ours, use our intuition too, use all our faculties. We
rely far too much on ill-defined terms and the often faulty
reasoning that labours in their wake.

Sharing our insights somehow, to compare, respond, explain,
go on exploring, we need to find a common language, certainly.
But mere words won't do. To capture deeper truths it needs
symbols. Pictures that can be expanded on, and endlessly
redrawn around the same intangible meaning. Stories that can be
interpreted from an infinity of angles. The archetypes, the life
principles that 'ensoul' us (lying at the very root of our every

move), can not be handily compressed into a word or two, filed under A, F or T. That is why the names I have given them are unimportant, makeshift things. Change them, if you like. What matters are the many potential flesh-and-blood stories each of these abstract patterns stands for. It is from among these that we constantly have to choose what to 'be' – what to live.

Lots of Love

Another word with no apparent boundaries or clear-cut meaning: love. The one thing we can say with certainty is that we automatically associate it with emotion. We feel love, we say. We feel it for our parents, our children, our current partner, for our country and leader or party, God and the latest football hero. Not to mention loving that sunset, a tasty roast, fast cars, cats, underdogs, Greek holidays, children's innocence, Brahms, swimming and the neighbours' new wallpaper. But does 'loving' them all mean we relate to them all alike? Hardly.

This is an even worse confusion than the one between one type of 'greed' and another. We have seriously run out of distinct words. Lust after, empathise with, desire, need, admire, lean on, appreciate, take advantage of, feel comfortable with? We don't attempt to be precise, for the simple reason that we don't really understand what we are doing. Or maybe we would rather not know too much about it anyway, in case we end up disillusioned with our motives.

The first misconception we need to dispel is that 'loving' is always *primarily* to do with feeling. As a matter of fact, there can't be many moments of the day when we are *not* exercising our emotional faculty, consciously or unconsciously. We feel in the course of using our senses; we think at the same time as we feel; emotions accompany our intuiting, and intuitions our thoughts. Or, as I have put it, our different motivational strands with their characteristic main functions are all intertwined: they support and inform each other. Our various functions all go on at the same time, this one in a lead role now, and then another. Whatever we do, feeling, thought, intuition or the use of our senses will somehow be involved in it. This may sound perfectly obvious, but we are nevertheless apt to forget it when it comes to assessing the origins of our actions.

'I love you!' some ardent young Romeo proclaims to his Juliet, awash with great surges of emotion. What he feels at this moment actually comes from the Priest in him feeding an all-embracing empathy into his Hunter-type behaviour, *which is what actually drives him:* the intuitive search for something worthwhile to call his own, in this case a beautiful woman, a 'good' woman... or possibly a rich one. And while he does whatever it may take to gain her favour, he remains emotionally uplifted far beyond his normal, earthbound experience, infused with an uncontainable love for the whole world – typically even the cleaner gets a kiss in passing.

That is the ideal version, anyway. The same role negatively interpreted finds him rather lacking the romantic touch. Instead, he is plainly hysterical (a Priestly negative) on account of some woman who, just because someone else fancies her too, suddenly strikes him as a desirable sex goddess on no account to be missed out on. He immediately offers to fight the other man for her: he simply has to add her to his never-ending string of conquests, emotion all the while boiling over, much shouting and bloodied noses. Again, it would be a gross misinterpretation to put his behaviour down to feelings, out-of-control feelings, an emotional problem or imbalance. His feelings are not the driving force. The Hunter impulse is what motivates him, and fiery forward-driving intuition is the function he primarily, consciously, uses. Or in this case abuses, making a bad job of it.

But whether he is being a perfect gentleman about it or an objectionable lump of the worst kind, we are looking at a quite specific sort of 'love'. We might think of it as a case of desire rather, or lust, but actually *need* strikes me as the better term here. The desiring, the aiming-at, is truly about something that is missing, something new needing to be gained, in the course of this most basic search for self, identity. And of course occasionally 'I need you' is precisely, realistically, what is said. Not that it ever sounds as good as the bit about loving!

If we take a look at the Hunter's archetypal Feminine counterpart, the response he gets, we find a rather different picture. 'Well, I love you too,' replies our Juliet, still a touch uncertainly, to her Romeo's fervent declarations; and it will have taken her a while to get round to even that. Her hesitation is due to the Artist in her, who has her keeping a circumspect distance: she expects to see basic standards met, weighs things up, bears consequences in mind too. She wants this love thing fully assessed and put in perspective first. Of course she can see the positive potential in her prospective partner, and their relationship. But it will take more to persuade her than just a lot of effervescent ardour. However, in the end she too needs: not just to gain, to be released from her Artist's limbo of waiting and to get herself a life at last, but also to 'properly' relate in the process.

Again, there is always the shadow side. With the Artist impulse allowed to rampage out of control, we find a woman prepared to 'fall for' any chap who happens along. In love with sweet love itself (never mind the details, or the consequences), she hurls herself into the first possible relationship regardless. Not surprisingly, she tends to end up with the lout, possibly a black eye, and more than probably deserted for the next target woman in his life. And holding the baby.

Hunter and Artist show us two instances of what I would call 'need-love', in its specifically Masculine and Feminine versions. What is immediately striking here is that 'she' could easily go on relating in different ways to the same person indefinitely, and still fulfil her need for constant self-renewal. 'He', on the other hand, in order to find himself anew in action, always needs a fresh aim. Another woman, rather readily suggests itself.

If we are thinking in terms of a real-life couple now, two people conducting their relationship at this level – one acting the Hunter part, in pursuit of something valuable (woman as Work of Art?), the other being the Artist, who responds by assessing and improving what she finds herself faced with (Beauty taming the Beast?) – then we can't help noticing that they will automatically be mismatched, in terms of their long-term commitment. It seems clear that if they are to have a future together at all, at least one of them needs to start drawing on other impulses at this point, a different kind of 'loving'.

So once the hectic courtship is over, with any luck we find a transformed couple. No longer Hunter and Artist, perpetually seeking, they will now be playing the roles of Creator and Mother, settling down to a life of giving of themselves.

The emphasis now shifts from the keen searching of the ever needy extravert, to the more relaxed field of mutual acceptance and reassurance among introverts. As Mother, what the partner in the Feminine role looks for is emotional acceptance, and a chance to carve out a sheltered niche for herself, within the context of a shared life. Beyond that, she has her independent inner life to sustain her, of course. The Masculine partner, in the

Creator role, does not have this kind of independence: he constantly 'looks into the mirror of his partner' to find his inner worth demonstrated to him there, or we might say his self proved and validated, by the way she reacts to him. He needs her a lot more than she does him. All the same, gone is the passion of his chase, the blood-tingling tension of one drawing too close while the other keeps almost coldly aloof – now they are comfortingly patting each other's backs. Maybe we could call this 'fulfilment-love'; though, again, the two versions of it differ considerably.

And of course there are always the negative interpretations of the same roles, as well as the mixed sort of marriages that ignore the more natural pairing of Hunter/Artist (both extraverts, immature, pursuing primal needs) and Creator/Mother (both introverts, more mature, in search of fulfilment). Mother at her worst, for instance, may well imprison the Hunter in her tightly spun web of emotional blackmail, capture her man for good that way. Meantime an unrestrained Creator is likely to find himself a whole bevy of females, besides Mother, to tell him how wonderful he is – what's to stop him? – or, having taken in the Artist with magnificent presents, he then proves far too wilful to contribute to their relationship the kind of input she might reasonably expect. Or take the pretty picture the Artist makes, or makes of herself, all hair-do and smiles: this will attract the Creator like nothing else, making him 'feel good about himself'... till he finds the image to be false, or inconstant, fading. Then again, a nagging Artist who expects perfection at every turn can reduce her Creator partner to a state of, not just worthlessness in his own eyes, but practically non-existence too. Thus can the course of love run unsmoothly.

So here we have two very different ways of loving, one meeting raw self-ish needs, the other providing mutual support, reassurance, completion of self in the presence of other. And only one of the four patterns involved, the Mother in us, is actually about feeling! But where is the sex in all this? Surely we have a sexual impulse as such that more than anything else drives us into the other's arms?

Yes and no. Experience tells us that a sexual charge can attach to anything; sexual activity can take any number of forms, left to its own devices. Urgent, forward-driving, simply demanding to be *acted out*, in itself the sexual impulse is actually quite amorphous.

Just like the Hunter impulse pattern, in fact, with its stress on action, universally adaptable action. From that point of view we could file 'sex' under 'Hunter', but at the same time we have to recognise that the Hunter in us isn't only about sex. Neither does the Maker in us, say, exclude sexual activity from his repertoire... he loves his dependable physical comforts after all; and the careless conquests of the Eternally Spoilt Child could well take the form of sexual exploits too. So where does that get us in our quest for our 'sex drive'?

Let's try *instinct* then; surely at least that can be pinned down? We would be looking for something impersonal, something given, 'inherited' rather than acquired, which right from the outset guides our behaviour. Both the Artist and the Destroyer in us obviously fit the bill here: both have 'prior expectations', derived from something beyond the personal sphere. The one, as we have seen, is the archetypal Feminine opposite number of the Hunter: guided by 'instinct' herself, she guides him in his amorphous, universal search. And the other – interestingly a unique mixture of the Feminine and the Masculine, Fire and Water, intuition and emotion – this is the one who strips off all the layers of the merely superficial in order to get down to the bare essentials of life, who can be said to bring an underlying 'code' with him/her into a relationship so close it amounts to symbiosis.

The Destroyer, of all things, as main procreative drive? We might bear in mind that before sex was ever invented, when organisms just split off bits of themselves by way of producing their offspring, they did not face death either. Sex and death came as a job lot, derived from the same root, call it a life principle or a motivation pattern.

Sexual behaviour, then, can follow any pattern in the exact form it takes. Strictly speaking, there is no 'sexual impulse' *as such*, though it can be seen to be part of, one interpretation of, the general Hunter impulse. As for our 'sexual instincts', on the one hand there are the purely Feminine ones (Artist) designed to give direction to the Masculine Hunter's otherwise vague search. And on the other, there are those satisfyingly hermaphrodite ones (Destroyer) that get down to the real business once the preamble is over.

No wonder the fairy-tale huntsman, for ever lost in the woods, can reliably count on a pure-white hind to come to his aid and lead him to the castle... and after much probing and testing of their respective worth or origin, they turn out to be each other's prince and princess after all. Happens all the time.

Let us leave 'him' and 'her' to it, though, and have a look at other forms of loving. Mother love, for instance. As we have already noted, the Mother pattern really is primarily about investing one's feelings: finding a measure of emotional acceptance. Embedding part of herself, of her emotions, in her children, the mother really does feel for them, suffer with them, as well as directly experiencing their joy as her own.

Of course it works the other way about too: the child 'loves' his mother in the same way, feeling personal loss at the mother's disappearance, personal pain witnessing hers, needing the sheltered place she can provide, her embrace if nothing else, for his feelings to be able to emerge safely – just as she needs his unconditional acceptance for *her* emotions to find a home in the world. In short, both mother and child relate to each other along the lines of the Mother pattern. This makes it a very special relationship. So far the loving couples we have seen have been motivationally rather mismatched, at odds, striving for or expecting quite different things. Here at last is a pairing based on mutuality: in motivational terms they are equals.

In practice of course they are far from being equals. The mother will have learnt to control the investment of her feelings, know for instance when to retain them inside herself, for the time being, and how to take refuge in her independent inner-emotional life when the going gets too tough out there. Not so the child. He is still all over the place with his feelings, just as she was, initially. Pouring out his own sensitive emotions regardless, he is only liable to have them hurt. He depends entirely on his mother's in that sense equal need of him – in order to fulfil all of her given potential, as an also *extraverting* introvert, finding a reception and application in the world for her inner feelings – and he begins to practice these things by following her example. Just as well we have such a needy and fragile Mother in us; what would become of our children without her?

None of which is to say that a *father* couldn't act as Mother and be the mothering parent, of course. Then again, he could just as easily take on the role of the mothered child.

One often sees older couples especially adopting this kind of mother-child relationship, maybe reversing roles as they go, taking turns at caring for, being looked after. Since it is the only really 'good match', it is perhaps no wonder if couples hit on it eventually, worn out after years of being at constant cross-purposes. One might see this as inappropriate, an infantilisation of one or both partners. But who is to say what is appropriate? Individually speaking, anyone can take on any role, and there is plenty of scope for all sorts of likely and unlikely (mis)alliances. So why not Jack and Jill, both in their slippers, being Mother to each other?

All the same, so far all we have seen is some kind of self-interest served, with more or less in the way of benefit going to the partner. But isn't 'love' all about giving, giving, and giving, never mind your own interests? By and large: no.

We could take a slight detour via 'joy' and 'inspiration' though, in search of the only truly selfless forms of love – and we might even see fit to ditch the inverted commas at this point. It may be recalled that The Eternal Child in us, as well as the Revolutionary (introverting introverts both), have things to give free of charge: needing nothing from the world for themselves. They receive gratis whatever they may require, in unlimited measure. So they can afford to be generous, just loving to give, in all simplicity, beaming with childlike pleasure at another's joy; or automatically showing their solidarity by sharing, assuming equal rights with any other.

One might object that where giving and sharing cost nothing, it can't really be counted as loving. But the giving itself is not the point of these impulses. Their ultimate function is to lead or draw us inward – where *all* can find the wellsprings of such easy generosity and unlaboured at-oneness with our fellow human and other living beings. If that isn't love, what is?

The Priest in us too, it will be remembered, eventually makes contact with an inner, transcendent source of contentment, finds a dependable base for her fragile feelings there, and subsequently acts self-lessly. She becomes a channel, a conduit for a greater Love, a vehicle for an all-inclusive empathy that goes beyond the realm of personal feeling. If we interpret that a bit more loosely, we may be able to see a different 'motherly' pattern here: a 'maternal instinct' in fact, informed by the same code that serves Artist and Destroyer as the basis for their conduct, only here accessed along emotional lines, lived out primarily through feeling.

Surely in these last patterns we find the true homeground of that uncertain L-word. This is what we actually mean when we search for 'love' in the world: something totally freely given, something that won't depend on our behaviour and will never be withdrawn, something absolute. And of course we won't readily find it out there, in the world around us, except – hopefully – as infants, children. As independent adults we have to realise that it is ours to enjoy only after a long process of growing up, growing inward, becoming grounded in a non-material way, via the Priest in us, for instance.

But there is the Priest's shadow side too, of course: enacting that, we remain permanently immature, entirely dependent on vicariously experienced emotional heights (that don't truly transcend, only tower) and depths (which aren't truly 'inner' either). Hysterical adulation of a pop star, or a mighty collective grief at some royal's funeral, this is the sort of shallow emotional reaction wrung from us here. We do love a good cry.

And the perverse love of pain is another thing we find here: not actually of the pain itself, that is, but of the borrowed or plugged-into emotion that goes into the inflicting of it. The outburst of (perceived) aggression that momentarily satisfies a twisted emotional appetite. The (outwardly professed) sorrow of the coldly chastising parent. Or the real rage of a deeply disappointed partner. 'I just love it when you're angry,' becomes the perverse response to 'I hate you!'.

Hate. Another word we could chase round and round, tracing umpteen different explanations, sources. The Maker hating new opportunities foisted on him, the Hunter hating to be deprived of them... all sorts of things 'hated' for a multitude of reasons.

Words? Take them with regular pinches of salt. They explain nothing.

The Battle Between the Sexes

It should come as no surprise now if I say that to speak of *a* Masculine and *a* Feminine archetype is a mistake. There are clearly more than just one of each. We have already looked at several, more or less successfully bonded in pairs, in the last chapter.

Consider also the diverse cartoon figures that crop up again and again, meant to typify womanhood or manhood as we live it, in its many (absurd) versions: the wide-eyed waif, for ever more girl then woman; the amply curvaceous flirt, all paint and artifice; the frighteningly big woman with her hair in tight curlers, rolling pin at the ready; the thin (usually drunk) little child-man in his crumpled three-sizes-too-large clothes; the dark, wolfish menace of a man typically lurking behind a bush/door/corner; the quite unsinister musclebound male simply going about his gung-ho business... We can now identify them as, respectively, the Priest, Artist, Mother, Eternal Child, Destroyer and Hunter impulse in us. (We can also see apparently unrelated figures as deriving from the same motivation pattern: the Braying Aristocrat on his high horse, the Wise Old Man or Wise Fool, the Fat Friar with his wine-reddened nose, the unsuspecting Little Man due to encounter Mother's rolling pin – these are all poses, roles, functions belonging to the Eternal Child in us, variations on that theme.)

What I am saying is that there are quite a number of distinct Feminine and Masculine archetypes that we – actual, rounded, flesh-and-blood people – live, act out, in the course of our daily lives. I will deal more fully in Part Three with the question how such factors as biology, ethnicity, life phase, job, choice or compulsion relate to *individual* behaviour. For now, I am taking a look at some of the things we can say of men and women *as such*, general insights we can derive from our more obviously 'sexed' motivation patterns.

Starting with the two natural pairs Hunter/Artist and Creator/Mother, what is immediately striking is the way they fit hand-in-glove: positively or negatively, there is an overall balance to each pair. However, if we consider them singly, and if we translate the abstract pattern into the real-life role of young man or woman, then suddenly we begin to notice the inequalities, the (dis)advantages, the unfairnesses that men as well as women complain so bitterly about.

The young man (Hunter) gets to do all the brave, adventurous doing; his female counterpart meanwhile (Artist) is stuck with the job of being endlessly circumspect. He the hero, and she the ditherer. It's not fair! Then again, he can slave his guts out, get covered in mud, and somehow it's her god-given function to stand a good way off, throw him the odd spanner and *criticise*, is it? It is. Not fair either.

Things are arranged no more justly where the Creator and Mother are concerned. He gets all the glory, shines in public; she gets the run of some quiet backwater for her more delicate undertakings. Why does her kind of work never warrant a mention in the papers? On the other hand, being strong inside herself, she can stand on her own feet – while he has to keep running to mummy for reassurance in between making guest appearances on TV. And she can't help laughing at this big important little boy of a man who reckons he is her master; which he duly resents, more puzzled and lost than ever in his too-big boots. He should just swagger less, she says. She should stop nannying him unnecessarily then, he replies, she only keeps doing it to feel needed. The arrogance of men, she cries. And cries. He grudgingly lends her a hanky, beaten yet again. Acrimony all round.

It is just as well we don't, in real individual life, live out such unalloyed, cartoonish scripts – by and large. And of course our young men aren't all forced to behave purely like archetypal Hunters, for instance, whatever one may say about society imposing gender roles on the individual. Nevertheless, it will be true to say that young men as such will act out of this pattern of the ever youthful Masculine archetype much more than they do all the others. It is not a piece of unwarranted stereotyping then to examine a pattern for what it will tell us about a collective, a type, created by circumstance of age, job, social position or whatever.

We say: 'Young men need a job. Gives them something to be proud of, keeps them out of trouble too.' Understanding the Hunter pattern allows us to examine the situation from a new angle, though. For a start, pride is not really the issue, nor is having a job in that sense, or even an income as such. It goes much deeper than that: as we have seen, for the Hunter not doing literally equals not being. Seen in that light, expecting young males to stay inactive for any period of time makes about as much sense as telling the seeds in the ground not to germinate, shoots not to push up through the soil – you can condemn a man to death, but you can't realistically expect him to go into voluntary suspended animation.

Deprived of positive, legitimate things to do, young males soon find some other... not 'outlet for their energy', but *chance to actively find themselves*, become somebody, through action. They need a positive goal, an aim in life, in order to have a life at all, else they soon plan mischief (ie pursue negative aims). And *characteristic* action being what defines them to themselves, they will then of course repeat their mischief, no matter what the judge threatens them with. It can't be worse than the psychological death inaction would spell, anyway.

Liberal thinkers have long realised that giving youths something positive to do is the only cure for persistent offending. What has been missing is the right language or imagery to describe the situation. 'They have all this energy to get rid of, they need to let off steam', only invites the answer: 'They will just have to learn to control themselves, sit on it. Bit of discipline will do them no harm.' Having energy, and either expending it or bottling it up, is the wrong image, it misrepresents the situation. If we could say instead 'They have nothing, they are nothing, only a strong impulse to do something, in order to become someone', then that immediately conveys a very different reality.

Of course one can't literally say of an individual young man that he 'is nothing'. Yet in order to deal with the problem thrown up by a specific impulse pattern, we need to consider that pattern in isolation, treat the young man as if he were indeed a Hunter incarnate, because that is the pattern he is currently living out most strongly, maybe almost exclusively. And if we are to ask him to stop acting offensively, act a bit more circumspectly, to use some Artistic judgement, bring some Thinker's discrimination to what he gets up to, and to develop a more mature Priestly empathy, rather than get caught up in the vicarious emotional experience of the crowd, the gang, then hadn't we better make sure that he is surrounded by lots of positive choices and examples that will help him make the best of his current role in life?

And having approached the problem of youthful delinquency from the Hunter angle, we would do well to enquire what else might contribute to it: the Revolutionary in us, for instance, ultimately needs an opening to contribute something uniquely his own, to be able to make a difference. And the Destroyer needs opportunities to attack what goes totally counter his perfectly valid vision of better things. While the Eternal Child will give of his best only in an environment that does not tempt him into rip-roaring consumerism and manic hedonism. So what are we are doing, as a society, to give our 'bad boys' a chance?

Women, of course, are never considered a problem. They just stand on the sidelines, shaking their heads in disbelief at men's coarse antics. Snipe a bit, subtly, with words rather than guns. – In fact, if one has ever witnessed a woman verbally demolish her man, coolly and with a precision bordering on the fussy, one knows just what the Destroyer looks like in its female incarnation. Fists can be dodged; lethal words always find their target.

If Hunter, Creator and Eternal Child can be said to stand as the representative motivation patterns of the male, then men are not really in a strong position vis-à-vis women. Artist, Mother and Thinker certainly have the edge over them: keeping a cool head, looking where they are going, planning, calculating pros and cons, women maintain a critical distance or at least balance outward action with self-sustaining inner being much more easily than men, as a gender, ever can. And where men's violence is overt, physical, all yelling, pain, rumpus, women's violence does manage to look soft and innocent in comparison. Even the harsh regime of the Bad Mother, the cruel maltreatment of imprisoned feelings, fails to register, officially: it lacks the kind of eventful impact a good pub brawl has. As a result, female violence is hardly ever mentioned. The way they shrewdly provoke and then glee-fully slap down; ruthlessly manipulate others' feelings, extort responses; cleverly impose their set views, brainwashing those in their care; destructively criticise every move or heartlessly dismiss what doesn't fit a prefabricated mould; narrow others' choices, denying their individual differentness and essential freedom, withhold help in order to keep their victims in a state of permanent dependency... Ouch!

Woman is right to call Man primitive and brutal. Man is right to say of Woman that she is sly, not to be trusted. Woman, on the whole more complex and sophisticated than Man, easily looks down on him, sees in him a truly perennial child: a hunter-about-for-things who never grows beyond the utterly needy stage; a creator of things without much real insight into them; or even at his most advanced a contemplative sort who, lacking worldly nous, stays in that sense childlike too. Woman towers quietly over Man, guarding her inner thoughts (Thinker) and feelings (Mother), or calmly tapping into basic instinct and thus confidently calling all the shots (Artist).

At the same time it has to be said she is also *wrongly* accused of being devious and deliberately untransparent, simply because Man, as Hunter and Creator, lacks the insight to know her for what she is, in herself. His love (!) for her is not so much blindly unseeing, as lacking in understanding (while she of course, as Artist, is apt to turn a deliberately blind eye to what she would rather not have to deal with).

At the archetypal level, Woman is ever beyond Man's comprehension. Something to be feared, warded off, branded 'different' and potentially evil. Assaulted by way of a deterrent measure, and for the same reason routinely kept down, locked up, banished to behind veils and categorically closed kitchen doors. Denied any standing or chance of an even moderately powerful position. It is the unknown, the darkly incomprehensible, that is being abused and banished here: Woman as Witch; worse, Woman as indispensable Muse, transforming Beauty, life-giving Mother and inspiring Angel of Mercy *but at the same time*, hidden away somewhere amid her complex nature, darkly powerful Witch.

This is the sort of generic strife between the sexes that has been enacted all over the world for millennia; still is, especially where more communal forms of living continue to be the norm, gender roles being rigidly assigned, and not much scope allowed for their individual interpretations either. But all that overt violence against women should not blind us to women's equal capacity for making others' lives a misery with their apparently subtler, often covert forms of violence. And exploitation by (rather than of) women, too, can go unnoticed for long stretches, not being of the obviously grabbing, pompous, noisily demanding sort that Creator and Eternal Child might go in for.

Take the Artist, for instance. Determined to pick only the sweet and pleasant bits out of life, simpering and nodding and decoratively standing by while others shovel the dirt, flattering all and sundry into making life pleasant for her, while hiding the stark truth behind fancy frills, she knows how to lead her man by the nose and make him pay: the gold digger par excellence. Hunter and Creator never know what's been hitting their pockets till it's too late. They are simple, up-front, too totally extraverting to dream of looking deep or beyond; surface appearance is all they can relate to. And the Artist is a champion at forcing a pretty appearance on things, including herself.

But there is also the contorted exploitativeness of the Priest, another great Feminine archetype and the motherly instinct personified, as we have seen. She can be the ministering Angel, Woman as pure and otherworldly – that is after much inner struggle, rather than naturally, as Man tends to assume. But equally, in her negative manifestation, she is the Slut who will sell herself cheap; or the Helpless Waif, who is really a very efficient leech.

Most twisted of all, she is Woman as Battered Object: with no inner feelings of her own but for ever plugging herself into others' emotion, even supposing it is rage and deepest contempt. In other words, the Poor Little Woman who essentially, perversely, gets what she wants, despite appearances to the contrary. She 'asks for it' alright – but then let's not forget the Destroyer's penchant for blaming the victim either: rightly or wrongly claiming that those violent outbursts were *provoked*, and by the least little imperfection.

Lastly, we must not forget that the Priest pattern can also manifest in an active negative form. The worm can and does turn and then becomes as coldly and cuttingly destructive as any Destroyer, in search of her elusive inner peace and harmony.

Man, Woman: so many roles, so many faces, a vast spectrum of appearances. As we can see, the good in the one can enable and complete the good in the other (the Artist perceiving and supporting the Hunter's potential, the Hunter working to make the world a more Artist-friendly place, etc), just as the 'evil' in both dovetails too. Obviously, even speaking of men or women as such, we would be hard pressed to make any categorical statements without having to supplement them with 'But on the other hand…'.

Except maybe to say this much: women do have so many more hidden facets, possible reserves and apparent reverses than men, leading to mystification, misinterpretation, fear and misogyny on the one hand; contempt, cunning and subtler forms of abuse and exploitation on the other. The one feeding nicely into the other. We have had this battle between the sexes for all the centuries we can remember. And we will continue to have it, unless we learn to live as complete and rounded individuals, with both our Masculine and Feminine impulses to draw on and interpret widely – and, if we can come to understand them better, more positively.

Money, Money. And More Money

If it is not sex we are obsessed with, then surely it is money. Whether bundles of cash, or wealth in the shape of choice possessions, a rich life style: houses, cars, furnishings, clothes, meals, holidays, all sorts of things, above all *lots* of things. So why do we insist on draping gold chains around our necks? Take to driving stretch limos? Need a yet bigger mansion?

I'm sure the reader, at this stage, no longer expects a simple answer! We acquire riches from many different motivations, some of them quite contrary in nature. For instance: the Hunter tends towards proactively grabbing the biggest and the most for himself; the Maker, on the other hand, looking for security more than anything, may end up ensconced behind a pile of identical, accumulated stuff. Both become rich, but for very different reasons (and neither do they relate to what they have in the same way).

I would identify three main such reasons: success, security and ease. Most of us would probably suspect the desire for success to be the main driving force, followed perhaps by ease, but if we consider our twelve 'internal figures' in their various possible wealth-accumulating modes, what we actually find is that by far the largest group (five) do it to gain some form of security. Only two could be classed as success-seekers, and another two can be seen to be in pursuit of an ease-y life.

That leaves out three and I will just run through them here. The Revolutionary in us of course never does care for riches; he doesn't hang around for things to build up. And the Healer, for his part, may go in for spells of frantic collecting (basically seeing the whole world as a piecemeal reflection of himself, he doesn't want to lose or miss any part of it), but then the more he fusses over every single bit, the more he misses the larger picture. At any rate, his short-lived coin collection will hardly amount to what one would call wealth. The Thinker in us, likewise, may get obsessed with small details like pennies and think herself shrewd, but then she goes and spends the pounds freely 'with the other hand': hopelessly divided against herself, but no doubt able to give some perfectly rational account of herself.

Success itself is a word maybe best applied to what the Hunter gains. He succeeds at his worthwhile endeavours, whatever particular form they may take; or he 'succeeds' only in so far as snatching things from his competitors is concerned, things to amass, without even valuing them. His negative aspect is that of the archetypal business whizz kid, frazzled with the need to achieve yet more, the poor rich man who never thinks he has enough. Ownership, for him, is quite the wrong path to take. It is the quality of his doings that should really count, not the quantity of things in his possession (nor the *size* of his biceps, or the *amount* of power he can exert, needless to say). At his worst, he is a perennial would-be achiever whose wealth gives him no pleasure at all.

Another kind of succeeder is the Creator, though here the measure of success is not active achievement so much as self-establishment: being recognised, getting some positive feedback, finding himself acknowledged, all so that he may know himself for what he is. Image is a word that springs to mind. The greater and better his image in the world, the more alive to himself the Creator in us will feel.

A negatively used Creator of course has all the world doing his work for him, and then refuses to share out the fruits of that labour fairly. He and his entourage get to swan about in furs, use private jets, seriously admire themselves in the gold-plated taps on their baths. They hog everybody's attention and set a standard of notice-worthiness, so to speak, that is hard to achieve for lesser (ie less wilful and exploitative) mortals.

But we are all of us Creators; we all need to be 'public figures' of some sort, have some kind of image in the world. A persistently bad example set by the really public public figures only starts everybody worrying about the Joneses. None of us want to look comparatively shabby in our neighbours' eyes: to the Creator in us it equals knowing ourselves to be somehow shabby in ourselves. But if we think about it, 'looking good' at its most positive is not about how much ill-gotten plumage we manage to wear. It is about generosity, responding to need, being seen to be fair and 'things' like that. Handsome is as handsome does. Something we too often forget in our pursuit of a mutually acceptable public image, standing, status, maybe even our five minutes' worth of fame. Again, the issue of 'power' comes into it: power in this instance to be, stay, stand steadfast as oneself in the world – rather than muscle applied to the task of becoming 'somebody'. Success already shades a bit into security here.

The concept of image is something we might also associate with the Destroyer. The positive expression of this impulse quite rightly makes us do without, rather than pick up worthless things. But negatively used, the Destroyer has us amassing rubbish almost for the sake of it – while taking a perverse delight in kicking it around, accusingly. And a bit further into this pattern, we then end up with both the good and the bad (and we never do in all honesty forget the difference) strictly segregated: in other words, we acquire a façade, a mask. This may be the grottiest look we can manage, fixed scowl and all, if we live in the kind of neigh-bourhood where the local bullies favour it. Or it will be the smooth, flawlessly polished, show-them-you've-got-it glittery exterior imposed on us by those slightly subtler bullies of the Establishment: a thin show of riches, hiding our more extensive 'poverty' underneath. An up-front wealth we parade most conspicuously, by way of deceiving others into thinking more highly of us than we merit, as we know perfectly well. This may give us influence, power, beyond what we deserve, but above all it helps keep us safe from suspicion, criticism, attack.

By now we are well into the area of *security*: fitting in with the predominant mafia, not sticking out in a crowd, avoiding hassle. The most security-conscious pattern of them all is of course the Maker, for ever worried about losing all those concrete things he is personally identified with. He might learn to take a more relaxed attitude and come to identify with his skills, his know-how, his acquired potential, but at his most grindingly, insistently materialistic he ends up surrounded by such a mass of possessions he can literally hardly move. Things in unnecessary duplicate and triplicate are a sure symptom he has been getting the better of us. Twenty unused tea-towels salted away in the cupboard? Think again what they might be doing there!

Other internal figures with a keen interest in security are Boss, Mother and Priest. The Boss, needing to prove her abstractly thoughtful, highly principled self in action, will go for status of a rather less flamboyant kind than the Creator's. But while at first she may only think of getting her feet firmly enough on the

ground, she soon stands in danger of sinking deep into the practice of a crassly reductionist materialism, fetching up typically as
an over-achieving workaholic with no time to spend. The fat
savings account has its shallow roots here.

Moving on to the Mother (who should be a familiar figure by
now, with her need for an emotionally satisfying reception in the
world), we could say that she looks for 'happiness' rather than
for status as such. Mind you, her unfortunate penchant for
supporting the status quo, underpinning the established order,
no matter what, might have one fooled. Of course she is not so
much upholding anything as finding some secure material
support for herself, her own feelings-in-the-world. All the same,
the upshot of it is that if the powers that be require us to wear
pearls or stripey ties around our necks, then as far as the Mother
in us is concerned, pearls and properly tied ties it is. That way
everyone will be kept 'happy'.

Reasons for obedient outward conformity are mounting up
rather, and all because we refuse to be obedient to our best potential, our truest inner nature, all those positive interpretations of
our inner scripts.

The most slavish of them all has got to be the Priest in us,
though, in her worst passive mode. She would grovel and literally lick one's boots, in return for a show of rapture, or else an
eruption of ugly feelings, as long as it promised her being swept
off to dizzy heights/abysmal depths, whichever. But she will just
as happily be a man's clotheshorse or a mobile display case for
him, to show off his fortune. Dripping borrowed jewels, living in
borrowed bliss, her life is a perfect fake. The jewels may well be
fakes, too, for all she knows. It is this Priest in us that has us
gawping insatiably at TV images of the personally unattainable:
rows of sparkling chandeliers, with the high and mighty of the
world dining richly below. Fantasy wealth, for our stray and
world-stranded feelings to feast on.

It is basically the Priest's inability to find inner security that
makes her seek refuge in the unassailable 'status' of a slavish
follower of anything, anybody, anywhere. But though her
emotional craving is not just for (apparent) wealth – witnessing
the very depths of poverty, wallowing in a shallow frothed-up
mass empathy with the most skeletal of disaster victims, is equally
a kind of emotional sustenance to her – still, essentially, we are

beginning to move closer to a desire for *ease*.

This is the last of the reasons why: why we want, even need, a thick wad of bank notes to hand at all times, an extra-plush car outside the door and a smart chauffeur to go with it. It's what the Artist in us is all too prone to specialise in: making sure she has it easy, always taking the way of the least resistance, and homing in on the sticky buns while artfully dodging the plain bread and butter of life. Self-indulgence is her middle name, no matter how hard she tries to make out that she is the victim of her own delicate disposition, not designed for the coarse, hurtful or unvarnished. In the grip of our Artist impulse gone wrong we have nothing much of true worth to contribute. We only add (metaphorical) pink bows and icing, thus prettifying an often ugly reality. And while we may not accumulate wealth for the sake of it, just finding enough 'cushions' to keep us comfortably insulated from hard reality still adds up to an awful lot of soft furnishings, drapes, ornaments and dinky accoutrements, to say nothing of all the clutter that serves merely as 'padding'... lest something impinge painfully on our pampered existence.

For a taste of the very heights of luxury, though, we have to turn to the Eternal Child. Having an easy life – that is to say inside himself, in touch with more transcendent joys and values – is his birthright. But the moment he throws himself into an endless round of manic 'fun' (and disappointment) in the world of concrete substance, he becomes hopelessly addicted to physical pleasures of the most primitive kind. The very bigness of a thing delights him. Noise. A dazzle of colour. And nothing less will do him than that antique door knocker the size of a saucer: something to shake the foundations! True, there can be more than a hint of one-up-manship about him, his mega-conspicuous consumption leaving others in no doubt by how much he transcends the lowly status *they* were born to, as it were, but for the most part he is simply chuffed with the limitless and the totally unrestrained.

Of course I am not saying that having fun is bad for you, or bad of you. But outward enjoyment should somehow tie in meaningfully with an inner joy – not take its place. Strictly speaking, the one should be an expression, really just a taste or a token, of the other; else we will have to admit to a degree of inner emptiness. We should en-joy the world in the sense of bringing joy to it, not squeezing it for what pleasures we can derive from it. *Doing* fun things, rather than *having*, buying, consuming prepackaged things labelled 'fun'. Celebrating, not just for the heck of it, but in a sense ritually, symbolically, as a reminder of better things. Better things to come, as well: looking forward, anticipating good times ahead... just in this simple act of 'living in hope' we often find a boost to flagging morale. But of course we are just as likely, and free, to allow the Eternal Child in us to throw such intangibles to the wind and get stuck into the hard stuff instead.

His is a consumerism gone wild. Shop until you drop, party till your ear drums have packed in and you've drunk yourself under the table; then pick yourself up and start all over again. Or – and this is really daft – gamble all your money away just for the bursts of hope it gives you (even if this one is a forlorn and unrealistic one), and then start making the next new fortune by haphazardly prevailing on others to part with some of their cash. In purely financial terms, we are looking at a boom/bust cycle.

In personal terms, we are looking at obsessive, manic, addictive, compulsive behaviour, based on no underlying need at all. The Maker in us has every good reason to get stuck into the material side of life. The Creator, too, needs to substantiate his unknown self in order to get to know it. The security-minded Mother, the down-to-earth Boss, the insatiable Priest, they can all find half-plausible explanations. Only the 'free spirit' Eternal Child has no ready excuse for getting sucked into such abysmal dependence on worldly wealth, extravagant living, all that big-time sensual enjoyment. –

To recap, and looking at it in the round, there are two processes at work. One has to do with simply overdoing our concrete efforts. Looking for *too* lasting a result, too established a position, and so on. Pinning things down inflexibly, when we ought instead to allow them to die a bit, bit by bit, so that new variants and versions can constantly take their place. And overdoing things in a dramatic sort of way. But also playing safe to an absurd degree.

The other process has to do with the inappropriate or excessive concretisation of something essentially abstract: inner values and processes, the whole inner life as such. No matter how seemingly abstract a form our wealth may then take (bank accounts; shares; bonds; half a race horse, on paper) it is still a crass embodiment of something that should be left to lie beyond the physical part of life. In this instance we are not only going too far, but going in the wrong direction altogether, as it were.

Whether Hunting, Making, Mothering or whatever, too often we cling, instead of letting things flow through our hands: creative, responding, sharing. We get attached, bogged down in the safe. Worst of all, we project 'inner things' on to things out there, allowing them to slip from our inner-self grasp, even going so far as to press them on an unwilling world all too palpably.

Inappropriate concretisation makes us all into addicts, passive consumers, conformists. It makes slaves and hollow shams of us. And bullies, extortionists, practised tyrants. It has us chasing witless from one so-called success to the next. And for all the fine fronts we put up there is one word to sum it all up: corruption. From Latin: a breaking to pieces. The sure fate of *things*.

War – and Peace

Mention war and the automatic assumption is that this is conflict writ large. Competition gone ballistic, rivalry cranked up to the level of deadly enmity: the epitome of us-or-them behaviour. True in some respects, but is anybody really suggesting that this is why eager young men join up in droves – because they are spitting fury, fired up by a blazing personal hatred and a huge appetite for slaughtering their opposite numbers?

The polite word for war, as in ministry of, or budget for, is of course defence. And, sometimes, that is just what it is. Attacked as a group, we need to defend our right to be, be ourselves, live out our own characteristic cultural values, collective habits and beliefs. This should awake the Hunter's courage in us all. That is to say our individual integrity of action, our personal identification with the way we act/live, should make it impossible for us to simply abandon our ways at the say-so of a potential invader – individual courage in the service of collective integrity.

Conducted at a one-to-one level, conflicts, even outright stand-offs, can always be resolved in better ways than one party shooting the other dead first. For instance, resolutely standing for what one is, unflinching, may earn the other's respect. Being prepared to adapt, give a little bit (adjust in the course of one's own becoming, that is) may help negotiate a peaceful settlement too. Non-violent resistance could prove persuasive; or it might ask for the ultimate use of courage, self-sacrifice. All of which is looking at the saintly side, rather – in less exalted mode of course, the Hunter in us characteristically has us scrapping endlessly over things, rights and areas declared 'mine, mine alone'. Nevertheless, it seems fair to say that at the individual level we can avoid the use of undue force relatively easily, if we really try.

This can hardly be said when it comes to nations going to war. The call to arms is in many ways just that: an offer (of 'action'), a promise (of adventure in new fields… with the word 'battle' writ small), a matter of subtle seduction even. Often enough, where the real courage lies is demonstrated more aptly by the few despised war resisters than by those many who are readily beguiled by crowd sentiment and the excitement of bugle calls.

What the traditional deeply moving music and high-flown rhetoric (the Priest at work again) is supposed to arouse is actually far less to do with belligerence than with a comfortable feeling of belonging, an at-oneness with something larger than self, and the longing for a greater common good that transcends mere personal interests. In other words comradeship (as in male bonding), the allure of collective idealism, the pursuit of something if ever so hazily noble, the personal need to be actively of service: this is the real mainspring of warfare, whatever particular (say) economic conflict between the leaders of the respective nations may have sparked the thing off. Indeed, without that particular spark to hand, would the collective need for 'heroic action' not have found itself another? History appears to be littered with fairly flimsy excuses for making enemies of other nations.

Certainly nations, just as people, can have conflicts of interest that escalate. But it isn't the individual soldier's conflictingness, so to speak, that gets him caught up in his country's war - it isn't one man's personal hostility added to another's and another's that gathers and fuses an army - instead, at its best, it is a man's legitimate need to do things *not just for himself;* and at its worst, his readiness to be badly used and misdirected, apparently for his own self-ish good.

Other motivations than the Hunter can play a direct part in a war or civil-war situation: the taste for destructiveness that is born of disappointed high expectations (Destroyer); the automatic disruptiveness that results from too strong a commitment to making the world a better place (Revolutionary); the desire for an overriding harmony that will simply brook no dissenters or threats (Priest); the reforming zeal that comes with knowing the answers without even hearing the question (Thinker). And subservience and plain conformity too will set many marching in step, though these can hardly be rated as primary causes of war. Just looking at the active motivations that lead to warfare, there seems to be a lot of idealism gone wrong at the back of it. The headlines may scream about this or that official conflict, presenting them as the reasons for the whole hate-infested nonsense, but what if these are no more than the secondary symptoms? Fronts, excuses, rationalisations?

But if it is twisted, mistaken or overdone idealism that is the main root problem, whether within the context of the individual's search for identity or whatever, then ultimately we will need to do better than attack the apparent reason with various methods of 'conflict resolution'. Getting to the bottom of the malaise will require dealing prophylactically with our sick ideals. Above all, we need to treat the lack of realisable dreams as a serious affliction. The absence of viable aspirations, even plain down-to-earth achievable goals, should instantly set alarm bells ringing. Really, we are back in the realm of giving the potential hooligan something worthwhile to strive after, and something better to worship and idealise than a bloodthirsty god, a would-be superior nation and a twisted, destructive hero image.

If we nurture in each individual the seeker for better things, by giving them the opportunities they need, they will not be readily available as either gang or canon fodder. No canon fodder, no war – whatever the generals may decide. (And, yes, even today's high-tech wars need willing button-pushers and trigger-pullers.) Hitler, let us remember, was elected to power by a smashed, down-trodden and impoverished nation: a bunch of no-hopers in need of a vision. If we are to believe in a war to end all wars it would need to be a War on Want more than anything else.

But do the poor and needy, seduced by doubtful visions, really go on to commit *atrocities?* Easily and with no more than a sheepish shrug: the Hunter in us, it may be remembered, when misused, fails to identify with his own actions, simply disowns them. They somehow don't count: it wasn't *really* (what he experienced as being) him that did it. This is easily rationalised as 'But I was only following orders'. If he had had prior opportunity to find-himself-in-action, positive work that 'counted' and hence gave him some self-esteem, he would not have followed those orders so indiscriminately.

That is one take on war and peace, the view from the willing-hero Hunter angle. The Artist archetype provides us with another approach to the question how to try and avoid getting ourselves into a warlike state. The first thing she can tell us is that *keeping* the peace is a rather more viable undertaking than trying to *make* it once hostilities are already under way.

Genuinely maintaining peace is a far from cosy option, though, and nothing whatever to do with encouraging everyone to smile a lot, placating any potential enemies in the process. One thing we can well do without is false peace in its many innocuous guises. The Artist's own bogus peace for a start, with her penchant for papering over the cracks; but equally the blind loyalty, the obeying, conforming and even just innocently going-along-with that we do at the behest of so many of our other impulse patterns: the risk-shunning Maker, the feckless Priest, the purely success-oriented Boss, the Mother who refuses to budge from her entrenched position and the Healer who reckons one thing will do just as well as another, to name some. It may sound exaggerated, but all those apparently harmless attitudes ultimately and inevitable will lead to war.

The Artist's job is to look with a knowing eye at every detail and how it sits in relation to others, how they might all fit together (peacefully), make a (healthy) whole. But this involves peering into the corners, noticing gaps, broken things and indications of rot: not just becoming aware of the obvious poverty, prejudice, injustice and so on, but actively searching and testing, just in case; finding the first sign of some potential trouble, and dealing with it there and then. Giving the place a good dusting down is more than an aesthetic exercise. If we can get the Artist's 'big brother' the Destroyer involved, to really delve deep for any evils to be nipped in the bud, so much the better. That is what the Destroyer in us is for, after all, to destroy the potentially destructive.

To put it rather bluntly then: if we want to maintain a genuine peace, we need to be prepared to upset and disturb, reveal, doubt, unsettle, change, reorganise, question closely, cause friction and *minor* disputes – even a small measure of hurt can't always be avoided. We face being less than popular for daring to 'make a fuss' when something is after all only a little bit wrong. But what is the alternative? Wait till it gets a whole lot wronger? And at what point does a compliant yes suddenly decide to metamorphose into a protesting no? Embarrassed, too often we keep stumm; soon pretend to ourselves that nothing really untoward is happening; end up not even noticing: the Artist's own shadow side, all gloss and grinning. If we are to make a job of this, we need to start as we mean to go on.

In the last analysis only a holistic view of the world will yield true peace; an inclusive view, that is, one that brings every individual and group into optimal relation to others, while banishing, ignoring or forgetting no-one. Total justice is needed. Justice that recognises and actively encourages the potential for some kind of good in all. Justice that does not pretend that our prisoners, mental patients, drop-outs, travellers, yobs or people in care homes have somehow exited society, via some magical plughole.

'Normality', for all the worshipful fuss we make about it, can never guarantee us peace and quiet anyway. Our cherished law and order never do hold for long. The so-called normal are only the ruling minority. Meantime today's dispossessed, abused and neglected are sure to be the militants, saboteurs, thieves and gang-members of tomorrow, in a climate of irritable hunger for opportunities. Small-scale, personal or group, conflicts are the result. But also the kind of vacuum crying out to be filled that I described above: a nice, normal society that, if one cares to look more closely, is potential canon fodder land.

The need for integrity in social life is badly, wrongly under-rated. There seems to be, on the face of it, no connection between being fair to our convicted life prisoners, for instance, and the whole nation avoiding military conflict. And yet the Artist in us, for one, would argue that there is, seeing everything in relation. There are in truth no unbridgeable gulfs between people, no Berlin Walls to keep us apart. Society, as humanity, is one and if we fail to treat it as such then we are failing altogether. To crudely revenge ourselves on offenders, rather than look for the possible good in them, is to fail. To simply prevent them from doing their worst, instead of enabling them to do their best – even supposing some of them have of necessity to do it from inside a maximum security prison – that is to fail, because we are categorically denying their human potential. We are robbing them of their birth-right chance to contribute positively to life, and robbing life of their unique contributions as well. How can such a funda-mental injustice not have repercussions: it bleeds all over our social attitudes and practice. It is a rot that is bound to spread, however insidiously.

Protest, vigilance and open criticism, implementing change for the better, for all: those are the tasks of a peace-keeping force. Being a pacifist is a properly confrontational sort of business. And unlike going to war it is not to be conducted in outbursts, in answer to sudden threats and crises. It is a steady job. A job for the Artist in us, above all.

Remains the question: can there be such a thing as a just war? I have no answer to that. Can there be a just peace? strikes me as the better question. And maybe the answer is yes; if we try very hard.

The Politics of the Inner Landscape

Injustice leading to strife, a multitude of small wrongs feeding into the largest wrong of them all – do we never learn from history?

An overused cliché, this 'learning form history'; something that at any rate could only work if we lived for ever. As clearly we don't, who is this 'we' we so glibly talk about? The next generation, and the one after that: all of them listening, not to the accumulated hard-won insights of their elders, but to the same raw inner promptings we are all intrinsically subject to. Looking through the centuries, we can see our basic motivation patterns rendered in a great kaleidoscope of styles, and with increasing complexity and subtlety too. Still the essence of them never changes. History will always be just people faced with the same old personal choices. The politics of the day, that's me struggling to make something decent of the Revolutionary in me, and you trying to keep your Boss impulse working along acceptable lines, and someone else not letting the downside of her Destroyer pattern get the better of her.

Utopia, as far as it goes, would be everyone striving to live out only the most positive interpretation of the various impulses they are heir to. But does that mean we can identify a single best-possible social/political persuasion, a perfect attitude all might reasonably share? Answer, emphatically: no. Our innate impulses at their very best may all be moderate, responsive and liberal in the most general sense, but at the same time our 'inner cast' is a hilariously mixed bunch: conservative establishment figures, enthusiastic egalitarian reformers, natural leaders, free-and-easy cosmopolitans and the unashamedly parochial among them. Strands of political shading we all share, in some degree.

You, however, might be more of a Creator type than me, and hence incline more towards the establishment-minded Right. And I for my part may have a larger dose of the Priest about me, basically all-embracingly global in outlook: consequently I might be expected to sympathise with the Left. Is that what determines the way we vote? No, because things aren't as simple as that.

Take two motivation patterns from apparently opposite ends

of the political spectrum: Boss and Eternal Child. The first is concerned with the upholding and implementing of set rules, laws, received dogma: the Boss in us finds it laid upon her to prove in action and apply in practice something she knows inside herself to be true, right and proper. In the wider interpretation of the pattern this may even be whatever parents, teachers and the law-makers of the day have decreed should be the 'given' everyone takes as their 'natural' reference point. Either way, the Boss in us is about publicly upholding it, defending it, doggedly making it work – whatever it may be.

The Eternal Child in us, on the other hand, is simply not made for this down-to-earth public responsibility stuff, the serious nose-to-grindstone plodding that goes with it. He stands for glorious fiery-fluid inspiration, the holistic or re-ligious view, freedom to share, joy of giving, celebration, holy days and simply holidays, liberation, latitude, liberalism par excellence. (Of course the basic 'internal given' is exactly the same for both patterns. Nevertheless, *in effect*, accessing it via the Eternal Child makes it diametrically opposed to how we view it and handle it through the Boss pattern.)

So here we have the rightful forces of legality and preservation, conservation; and the equally indispensable ones of liberality and progress, of change in the wake of a broadening horizon: two complementary life principles. One to build up walls, one to breach them. All very neat and tidy.

That things are not after all so simple becomes apparent the moment we consider the negative potential of each life, or motivation, pattern. True, the Boss at her most destructive will only become more status-quo-oriented than ever; she will basically be herself, only unbearably more so. In stark contradistinction, the negatively handled Eternal Child does a complete flip. Suddenly vibrant inner freedom no longer translates into a gift to the world: it becomes a dead privilege instead, an imposition, a haughty demand. You can't get more 'reactionary' than the Eternal Child at his worst, more exclusivist, snootily hierarchical and stuck in an inherited sacrosanct tradition.

Now let's just add that the Boss in positive mode can be quite subversive – undermining what has been unrightfully established, because she owes primary allegiance to inner Truth – and confusion is complete. The natural conservative at her best is genuinely progressive; the natural liberal at his worst is reactionary in the extreme. Even at this quite theoretical level there is no saying, no easy pigeon-holing. Now we can see where it all comes from: the unexpected sudden lurch into the opposite camp, the unlikely alliances we may form, the moment we are no longer being true to ourselves.

One of the most puzzling patterns in this context must be the Healer. Seeing everything around him as perfectly valid expressions of self – a self in search of its own integrity – he is the archetypal egalitarian in more than one respect. Misused, this impulse soon yields the figure of a fanatical subversive: the would-be equaliser who will allow nothing to stand out, and hence nothing to stand; who would unify the world into a simple, single mass; whose self-imposed job it is to painstakingly demolish whatever surpasses the lowest common denominator, by whatever means. First active social justice is replaced by pure ism, then social-ism slides towards the unattainable mirage of commun-ism, the once and for all 'healed' world of materialistic myth.

In the above we can see our purely superficial attempts at curing social ills, the endless cosmetic tinkering, the lip-service of a 'political correctness' that lacks all depth, because we have failed to let our Healer impulse take its cue from what is a *transcending* connectedness of all – transcending individual differences, preferences, situations, styles – and thus learn to go *beyond* juggling with surface appearances and other short-termist reactions.

But there is also the Healer's other shadow side, the one that doesn't try to artificially level out a world of natural ups and downs, or vigorously stir all the colours of the rainbow into one hideous shade called uniformity, but quite to the contrary passively tries to keep all things separate: this is the child whose pictures are painted entirely in purple, because he refuses to recognise any other colour. This is also the racists, the proponent of caste and class, an inveterate categoriser of people. He believes in this strict division, not by way of taking some systematic overview, but purely owing to his having an exclusive investment in whatever is familiar to him, fits inside his 'closed box' of a life, doesn't contradict his categorical expectations or (heaven forbid!) stretch his horizon. He can't allow himself to recognise any other sort of others, outsiders, strangers, foreigners – or to be precise: not for the time being, anyway, not for as long as he is left to inhabit that particular box. So he simply discounts them and manages, by hook or by crook, to stay quite absurdly, wilfully, ignorant about them.

The political persuasions of his rabidly 'socialist' twin have this incorrigible arch-conservative in fits. And so the one tries to make an obediently dead lump of society, while the other painfully fragments it. Two very different faces of the Healer tendency in us. You take your pick.

For an even more extreme attempt at 'communism', though, we can turn to the Priest. Her so innocent-looking emotional need for harmony soon translates, in the political sphere, into her either becoming the passive tool of any grand world-unifier that chances along or, actively, becoming just such a heartless despot herself. The Healer may have us being sneakily subversive, or (deliberately) blindly divisive, but the Priest goes one better: she methodically exterminates those who don't fit.

Another natural egalitarian is of course the Revolutionary in us. Capable, inside himself, of instant self-transformation, his attitude is to view one self to be as good as the next. His message is one of essential equality, a common humanity that transcends our superficial differences, the rightful community of all, because we are after all brothers under the skin. But once he loses his way, as we have seen, the picture readily turns into its opposite: not just demolition of the established order, but also violent social fragmentation, ending in outright civil war.

Pernicious 'globalisation', or wrongful divisiveness: both can be negative effects of the extreme Left... as indeed of the extreme Right, where we find a similar evil mix of unifying coercion on the one hand, and neglectful exclusiveness on the other. The Creator, for instance, in order to admire his multi-faceted inner potential reflected in a way that also shows him to be whole, should work for a society that is both respectful of individual difference and constitutes a true community, where the laws of natural fairness and generosity obtain. This would be the ideal, Creator-style; give it whatever political label you wish. Instead, too often he exacts mindless or hypocritical obedience from the favoured, the rich ruling-clique few, and wilfully ignores and neglects the rest: poor, disenfranchised, non-persons. He too frag-ments society – almost unawares, so intent on his power-juggling machinations is he – but culpably nonetheless.

And always there are the rank and file of political supporters, whether of the Establishment or its would-be underminers. We find them seeking only the utterly predictable (Maker, Mother); willing to prostitute themselves to any cause, however wild or daft (Priest); busily shoring up an absurdly inflexible status quo (Mother, Boss); ready to do anything for so-called peace and quiet (Artist, Priest); or loving nothing better than to gawp and identify with the currently high and mighty (Priest, Creator)...

Which brings us to a slightly different angle on 'politics'. (I trust I have disillusioned any reader who thought this was merely a matter of carefully considering the issues and making up one's mind.) As Creators, we all need to see our highest potential reflected in others, before we can own it. Individually, we can find such role models in parents and teachers, neighbours or indeed fictitious characters. But public figures have always fulfilled that function at the collective, societal level. As queens and emperors, as caesars, senators, courtesans, poets and prophets, tribal deities made flesh even. Latterly more likely as politicians, actors, sports personalities, pop-stars.

This raises the question what kind of public figures would serve us best. One of their functions will always be to live and die for us, while we view them with a Priestly adulation of their excellence and/or delight at their fall from grace. They are the target of our basest vicarious appetites, fodder for the voyeurs we are, and as such they can hardly be said to be fulfilling a positive function. But in so far as they can *show us*, that is to say embody something of our own Creatorly potential, stand for something that makes us want to follow their example, they do have a valid and important role to play.

But whom do we want to elevate to this publicly visible position of collective example setter, role model? The aggressive footballer or petulant tennis champion, the drug-addled lead singer, or the emotionally imbalanced ex-royal, all of whom regularly fill the front pages with misbehaviour we excuse on account of their prominence? The press is only too pleased to supply the hype that builds them up – only to pull them down again with Healerish glee (avid communicator turned destructive gossip: winkling out secrets, spilling the beans, peddling lies and slander). Or are we better served in that respect with our politicians, democratically elected to public office after all, even if they are one and all at the top of an especially greasy pole?

And then there are monarchs, time-honoured, with attendant princes and princesses – not just the stuff of last century's fairy-tales either: they appear to have a peculiarly tenacious hold over the public consciousness even now, cropping up with astonishing regularity in the most futuristic films. We should ask ourselves: why?

It has to be said that they at least have neither been spun out of thin air by the tabloids, nor have they had to poke their competitors' eyes out in order to get to the top (not nowadays, anyway). They have been given, rather than striven. They are born what they are to be and only need to actively, and most positively, be themselves: obedient to their given potential, realising it. Ring a bell?

In other words, and looked at in that light, those 'born to rule' – or born to prominence of any sort, like the sons and daughters of the already rich and famous – could be said to be potentially the most suitable figures to people the public stage for us, be our examples, because paradoxically they present the closest mirror image of *everyone's* situation: having to conduct, or 'rule', one's life according to one's given situation, one's innate talents, living up to one's natural inheritance in the fullest measure. These are by their nature Creator-type figures, and consequently will teach the Creator in us all how to handle ourselves, 'be ourselves' in the world. Ideally, of course, they would show us how to be fair and generous in the way we relate to others, for instance, while being entirely, proudly, ourselves.

This, not furnishing a cheap spectacle of expensive living to the masses, could be the positive role of royals and other such 'ruling families': to set a public example of *truly* graceful living. Our strangely enduring taste for contemporary myth and civic ritual may not be so silly after all, then, but rather reveal a well-founded expectation – if mostly unmet!

As a society, we do seem to need some public vision to help us find ourselves, 'playful' enactments on the public stage of what we are all, individually, 'born to be'. But 'rulers' who should actually do nothing of the kind? Who have neither sacred nor secular authority of any sort, but are expected to stand as prime examples in the public eye of how simply to be oneself? Some job!

Then again, the dangers of such public Creator figures becoming overly grand and self-regarding are obvious. Demanding autocrats who play the role of irritable tyrant to the hilt: they make not just bad role models, but absurdly childish ones, when one considers it closely, with their endless shouts for attention. Their ever-needy example leads directly to the infantilisation of the many by the privileged few, stifling the very basis of democratic processes with an invitation to do no more than stand and stare, spell-bound.

So – given that the truly admirably behaved will never make it to permanent prominence – will we be safer, after all, as a modern society, 'looking up to' a clutch of duly elected cut-throats and a rag-bag of talented ruffians and plausibly packaged train robbers, all of them mercifully exchangeable? Or not? Discuss.

Doing the Splits

We have seen in more than one context by now just how easy it is to become divisive. The Hunter in us perceives rivals and enemies at the drop of a hat. The Artist blithely separates the nice from the nasty, as superficially judged. Our Creator impulse, if we don't watch it, will partition society into the favoured and the rejected, ie the rich and the poor. Or take the Healer, who should of course be healing any rifts as they occur: he can be one of the worst offenders, consigning everyone to separate castes and classes, or maintaining that 'business is business' and nothing else should 'come into it'. All examples of what happens if we misuse our impulses, fail to get our act together – and in the process break up the essential one-ness of life around us. However, the break inevitably affects us too.

I'll be coming to the various inner splits we can develop in a moment, but I'd like to work my way in from the outside, as it were, partly in order to show up the continuity between 'inner and outer self', but also to demonstrate how careful we must be in interpreting what to actually call inner-life (and what to see as no more than personal, and possibly hidden from public view).

Starting at the shallow end, then: neither Hunter nor Maker impulse go deep in us. As personified archetypes they are all about strenuous activity, doing in order to become. Settled inner being is not in their repertoire. And yet even they are apt to show signs of internal splitting – internal, rather than inner, if I can put it like that. To wit: the Hunter at his worst does not own, or properly identify with, his own actions. The Maker, for his part, huddles inside such a quantity of accumulated stuff that he is no longer properly in touch even with his own 'skin', never mind his surroundings, or the effects of his doings on others. By extension, one could say that habitual repetition has made him blind and deaf to circumstances around him.

Going a step further, we find the Destroyer developing two very different faces. Mr Clean on the surface, yet grossly corrupt underneath. Or swaggering hoodlum, for ever stroking the cat strictly in private. His sorting right from wrong, without rightly relinquishing wrong, only has him cutting himself in half. The two sides or faces of him take it nicely in turns (shocking outbursts, radical swings in behaviour, leading a double life etc) but that won't make him whole. He neither goes to pieces, nor does he hang together as such, he just does his living in a painfully divided sort of way. On top of which he quite fails to realise that it is his own approach to life that splits him. He blames it all on others, who never allow him to be what he should be, but for ever corrupt him. Not to mention mysterious forces that take hold of him and make him do things his better half would never contemplate.

The failure to identify with one's own actions takes a step further inside with the Thinker pattern. Here we have a clean split between inner being/action out there. The newly introjected self is tucked away in a state of would-be perfect intellectual isolation. At the same time, action becomes rudderless, not directed by inner conscience, not answerable to what one thinks one really 'is', inside oneself, but thoughtlessly obeying the demands of ongoing life. This is your archetypal hypocrite: head pronouncing one thing, hands blatantly doing another.

The Mother in us goes yet another step deeper. As an intro/extraverting introvert she brings established inner being to life in the world around her, pouring herself emotionally into this task. If she pours out too much, decants her self wholesale (to all intents and purposes imposing herself), then very soon she will feel fractured and pulled about by the disjointedness and constant changeability of life. Foolishly, all she can think to do in response is to disown parts of herself. She denies having certain feelings, she consciously cuts herself off from them, lives as a truncated version of herself. But the very things she denies being will sooner or later burst in on how she normally conducts herself. Like the Destroyer, she will claim to be possessed or somehow directed by something alien and other. With her, though, the process goes much deeper: she is actually betraying some parts of her established inner, subjective being.

The Mother's situation is quite complex: instead of projecting her inner self, appropriately, only *a bit at a time*, she abandons innerness (the only 'place' or state to find safety, wholeness, perfection in) entirely. She projects all of her inner life out, into a bitty world, where of course she will now promptly 'go to pieces'. One might be tempted to say that her life has become so objectified, so externalised, that it can hardly be counted as an inner life at all any more. And yet what is being broken up and abandoned in part is her inner self – so we are looking at truly *inner* splits here, not just a split attitude to action, or a parting of the ways between being and doing, but a fragmentation of the very essence. Even if it is only an 'apparent', superficial fragmentation, instantly curable by emotional de-investment and a return to inner-life wholeness.

If we have escaped confusion so far, with the Revolutionary in us we may find ourselves stretched. An inner self, again projected outwards... but failing to find a place for itself in the world. (He is a natural misfit, remember, whose proper role in life would be to act as no more than occasional inspiration). An inner-self that hovers somewhere neither in nor out, suspended in some kind of unreality. Meantime – what to call this: a case of active-self that has hived off from inner-being as such? – in practice, destructive act follows destructive act, in an effort to make room for this hopelessly projected, endlessly waiting self. And the Revolutionary in us, too, blames others for his misfortune: he won't of course admit to 'mislaying' his own self, which is quite mad enough as it is, but then goes and blames others for somehow stealing it!

We approach life wrongly, and then make out that it is doing awful things to us. A prime example, in fact one of the most talented splitters, is the Healer in us. We have already noted how he chops up the world into categorically unconnected classes of people etc. But as he does so, he also divides up his own self into areas that don't connect as they should. Now we have to be careful here: with the Healer (as with the Creator, extraverting introverts both) projecting all of his inner being outward is actually quite the healthy, proper thing to do, not an aberration at all. 'Going to pieces' is his natural condition. Of course, finding his inner being reflected piecemeal, he should then constantly, actively, unify these scattered reflections, to realise his subjective integrity. But if he refuses to do his work, and pretends that small, momentary parts of him are all there is to him, then he too is deliberately disowning large areas of what he is.

The delightful thing to notice, among all these crazy goings-on, is how they tend not to work, but incorporate their own downfall. The Healer may stubbornly insist on being only a fraction of himself – but then he hops from being only-this to being only-that... and thus he eventually gets round to being it all, after a fashion. Likewise, the Mother has her periodic 'inbursts' of what she otherwise flatly denies being. And the Destroyer has his reverses of 'face', outbursts of unsuspected nastiness, sudden revelations of soft spots. The Thinker, as we saw, when faced with a stalemate situation simply 'converts' to the opposite side by turning herself inside out: the undone becomes the done, the previously unthinkable the new dogma. And so it goes.

Only the Revolutionary, having well and truly mislaid his self in the process of trying to impose it on other out there, goes on and on being divided between unreal, absent self and only too real here-and-now action.

He does have a companion, though, in the Priest, one pattern we have yet to consider in this context. The Priest, as an extra/introverting extravert should in time come to introject what she has become. She should then stay inside herself and – just to make matters more complex again – quite rightly divide herself into fulfilled inner being and self-less action in the world. If she fails in all that, she comes to lead a vicarious existence *inside* others, so to speak: parasitically partaking of their inner, internal, personal, or at least normally private lives. She thrives on others' feelings, whether sympathetic or not. She doesn't split or lose her inner being – passively, she simply never gets herself one (of her own) in the first place. She just goes on and on being others.

In her active incarnation though, equally 'heartless', the Priest tries to force the whole world to feel good to her; good enough for her to own, identify with, and eventually to introject this identity. In the process, she wreaks just as much destructive havoc as the Revolutionary does trying to make the world a fit place for his arrogantly superior self to inhabit. And she too manages to cut herself off from herself, in a sense: refusing throughout to employ her main, conscious function, feeling.

These are the things we do – daily, in small measure – and observe, if not in ourselves, then certainly in others. The question is, can we rely on our experts in mental health to know how to cure us of any of these madnesses? Does a clinical term like schizophrenic (literally: of split mind) tell us, or indeed them, much that is useful? At what point is someone to be considered 'insane' (literally: not healthy, ie ill)? To put it bluntly, it is excessive wilfulness that makes the Revolutionary in us go totally crazy. But is wilfulness a *disease?* Or are the conditions that may be provoking it ill, in that sense?

At the same time it is deeply worrying that so much genuine madness can be accounted as sane: warfare as job opportunity, social exclusion and inequality, hypocrisy and blatant pretence, glossed-over corruption, thoughtless obedience and conformity, cruel perfectionism, dogmatic repetitiveness and the sort of enforced stability that stifles life with all its natural changes, both inner and outer… One could draw up a long list.

Doing such crazy things to others, we automatically do damage to ourselves; and committing psychological atrocities against ourselves, we are bound to do the wrong thing by others as well. That seems to be the gist of it. So where in all this does it get us to apply labels to 'clinical conditions' termed neurotic, psychotic or indeed psychopathic?

Instead of seeing illnesses suffered, should we not rather note behaviour *done*, so to speak, and then ask ourselves: why is it done, for what purpose, with what aim in mind? Can we offer the 'sufferer' a saner route to the same goal? After all, as we have seen, all the potential 'madmen' inside us – the downsides of our inherent behaviour patterns – are *trying to make sense*, if in a crazy, lazy, greedy (and all the other words we like to use) sort of way. And what external conditions might we need to address that only help pervert people's legitimate search for identity, in its various forms, and their different kinds of self-expression?

To come back to what I said at the beginning of this chapter: there is a continuum of outer and inner self, and indeed beyond either. Starting on the outside, we have our physical and social environment; then there is the sphere of the 'outer self': our bodies, our actions, and close identification with others; next there is our personal inner self; followed in turn by our 'inner environment', whichever way we want to interpret that: the spiritual side of life, source of inspiration, innate inner-knowing, the divine, or simply our common ground, where we can be essentially at-one with others. And none of these areas sit in isolation. Inspiration can feed into action, environment may stifle inspiration, action will determine environment, and so forth. To be whole, healthy, sane, we need to both look deeply inward and give careful consideration to the world around us.

In either direction do we meet other. And other is essential to self. To what we become in the first place, obviously; but also to what we 'are', livingly, dynamically: we can't help but interact, actively share our selves. Neither is the distinction between self and other set in stone. For a start, despite the tidy continuum I have offered as a thought scheme above, it all depends where the action lies, so to speak, which way we are focused. Viewed from the 'abstract' inner self, for instance, the physical body is already suspiciously other!

Which prompts one to ask: if we can't live in harmony with our own puzzling, demanding and often contrary bodies, then who can we live in harmony with? And it isn't good enough to see the body merely as a vehicle, a thing for expressing our (inner) selves with. From the viewpoint of a more dynamic psychology, we must also recognise it as being 'self' in its own right: acquiring, storing, adapting, even sharing identity. It is that operative part of self that serves most clearly as gateway to other. It is the lynchpin in the continuum: that crucial area, physical life, where what essentially belongs together can so easily *appear* to fall apart.

... and Other Psycho-Acrobatics

There is much else one could mention, just viewing our motivation patterns from an angle of 'mental health' – put in inverted commas to stress that mental health cannot truly be separated from social, physical, political or whatever other sort of health. Individual or collective symptoms of un-whole-some living can and do manifest in all sorts of areas and ways: from people 'having social problems' to their 'being mentally ill'. As I say, there are many such symptoms one could round up under any particular chosen heading. But rather than become endlessly repetitive, I'd like to home in on just two 'syndromes' here. I shall call them the *Bubble* and the *Yo-Yo*.

To start with the main proponent of living in some kind of 'bubble': the Priest in us. What she does – what we do via her – is often depicted as an attempt to return to the safety and comfort of the womb. In the very widest *positive* interpretation of the pattern (turning inward and towards the ground of our being, something like an Eternal Womb, if you like) we may find some truth in that. But taking this too literally, as a return to an earlier state of comfort, is something of a misunderstanding.

Wider interpretation or no, we always need first and foremost to consider the directions each pattern takes, and the aims they reveal. The two directions the Priest pattern clearly throws up are of (arrow pointing inward) 'dying to' the purely material environment, followed by (arrow now turned around) newly acting out, as an inwardly inspired agent. There is nothing here about turning one's back on the world, period; nor about passive self-abandonment as such. Ideally, that is.

When we look at the Priest's shadow side we also see, not a defeated return to an earlier state, but only endless attempts to newly gain: safety at last, stability and self-composure, after being washed to and fro, emotionally. Unlike the Eternal Child, for instance, the Priest has no 'inner sanctum' as a starting point, no sort of original paradise that she might long to revisit. Instead, we have to recognise that the search for an emotional safe-haven, tranquil regeneration, an anchorage of a different (and from the materialist's view point 'unreal') sort is, via the Priest pattern, built into us. We could call this our spiritual impulse at its crudest and neediest, ignorant of what it is searching for until it gets there.

But when all goes horribly wrong for the Priest, we then get the characteristic picture of living in a *Bubble*. For genuine inner-ness, she substitutes a skimpy separation from the world at large: an unreal, artificial safe-haven for her exposed feelings to shelter in. She comes to live in a dream, a make-believe world of cush-iony froth and fantasy. At the very least, she snuggles down to watch endless soaps. Negative options like that are roped in to play the part of a higher (highly emotive) or deeper (peering right into people's lives) reality for her; and being 'unreal' too, if in a different sense, they have to pass for transcendence.

She may pretend to herself that she feels truly transported, uplifted and inspired by romantic fiction, the unrealistic thrills of fascist politics or crazed religious cults, or the use of world-bending drugs, to put it like that. But all she does is to falsify the world, rather than personally let go of it/selflessly better it.

Her escapism merely subverts what we call reality, while never getting her any nearer having a proper inner life of her own. A bogus innerness takes the place of that. An imitation womb-like construct, if you want to call it that (though, being external, maybe more of a kangaroo's pouch!). A superficial intimacy with other 'believers' too: *Bubbles* like that are made for sharing. But they are only pseudo-worlds, specially crafted alternative universes that stud our common world like so many black holes, sucking us in with the force of their hollow promises. Life hurts less in there. In between punctures.

Such spurious inner-being and living, needless to say, doesn't get the Priest's job done. She never reaches that state both blissful and altruistically useful that has in a sense been promised her – that she is uniquely equipped to reach. And 'faking it' only leaves her, as well as others, impoverished, in the long run.

Corrosive escapism? Or just some harmless relaxation? Addicted, or only having a bit of 'recreational' fun? We might be less eager to pin labels on some if we acknowledged just how riddled with holes we are ourselves.

Another one to construct a pretty good *Bubble* is the Artist. Of course, unlike the Priest, the Artist in us comes equipped with innate insight and hence knows from the start what's truly good.

Pity then if she can't be bothered to work from that basis, criticising and actively improving. If she 'criticises' only in the sense of *subjectively* editing out – by simply disregarding awkward facts, not to mention twisting everyone's arm with her round-eyed expectations – then she, too, passively corrupts the world. She spins an alluring web of appearances that, as we have seen, is totally divisive. As the rot spreads, her real-and-yet-illusory world shrinks to become an embattled enclave, and pretty soon she has a conflagration on her doorstep... which she continues to studiously ignore. Like that, she will stay 'in denial' to the bitter end. Another bubble burst.

(If the words we use have to be understood to be fluid, shape-shifting, imperfect representations of something more abstract, so do our images. The Artist cuts the world in half, good and bad, 'black' and 'white': this is one valid image. An equally valid image is of a world strangely coagulating, with tempting enclaves of sweetness and light set against a sinister backdrop of outer darkness. I hope readers will feel free to experiment with images of their own.)

Moving on now, we find that not all that unlike a *Bubble* is the closed box or rut the Healer can end up in. In passive mode, he shuts out all other representation of self for the time being, thus simplifying his task of being all of a piece. The difference is that he doesn't share his box, and that he will keep hopping from one to the other. He acts like a *Yo-Yo*.

He presents himself as one thing, and the next moment perhaps the complete opposite. He denies being today what yesterday he insisted was exclusively him. At his worst, he makes no sense whatsoever to anyone but himself. And even that only by hook and by crook. But we'll do him no service at all if, trying to sort out his evident confusion for him, we then rush to help him 'simplify' himself even further. Complexity is his birthright and his cross, his job to sort out, for his own benefit and others'. An easier life, a diet of simple tasks, a monotonous environment, will only strengthen him in his mad resolve to find wholeness through undue exclusiveness, (self-)divisiveness.

One thing that could help cure the Healer would be the Eternal Child's special gift: the easy intuitive grasp of integrity, both subjective and objective. But the relaxed, playful figure who sings and dances the day away, trusting that all *is* well 'underneath', is

of course only the sunny side of this pattern. The Eternal Child
can be just as much of a *Yo-Yo* as the Healer.

To resort to a different imagery again, if the Healer oscillates
fast, in a shallow and totally erratic fashion, the Eternal Child goes
in for few and far between but much more serious oscillations,
really proper yo-yoing: towering ups, abysmal downs.

Yes he is 'manic', and yes he is 'depressive', but we need to
investigate what lies behind such labels. If we can for a moment
put to one side the up-and-down imagery, and examine the
pattern's given directions and aims, we find all arrows pointing
in: we see an inwardly fulfilled, happy and contented introvert.
His turning outward at all, with all he can contribute by way of
surpassing insight, is a rare and free gift. Or it may be a fun excur-
sion, a playful dabbling in other forms of life, a hilarious amateur
performance, bumbling, and yet shot through with 'good grace'.
But it may well grow into more of a taste for physical temptations,
soon to become a habit of letting purely material pleasures usurp
the place of inner joy. Ultimately, we see a pathetic dependence
on life at its most concrete, lots of it, on a lavish scale, to make
up for the loss of any kind of inner life. The arrows have been
turned forcibly round: fixed in the unnatural position of pointing
him outward, further and further, 'manically' searching ahead of
him for what lies in truth behind him, and in his environment for
what lies inside him.

His openly frantic pursuit of a consumerist lifestyle makes him
infectious and, if I may put it like that, a tempter figure worth
setting alongside the two temptresses Artist and Priest.

His high living is really more of a deep immersion. But even
when his exaggerated striving is simply for more as such – of
anything at all, to reduce life's incurable deficits – he seems to be
getting less and less out of it. He hits a series of snags, and before
one knows it he *seems* to have done a complete U-turn. No more
galumphing around; he crawls quietly into a corner.

Actually, instead of wallowing in creature comforts, he now
wallows in self-pity. The reason I put it quite so harshly is to
demonstrate clearly that though he appears to be going in a
different direction (hitting a low, after being sky-high) he is, if one
looks closely, still headed in the same direction. He is trying to
find solace in a material mock-up of innerness now, returning to
his bed maybe, but not to his inner space (and the infinite space

of Inner Reality accessible from there). If he had successfully, truly turned inward, then he wouldn't be sitting there still moping. He would be humming to himself, a great world's-misery-defying grin on his face.

His ultra-grim silences, huddling in a very small heap, being spectacularly lacking in appetite, are only a variation on the theme of inner emptiness, hollow existence, over the top self-projection into a sphere of life given importance far beyond what it is worth. Of course we will try to entice him out of his corner – and we can see it as a momentary *Bubble*, if we like: what's more, this one really is an attempt to retrieve the lost 'comforts of the womb'. But if we try to jolly him out of it by waving desirable, fun things under his nose, our efforts will ultimately only be counter-productive. He needs to find his way back to that inner place, to that fortunate condition of being inwardly settled: to reconnect with his roots, get in touch again with the all-providing Creative Base. Offering him tempting titbits to consume is definitely a move in the wrong direction.

Yo-Yo or *Bubble*, boxes, ruts, pretend worlds where all is well or everything is possible – in the last analysis these words and images are no more than aides-mémoire and something to stimulate the imagination. All these separate 'syndromes' overlap, merge into each other. The Eternal Child has boxed himself into a wild-fantasy world; the Priest in her established rut of make-believe swings from false emotional heights to vicarious depths; the Thinker, for that matter, rigidly encapsulates herself in a tightly abstract corner, then reverses her position at a stroke... I think you get the picture. The outcome, in any case, is pretty much the same.

Bubbles burst. Boxes become stifling and ruts untenable. Would-be ideal worlds end up as passing, disappointing phases – or else lead straight to a bitter end. But before we get too excited about analysing the exact ins and outs and ups and downs of all this madness, it is as well to recognise that what we are dealing with, basically, are disorders of the volition.

Wanting too much, too fast, *over*doing the given task, going over the top. Ending up trapped and mesmerised by our own, too forceful attempts. That is what turns all those inherent promises into manifest failures and disasters. Inevitably, a lot of it is stimulated or exacerbated by environmental pressures and pulls, bad examples etc. This is why it is absolutely crucial that we confront our sanctioned forms of madness, public and private.

We also have to admit that, at the individual level, we can't tackle the upbringing we have already had. The damage is done: habits that have become entrenched, mental boxes that obscure our true horizon, splits, swings and strings of perfectly predictable reverses, a keen taste for fantasy worlds, the lot. There is nothing, though, to stop us *willing* to learn to use the same, abused motivation patterns positively. It would of course help if our well-wishers could refrain from trying to help us in all the wrong ways.

Murder's Own Logic

Some of these internal figures only tempt the unwary, beguile, mislead and fool those around them. Others are capable of much worse. Take this one, for instance: utterly demanding, he expects everyone to dance to his tune. If one stumbles, it is a personal insult to him that may easily fill him with a murderous rage. So he banishes all 'failures' from his sight, but then he immediately becomes suspicious: isn't everybody imitating him rather well? What are they after? Who are they anyway? Someone trips, falls in a heap, and his paranoia is complete. – It may look like ruthless brutality, but really it is *fear* that motivates him to kill without a qualm. And that is only the so-called Creator in us!

The thing to understand about the Creator pattern is this: his 'getting others to dance to his tune', pompous and arrogant as it may seem, still puts him in a terribly vulnerable position. Others receive his mysterious 'inner script' into their lives, act him out: from his point of view they *are* (being) him. Any shortcomings, disobedience or attempts to usurp his position have him genuinely trembling. This is not just loss of power, loss of face, position or possession: it is a loss of self he fears. No use arguing that it is only a visible (apparent) loss of self, when it is precisely in being reflected that he finds his only knowledge of self, grip on himself. Threaten the image out there, and you threaten everything.

In a sense, this is the pattern behind them all. Putting his 'script' in others' hands as either a gift to be worked with or a demanding imposition, he sums up the essence of the whole arrangement: life as a process whereby self becomes other and other self, and everything happens in mutual dependence. Unity and diversity come together in relationship, the very key to life.

Where the Creator's relationships go wrong, they do so in the most dramatic way. He will kill his own flesh and blood, or anyone dancing close attendance on him, even though it is a kind of self-mutilation. He kills them spontaneously, on the spot, for outraging him with obvious failure: a ceaselessly crying infant, or one that is ill, deformed, the 'wrong' gender; those who badly let him down, and those suddenly discovered to have been 'worthless' all along. And jealousy is what we call it when he suspects the imminent theft of his most treasured piece of mirrored self. In a frantic attempt to hold on to it, he kills the rival. But if on top of that he doubts his partner's loyalty, he will go on to commit a double murder, even while he feels that he is doing violence to himself. Also, in addition to all this rather frenzied slaying, he will plot and scheme with murderous intent against any he suspects of similar intrigues against him. Truly, his convoluted and downright crazy suspicions are a measure of his inability to understand himself, others, anything, in the absence of successful co-existence.

It is fear that is the basic motive behind the Hunter's capacity for slaughter, too. Again, we call it jealousy when *he* tries to safeguard his self from harm. But in this instance it is a self still in the making, being sought, a future self, a project... at its worst an endlessly projected self that never gets any nearer coming together. Losing as much as he gains with his ill-judged and hastily executed actions, and not much better than the Creator at knowing what other is about, the Hunter too gets chronically suspicious that he might be about to be robbed of his self – the raw material for a self, that is, his growth opportunities, his chance to be somebody, his personal future.

Less abstractly speaking, we might as well say that this anti-Hero chronically fears for his life (or that he is a complete coward). Yet to get the true flavour of it we must bear in mind the whole complex situation. Above all, unlike the Creator, he stands to lose to his competitors what he hasn't yet got. Where the Creator is outraged to find his existing identity under threat, the Hunter suffers from the *frustrated rage* of the novice self-seeker.

His is a different kind of paranoia altogether. He simply loses his head, scrambling to be first on the scene, desperate to get a toe-hold on the next rung to self, lashing out in passing at any rivals seen to be attempting the same. The Creator will test and probe suspiciously, ask questions first, and then go for the kill. The Hunter shoots first, just in case (there is no time to lose!) and then looks sheepish if anyone asks questions. His violence is no more than a primitive panic; he simply 'loses it'.

By the same token, the shock of suddenly finding competitor-enemies right at his elbow makes him turn even on long-standing friends and allies, should they suddenly step out of line, try to get ahead of him. But whatever the situation, if one wants to disarm him, and do so peacefully, one only needs a chance to talk to him long enough: show oneself to be on his side. Alternatively, one could try pointing out a better target for him to 'attack', suggest to him that he might actually gain something (one's respect, for instance) pursuing that instead. For the unscrupulous he is of course an ideal tool to send hurtling off on killing missions: determinedly forging ahead, thoughtless and eminently suggestible, easily manoeuvred and manipulated.

Whether he kills outright, or just causes minor injury, is basically down to chance and to what kind of weapon he happens to have to hand, or has been equipped with. Unlike the Creator, who is knowingly bent on exterminating unacceptable self-representing others, all the Hunter wants is elbow room and a clear road ahead of him. Unless we put it specifically into his head that progress, promotion, has got to mean a lot of cracked heads or corpses.

None of the above, though, comes anywhere near what the Destroyer is capable of: *deliberate cruelty*, that is to say enjoyment of murder, lust for it, murderous sprees that leave him perversely satisfied.

Disappointed idealism is of course what *he* is about – weird as it sounds. He approaches others with the same (innate) high expectations as the Artist but, owing to his much stronger holistic and emotional forward drive, gets instantly and intimately involved; is badly disappointed, many times over; may rage for a while at all these 'broken promises'; but in the end comes to find some kinky satisfaction in nicely predictable disappointment itself, in successfully winkling out the worst, proving wrong and bad and worthless: trashing.

It has to be said that, as an extravert, he is only destroying his own chances of finding much good to identify with. And his violence is automatically a matter of self-disgust also (not a product of it, mind). His murders are a bizarre self-mortification, by proxy. In other words, there is no dividing line between his sadism and his masochism. As we have seen, he combines good and bad under one hat, even as he divides the one from the other to the point of having two faces: both are he. Equally, he attacks both the apparently faulty and the apparently faultless: the one because it is overtly 'bad' (eg as a serial killer of prostitutes), the other because of its very sweetness and innocence – which only makes him want to test it to destruction, or ultimately spoil it if he possibly can (eg as a compulsive child murderer).

We should be clear that murder, the more elaborately grizzly the better, is only the most extreme form of 'spoiling' he goes in for. It may all start with a perfectly legitimate 'policing' that gradually deteriorates into gleeful harassment, becomes a more sharply focused doing down, and ends as destructiveness for the sake of it, rape as the only possible satisfaction to be gained, torture as an art form, executed with the nearest thing to tender care he can muster.

Since we are on the subject of rape I would like to take a detour here. It seems to me there is much we confuse and misinterpret when it comes to 'rape'. Originally, the word simply meant seize, as in unilaterally take hold of, against another's will. This is the sort of thing the Hunter is past master at: conquest-rape, if you like, an overly forceful attempt at gaining-for-self that simply fails to grant the other any right of veto. And if she resists, she might find herself re-cast in the role of enemy, rather than desirable goal, and take a beating on top of it all, to say the least. All the same, this cannot be compared with the Destroyer's chronic rage at a 'withholding' world and his twisted, inverted expectations that make him delight in spoiling the 'pretty' (as probably false) and routinely punish the 'ugly' (for being imperfect).

We might just, in parenthesis, add the thick-skinned Maker and a blusteringly demanding Eternal Child as 'inadvertent' if de facto rapists – and of course the Creator, with his inability to conceive of No! as a possible answer.

If these are the professional abusers, what about the professional victims, though? The Artist, in her most negative interpretation, is concerned only with getting a smooth ride in life, for which purpose she offers a fixed smile, a permanently pleasant picture, regardless. She is an arch flirt, all artificial eyelashes and false promises; in fact, just the sort of shallow, worthless conduct the Destroyer loves to hate. But she only hopes to attract the good things in life, nothing specific. And she is perfectly happy to 'forgive' a lot, ignore a lot that is... up to some unpredictable point where her cultivated naivety and shrewdly selective awareness quite desert her. She simpers yes, yes and yes, or grins a feeble well-not-really, giggles a no that sounds more like yes – long past the point where she should be saying properly no – and then suddenly screams rape and blue murder. If she maintains that she never saw it coming, she is not telling the truth, unconscious though her self-manipulation may be. On the other hand, if she protests that she didn't ask for *that*, she is being perfectly honest: she is only trying to keep everybody sweet, smiling and generally 'happy'. The better to find her own superficial happiness.

The perfect victim, though, will be the Priest: she won't even complain. Quite as twisted as her attacker, she may delight in, not the roughness and pain as such, obviously, but the towering rage, deep contempt, the whole splendid show of emotional life that she borrows for her own. (She is just as pleased to find profound sympathy, or intense outrage on her behalf, at the mauling she has had, but that is truly by the by.) Though she does not look exclusively for pain, we can still call her a masochist – truly nasty and degrading experiences being easier to find, one suspects, than surpassingly wonderful ones.

The Destroyer can of course equally be seen as a female figure, being a mixture of Fire and Water, intuition and feeling. It would be wrong to picture only a male rapist or serial killer. Predaciousness as practised by a woman also consists in spoiling, dragging down, corrupting, revealing someone's worthlessness. She may not carve her victim up into literal pieces to be dumped in the rubbish, but she will just as surely demolish him by other means. With that dazzling smile of hers (her all-perfect 'angel face') she could easily persuade him to take off his good suit, then coldly turn on him (her other, 'diabolical face') and falsely claim to have been raped! Character assassination, a subtler form of murder.

Whether we consider a Masculine or a Feminine Destroyer figure, what we are looking at is a slaughter of the innocents by the supremely cynical; but also always the possibility of a perverse dance of the *seemingly* innocent, willing colluders, with their unhappy tormentors. In either case, the tormentor is also the victim, every injury inflicted on others a case of deliberate self-harming, accompanied by utter self-loathing. And always, where the more 'private' face of the two is momentarily disowned, unspeakable things are done 'despite himself'. Or herself.

Others beside the Destroyer in us are capable of committing abominable deeds despite themselves. The Mother for one, so good at cutting herself off from what she also is, and consequently does. Or the Thinker, dividing herself into fine theory and dubious living practice. Murder may take many forms, and many of them sanctioned – like the Hunter being sent to 'his' war. Like the murders of the heart, of true vitality, of life's variety, truth, conscience and so on, murders committed in the name of stability, idealism, and even truth. And anyway, one may well ask: where does the Maker's simply having an incredibly thick skin end, and being a potentially murderous 'psychopath' start?

But if we want to see an instance of truly *heartless murder*, with not even a hint of self-torment attached, we need to look at the Priest in us, the active sibling of the professional victim mentioned earlier. Here we are definitely in psychopath country.

She is the one who busily reorganises life as she finds it, with a view to bringing about total harmony… for *her* to enjoy (and ultimately to introject: becoming emotionally all of a piece, inside herself). In the process, she will coolly edit out whoever doesn't fit in with that grandiose plan. She has no problem with ruthlessly liquidating any that might upset her. Despite being the 'emotional type', she finds murder easy enough – the trick being that she keeps the whole world of feeling at arm's length: she simply isn't emotionally identifying with anything, *yet*.

She is active, undoubtedly; but she is not actually, personally and for her own immediate benefit, *using* her main, conscious function: feeling. Hers is truly a dys-functional life, a performance so weirdly hollow it defies one's comprehension.

Strangely, she has a lot in common with that hothead, the Hunter. He too looks only to the future, his magnificent self-to-be, while failing to live properly in the present, not making a job of it, not owning his actions or taking responsibility for their effects. The Priest refuses to own not just actions but feelings. She stays emotionally aloof from the ongoing Project Ideal World that she keeps hoping one day soon to complete – and *then* feel for, and through identification-with to become. Become perfect, that is. Meantime, she is just as susceptible to manipulation as the Hunter, though minus his unpredictable mad-panicky spins. She can become a robotic killing or torturing machine that (ideally, from the point of view of her employers) quite fails to feel a thing. She simply, automatically follows any ready-made vision of a Better Order that one might suggest.

The Priest in us as victim, or as victimiser: two sides of the same pattern. We have already noted how the Healer can flip from passive to active, boxing himself in one moment, being all over the place the next. Now we can add that the Priest too can spring surprises like that. The worm does turn; the tormentor's face may well suddenly crumple in a picture of self-pity.

Maybe a reminder to the reader is again overdue, at this point, not to mistake a single impulse pattern for a whole complex, living person; we will be considering how abstract archetype may translate into 'real' life in Part Three. Also, when I say the Priest in us never feels a thing, no matter how much pain she is subjected to, or inflicts on others, it is of course emotion in and by itself I am referring to, not sensation (as of pain). As victim, she subsists on purely borrowed feelings; as torturer she is emotionally holding her breath, so to speak, a mysterious absence in her own life.

There is one more kind of 'murder' we ought to mention here, though: *suicide*. Of all our motivation patterns the Priest is maybe the richest in the variety of internal strands we can unpick. Let's go back nearer the beginning of her story, for a moment: before she finds her inner equilibrium, beyond the scope of daily hurts; or, alternatively, before she takes ultimate refuge in either of the profoundly insensitive states that are her two negative options. These are the early days, when she is still only too easily infected with participatory joy, or lachrymose mass hysteria, or whatever else may be going.

There comes a point when she is just beginning to get it together, learning to avoid unsuitable 'love objects' to introject, but never quite succeeding. She may not be circumspect enough. Or others may be misleading her on purpose. Things aren't what they seem to be but turn into bad surprises. Result: what she has deeply made her own suddenly comes apart, turns out rotten, upsettingly awful, the sum of it lacks peaceful cohesion, wholesomeness or 'goodness'. There is only one conclusion she can come to: she is no good at all, she is *bad*. It is obvious: she surveys her inner scene, and finds herself shocked. Why does she always have to attract such foul stuff! No matter that she has been lied to, deceived, betrayed (or forcibly subjected to abuse, for that matter), she still ends up blaming herself.

Inner stress, inner pain, at that point causes her to let go of it all. Yet again, she is emotionally cast adrift. But this time round she finds herself at the mercy of a world that forces her to become things against her will: negative things that she would know by now from experience to avoid, but can't, because there are no reliably positive options for her to choose, let's say. She is nakedly exposed to influences (quite literally: something that ends up inside her) she herself disapproves of. With that, self-loathing becomes a chronic state. Doing anything, living at all, becomes pointless: why actively work towards repeated self-undoing? Her environment, by being rotten, has proved *her* a hopeless case, a total disgust, many times over. Who wants to live with such a permanently unworkable, unloveable, un-ownable self? Waste of effort. Might as well chuck it.

The delicate question here is, how rotten is her environment, in fact – or is she actually being too 'greedy', trying to seize and have for her self too much (ie attempting to introject much more than is wise)? Simplicity, abstemiousness, humility, are the markers on the road to success for the Priest. A large emotional appetite, if I can put it like that, will only lead to disaster, in an imperfect world. Note: I am not speaking, in a vague sort of way, about 'being too much of a perfectionist'. I specifically mean looking for too much in the way of *material* perfection; total harmony, peace etc of a too *objective* kind.

The Priest in us may find much to feel genuinely suicidal about. But in one of her deceptively many incarnations she is of course also perfectly capable of putting it on like a pro, finding another handy Victim in Dire Straits role to slip into: faking it, her histrionic attempts nevertheless effectively tapping into a rich vein of sympathy. Carelessness, however, may just make this her last act of emotional vampirism. –

She is not the only one who can end up killing herself inadvertently. To live, one has to eat, naturally. Perversely, some refuse, as the next chapter will show.

Food: Glorious, Horrible, Food

Eating too little is not the problem for most of us lucky enough to live in parts of the world positively oversupplied with edibles. Eating too much is, and abstaining doubly hard where take-aways and snacks are so readily available. And of course we (wait for it) love our food. Tenaciously, boringly, fussily, fiercely.

So why all this to-do about our basic fuel? Why emote about the right kind of bread, the wrong sort of sausage? In so far as our culinary attachments and aversions are truly emotion-driven, the answer has to lie in the Mother pattern: food fuels not just physical growth but emotional development. That is to say, being fed is part of the whole experience of being 'cared for' when we are young. Our as yet unrestrained inner feelings find shelter; their outward expression is guided via graphic give-and-take lessons; our growth into more material existence as such is nourished: all at the same time.

No wonder then that we speak of *comfort food*. Just eating, chewing, licking and nibbling as such can be comforting. It may be associated with having been given lots of loving care and attention along with what it took to make us physically grow – or it may be a grim reminder that something to eat was the best and the most you could expect, and the more reason to value it, then and now!

The Mother's most glaring fault is to imprison feelings in some existing form, invest them permanently in the material status quo, including thoughtlessly accepted processes and procedures. This is how we get to have not only fixed (un)emotional responses, but also food traditions set in stone... and a knee-jerk reaction to broccoli. We can blame the Mother in our mother, but in the last resort it is always also the Mother in us, automatically accepting too much – while rejecting too much at the same time. And eating too much. More so the less we have the knack of living inside ourselves, releasing/withdrawing feelings appropriately.

We stuff ourselves, emotionally, into the world around us; stuff feeling permanently into matter. And instead of letting feelings return to their inner source, we stuff whatever they have got fixedly, undynamically attached to into our mouths. Inevitably, we get ever more matter-oriented in the process. And fat, if you'll excuse the word.

But not all eating has to do primarily with feeling. Comfort food is not the only kind we gobble down too much of. There is also what might be called *fortress food*. This is what the Maker in us looks for when he is still unsure of himself, needing simple raw materials to build himself up from, nothing too complex or surprising or at odds with his previous self-experience: keeping-the-larger-world-at-bay food. It is also what he comes to insist on at his most persistently self-repetitive: more-of-the-same food. So far, so defensive. But once he is safely ensconced in his ever-increasing bulk, he will mash up anything, pulp everything in sight into uniform food-as-such, anonymous grist for his over-heating mill. Before long, he is shovelling it in quite unseeing, surprised every time to find his plate empty. 'But I never eat anything, honestly!' is his cry when his excessive girth is under medical scrutiny.

(Note that our childish comfort foods and our primitive fortress foods may resemble each other even to the point of being identical in terms of consistency, ie mushiness. The psychological processes involved are nevertheless as such distinct.)

And then there is *attainment food*, as I will call it. The Hunter's unhealthy bulk is made up of that. Gaining and keeping, in a laying-aside and hoarding-for-a-better-future sort of way, is the Hunter's inappropriate substitute for successful activity in the present, for *moving on* from one small achievement to the next. Food, to him, should truly be no more than the fuel he burns in the process. Eat, digest, eliminate: move through life; and let life move through him. But if he cocks up at every opportunity, dreams only of mega-success in the future, blunders and bashes on all over the place but never actually 'gets anywhere', then he isn't moving properly, nor is life moving through him the way it should.

There are two interpretations we can put on this. Things rush through him and he never 'amounts to anything': he eats and eats but stays rake-thin. Then again, we can see him hanging on to things for the future: he won't let go of, everything stays unfinished business – hence he is permanently constipated, anally retentive if you like, and ultimately amasses a bulk he falsely dismisses, doesn't recognise as his. 'What do you mean, fat? Oh, that. That's nothing, really.' The ample belly, sticking out on its own, more of a puzzling attachment to an otherwise slim body, is never quite part of him – just as his deplorable actions aren't 'really' he; or just as he may actively end up 'beside himself' with fury.

And so the Hunter puts his faulty attainments all too literally 'under his belt' and builds himself up into something that may superficially resemble the Maker, but actually works along very different lines. Meantime the Eternal Child in us takes us down yet another route to obesity, consuming piles of what can only be termed *luxury food*.

Luxury, not necessarily because it is so choice, but primarily because it is not needed at all. The Eternal Child, remember, needs nothing from out of the material sphere of life. This is the pattern with which we can simply, innocently even, 'have fun' in the world; or else we can 'have our sport with it', insatiably using up its resources, wasting it, boasting of the waste even. Banquets, spurting champagne, roast suckling pig. But equally: plain too much of anything, inability to stop gorging, an endless chomping on things, failed compensation for an inner emptiness. This is a genuine hunger, but totally misplaced or misapplied; spiritual need mistakenly translated into feverish consumption.

So luxury food means excess intake, but also conjures up a picture of the privileged Eternal Child in us expecting to feed exclusively on oysters, choice morsels, all the jam and no bread. He is not the only one among our inner cast who can be picky.

Fussy eating, in that sense, already starts with the Maker, who refuses to touch things he is not familiar with. The Mother too, once her foodie affections have been fixed, demands the same time and time again. And then of course there is the Healer, wanting nothing but pasta for a month, then suddenly switching to chips. Not to mention his twin, who eyes with suspicion anything on his plate that sticks out as different and that won't be fork-pressed and mishmashed into submission. More mushy food!

So far, this is about warily fussy eating, refuseniks at the table. A different kind of fussiness is indulgence eating, already in part exemplified by the Eternal Child. But a purer example may be the Artist, who turns a deaf ear to doctors' warnings and continues to leave the healthy stuff for others to chew (too much like work, anyway), much preferring those reliably sweet things that melt in the mouth. She too piles on the pounds, witness to her lack of balance, poise, critical distance; symptom of her over-eagerness, her too immediate involvement. Or call it greed, if you must. Greed, not for much, but for the nicest, easiest, most pleasant.

And then there is the Destroyer, the other one with high expectations. Unlike the Artist's basic script, of course, his does not tell him to keep a beneficial distance, appraise things from a position of overview; on the contrary, it tells him to bring criticism uncompromisingly into whatever situation he finds himself in. It doesn't take much, then, to imagine him at the table: sniffing every drop of milk suspiciously, always ready to pour it away as not fresh enough, and instantly rejecting every slightly blemished piece of fruit wholesale. But of course he too is apt to get caught up, tempted to grab rather than abstain. And then we find him stuffing even as he looks disgusted, uttering condemnations through great mouthfuls: happy with his junk food, the more to have reason to moan. He wastes half his food from sheer contempt. His drinks make him shudder and look mournful. It pleases him immensely to be unpleasable. The role of fat slob is one he embraces eagerly.

But where the Destroyer eventually gets round to developing two distinct aspects, the brilliant and the murky, we also meet a very different figure: dining in style, only the best, splashing out on champagne in full view of everybody, a trim and elegant figure. This is food as status symbol, for want of a better expression. It is food as mask, as official declaration of what one is about (except that of course it is a false declaration, a partial truth only).

Slightly different again is the Creator's attitude to public eating; and *his* eating is always, in some measure, public. As the great provider, what he can put on the table shows off his (inner) worth, so it better be good. And where his own intake is concerned, well, in the purest theory he should be sustained entirely by others' heartfelt thanks: the only 'food fit for the gods'. But the less ideal the way he handles his self/life, the more he just wants to be waited on instead. Both childish and arrogant, he now takes the most exotic titbits as his due – this is truly status symbol stuff, meant to show him in the best possible light – and at the same time he is for ever petulantly demanding more. Never doing things by halves, he manages to be both fussy *and* insatiable. His resultant portly figure of course only strikes him as duly impressive. He is not someone to be overlooked in a hurry, obviously.

But the one who really can't be beaten for fussiness is surely the Thinker in us all. She isn't content with mere choosing and picking. She goes on to *do things with food*, taking it apart, then putting some of the constituent parts together again, in un-natural ways. Elaborately styling it, fiddling with ingredients: cuisine and modish presentation. Both Creator and Artist may make something of a work of art of basic sustenance, but the Thinker goes further, makes a whole science of it, weighing and measuring, considering nutritional value, counting vitamins and calories and whatnot. And having worked out such a diet to her satisfaction, she then goes on fiddling with that, rewriting it ad infinitum.

Such intelligent scrutiny of what she is about to 'introject', such conscious regulation of intake (and output, let's not forget: after the fancy diet, the laxative) can lead to some pretty puritanical eating habits. But there is always the flip side. And that's the Destroyer's other face as well, not just the Thinker's unthinking doings.

Coprophagia, the ingestion of faeces, may be an example too rare to merit mention. More within normal range is the all-dark side of the Destroyer, the hidden self behind the port-sipping persona: liable to indulge in compulsive 'crap' eating sessions, total junk, complete rubbish, as he knows perfectly well. And the Thinker too, once she has divided herself into head and hands, spotless self and active dirt-digging, is prone to some pretty unspeakable appetites.

There are a number of interpretations here, and we need to learn to be flexible, ready to consider different aspects, seeing the literal, but also extrapolating. What the Thinker takes into her body may be seen as something being internalised – and from that point of view she'll make sure nothing dodgy ever passes her lips, no matter how much vile stuff her hands may eagerly grasp: she keeps her insides clean, her head aloof, her mind pure. On the other hand, we can understand her as viewing her own body as being external to her-the-purely-intellectual-self: in which case she could eat garbage by the ton and yet never regard *herself* as polluted by it. She might draw up diet sheets for others; but when no one, including herself, is looking, her hands dive into that jar of sticky sweets with the speed and repetitiveness of a serious compulsion.

(Compulsion, addiction: an angle on behaviour that spans so much more than just what substances we take into our bodies – including what we force on others by way of principles, or expect from them in terms of applause, and so forth. This hardly constitutes a helpful category of enquiry in itself, being evenly distributed over all our impulses, and touching on literally every aspect of life. I will leave it to the reader to decide at what point unconscious wilfulness becomes 'compulsion', or what might usefully be termed 'addiction'. I suggest we treat such terms lightly, not as diagnostic labels.)

After these many separate species of both over-eating and selective eating, we come at last to not eating at all. For a start, there is the Eternal Child in us. Manically stuffing himself one moment, the next he hits a low: inappetence on a grand scale, not a morsel will pass his lips. Admittedly, he stands a better chance of regaining his inner contentment by abstaining from the high life, but not if he keeps moaning extravagantly and making an all too solid fuss. At any rate, he soon changes his mind, relaunches himself into his consumerist never-quite bliss with the same old over the top gusto.

The Priest takes her no's to life rather more seriously. As we have seen, she *can* suddenly throw it all away, finish with life just like that. Slow starvation is a different proposition, though. She might attempt it, for short periods, but her extreme neediness, acting like a vacuum or a sponge, instantly and automatically attracts new substance to fill it: an inescapable resurgence of appetite, or an outside offer of help perhaps... if only to force-feed her, whether she likes it or not.

To apply the anorexia label and really make it stick, we need to look to the Thinker pattern. This is where our body can so easily become other-out-there: an appendage that threatens to drag us down from our new-found intellectual heights. Body as suspect. Body as embarrassment. Body as something dirty or somehow just not perfect enough to identify with.

Where the Hunter reckons himself thin, despite evidence to the contrary, the Thinker thinks of herself as much too fat, no matter how rake-thin she (or should we say: her body) may have become. It is no use telling her to look in the mirror. She does not derive her self-awareness from worldly mirror images, like Creator and Healer. She knows herself inside herself – and not just as idea but as ideal, simply cutting off any conscious awareness of her 'lower nature'.

First she starves this undeserving physical self of attention. Then she literally starves it, to be properly rid of it. Her death-wish, though, is (to be precise) only a desire for perfection. She would not really regard herself as dead without her body, only more pure and exalted, for ever unspoilably gorgeous. Does it need warped religious dogma and the dictates of the fashion industry to feed such ideas into her head? Not really: she (un)naturally inclines that way. But it certainly won't help her any to be brainwashed along those lines; to be stuck, that is, with a mental diet of identically silly choices.

Bulimia, gorging and then making herself be sick, we can also recognise as the Thinker's province. Absent-mindedly letting her hands stray into the cookie jar for a good, compensatory if you like, feed – then realising what she has done. There follows self-disgust, purging, getting rid of all that sinful stuff. (And we should not forget the Priest pattern here, with its constant self-disgusted emptying out, only to automatically fill up again. This too could well take the form of unrestrained eating, followed by more or less deliberate vomiting or purging.) But if the Thinker keeps thoughtlessly eating, then she will never reach her goal of being ideally body-less. Seeing her physical self as something that actively works against her only alienates her even further from 'that thing'.

We have seen how the Destroyer too can manifestly have a death wish that is much more accurately described as a perfection wish. But he, incapable of staying aloof, will seek death in quite 'real', material terms, and in terms of other. We see in him a butcher fondling chunks of dead body, an image of beauty to him, a representation of the unattainable; or a gruesomely meticulous killer (who maybe courts his own death in the process). All this is quite the opposite of the Thinker, for whom all things bodily are simply anathema. To her, deadness, like everything else, has become an abstract idea – which *tries* to take on a life of its own, one might say.

But an exclusively inner, bodiless life is possible only to the Eternal Child and the ever self-transforming Revolutionary in us.

If the Thinker in us thinks she will manage it too, simply by spurning her 'base' physical life, then she has thought a thought too far.

More generally speaking, with the Thinker's mental isolation comes a conscious *body image*. At the extreme end of the spectrum, this can make something almost alien of what is really part of her whole self. But even less extremely, her body still becomes a cut off and outside thing, something to be treated in whatever way she thinks fit. She could enhance 'it', dress it up, alter it with surgery, feed it on fancy diets, hone it and tone it, supplement its bulk with artificial implants, go in for careful body-building – or punish it with gruelling exercises, neglect it, ultimately starve it out of existence, thinking to be so much better without it. She could even do several of these antithetical things concurrently. But that's the Thinker for you: self-contradictory to the last; illogical to the end.

'So Why Exactly is It Hurting?'

The Maker in us relentlessly makes us grow fatter and fatter, the Thinker in us thinks 'Body? Who needs it!' while the Mother in us throws her emotional all behind physical being – then finds it more convenient to banish large parts of it from sight... As if they weren't all bad enough on their own! Is it any wonder we fall prey to disorders, dis-ease? And whose health is it anyway?

Before we ask how our various motivational strands might work together, we need to practise interpreting them singly. This is not a matter of having set texts, lists, tables to consult, but something to be done imaginatively. Something akin to the decoding of myth. Archetypes are not dead givens: consulting them like oracles, the kind of answer we get depends entirely on how we frame the question. Or to put it another way, the more we know, the more these patterns will reveal to us.

I have no medical training, so I am very limited when it comes to the precise questions I could ask the archetypal patterns in connection with matters of health. But just to give the reader an idea of how one might work with symptoms, in search of the underlying 'fault', I'll try my hand at a few random examples.

To start with something quite general and widespread: infection. The first thing that springs to mind is the total lack of immunity to environmental *influences* we find, exclusively, in the Priest pattern. This in itself may lead one to wonder whether a state of emotional turmoil, upset or recent loss (of something previously internal, a subjective life content, or of something/ someone conducive to inner harmony) does maybe have a lot to do with catching infectious complaints, especially the more 'deep-going' ones.

However, the Priest can also stay or become relatively superficial, 'picking up' anything, for a short time. Hunter and Maker, too, are both entirely at the mercy of their environment for supplying them with their 'ingredients', and by their nature never run to any depths at all. There may be several insights to be had here into superficial and passing infectious illness. Let's just look at the Hunter pattern, though. Using it positively, you simply get on with life, move through it, soon get it out of your system, whatever it may be. Used negatively, the picture might be: reduced mobility, lack of exercise, inappropriate clinging and storing, accumulation of both objective 'riches' (fat) and subjectively unvalued 'rubbish' (build-up of toxins?), all encouraging bugs to settle, rather than shaking them off and leaving them behind.

Still on the subject of infections, when it comes to active *resistance* to things ready to invade us, we would seem to be firmly on Thinker territory. Now, thinking hard is obviously not going to stave off any colds; neither do 'dumb' animals lack disease resistance. But one helpful thing to note here might be the way this resistance is come by in the first place: through cautiously 'introjecting' only some of the relatively 'polluted' environment, while carefully, thoughtfully, keeping most of it out. Sounds like a healthy observance of cleanliness? It also sounds strangely like the practice of inoculation or vaccination. If we look at the downside of the pattern, on the other hand, we come across an excessive fear of pollution, having a thing about hygiene, shutting a multitude of so-called dirty things out... and then, unwittingly, picking them up all the same, all the better and the more suddenly and surprisingly. You regard yourself as immune one moment, and are brought low by something fairly drastic the next.

That too scrupulously clean a lifestyle will only serve to lay us even wider open to infection is hardly news these days, but not so long ago it might have been an insight worth having. I have no doubt that if medical practitioners took the trouble to work with the archetypal life patterns, imaginatively *and* in a scientifically informed way, they would find inspiration enough for new cures, integrated therapies, or at least novel lines of research worth following up.

Like this, if we trawl through the patterns, we can find quite a number of different 'causes' for infection – to attempt just one more angle: the Mother too tries to cut herself off, distance herself (in her case not from outside influences so much as from aspects of her own life) and then finds herself faced with precisely what she was trying to avoid: something that ought to be self, but which has become other to her, and which in effect invades her as something now alien. Rather than a case of infection, is this maybe the pattern, the underlying mechanism, behind auto-immune reactions?

One example of such a condition, where the body no longer recognises bits of itself and treats them as foreign invaders, would seem to be rheumatoid arthritis. Being physically stiff and unbending is a symptom that does of course tie in closely with one aspect of the Mother as we have got to know her, personified: as emotionally rigid. So we may need to ask in how far frozen, torn or disowned feelings could play a part in this context. Asthma, on the other hand – another condition that can be due to an auto-immune reaction – might correspond to the Mother's lack of in/outflow, to her habit of self-restriction, and in its wake those spasmodic 'inbursts' (emerging as outbursts), her panic attacks, and her feeling beleaguered or under attack in general. And there is also her strange dependence on minor irritants: things irritating, unsettling, slightly disturbing to her, that is, which are her very lifeblood in an otherwise lifeless situation. All in all, something for the experts to puzzle about.

This is not to say, though, that the rest of us might not try and come to some general insights. Take allergies, for instance. The Thinker's province again: being anti, reacting to life, nothing much ever agreeing with her unapproachable, unreproachable self. One general question we might usefully investigate is this: does the level of allergy-related illnesses rise in societies where 'choice' is not just encouraged, but perhaps – and I say this cautiously – elevated to a degree no longer healthy for the mind/body system? I am not suggesting that, literally, 'choice is bad for your health'. Rather more subtly, having twenty-five different soap powders to choose from might induce or encourage in us a level of Thinkerly pernicketiness that can only lead us down the negative road in terms of how we handle the Thinker in us, overall.

Speaking of mental attitude and its connection with health, we might like to take a look at depression – loosely rather than clinically speaking. The first thing to note is that, if we cast a look over the different patterns there are, again, a number of likely suspects. To start with one we have already considered in that context: the Eternal Child. At first sight, the problem seems to be purely a matter of something missing, something lacking. There is the loss of inner-life, the loss of that core joie de vivre that in no way depends on material gain, or physical well-being. But at the same time we can't help noting the insatiable, indeed manic, appetite for all too concrete living; and not just by way of compensating for the absence of better, inner things, but often directly leading to their loss in the first place.

But the Boss in us, too, must be a candidate high on our list of depressives. And here the first impression is, not of loss, but of being weighed down: so much to give (long-established knowledge, superior advice etc) and no one to take this burden off us. Though of course it is only a burden because we are trying far too hard to externalise our inner gift, ie force it on others to please our intellectually wilful selves. I can't help wondering, in this context, whether this Boss-type depression may not be an affliction more prevalent in older people, faced with an increasingly unlistening, 'disobedient' world. The Eternal Child-type, on the other hand, might be more what we go in for in our robust prime.

Thirdly, there is also the Priest's potential for getting us into a completely world-rejecting sort of state, as already discussed. Given the fragility, the raw beginnerdom showing in the Priest pattern, this could be the most likely 'cause' of depression in our youth.

These would seem to be the major roots of depression we need to keep an eye on, then. And it may be interesting to note just in passing that they take the appearance, respectively, of wanting to take too much, wanting to give too much, and wanting to accept nothing.

But maybe we should also briefly consider the Mother impulse under this heading: embattled and fearful, avoiding the full truth of what she has disowned, beset by anxieties and wary of what lies round each corner. If she looks a bit frazzled and worn out with it all, others may well be tempted to stick the label 'depressed' on her. In fact, when she first tries to press her feelings wholesale on a world not fit or willing to receive them, at that point (or phase) she too will find herself painfully burdened with 'too much to give'.

Veering off on yet another tack, what do we make of the Healer huddling in his box, querulously refusing any input? Viewed purely from the outside, one could easily mistake him for suffering from depressive phases, in between his headlong dashing about. – Plenty of food there for self-searching, close observation, and possibly investigation along lines not considered before.

Finally, for something totally different again, let's turn the spotlight on accidents. These aren't exactly classed among diseases, as such; we reserve that status for the breakages and assembled ills in their wake – but should we? We can look at the Eternal Child in us stumbling around in a puzzlingly concrete world, and say: nothing wrong with that, a measure of clumsiness is completely natural. But the artfully accident-prone Healer in us is rather a different matter.

Whether he actively deconstructs life, or passively fails to look where he's headed, as we have seen before: the Healer in us is naturally his own undoing, and in how far he manages to piece or pull himself together, learns to hang together, is the measure of his success. From that point of view he is 'disorder' writ large. And since this is an impulse associated with the thoughtful use of the senses, we could expect to find, specifically (and in addition to those not so 'accidental' accidents): afflictions of the nervous system, the sense organs, speech. There will of course be two distinct form these could take, to go with the Healer's two downsides. One would manifest as an all-over confusion, a general disruption of functions, a muddling up and slurring of boundaries. The other possibility would show up us a pattern of distinct comings and goings, 'illogical' fluctuations and puzzling reversals.

I won't attempt a comprehensive list of such disorders, but a few things that spring to mind are: skin rashes, twitches and hiccups and tics, all sorts of cramps and spasms and fits, disrupted mobility, 'freezing' followed by involuntary dashes (going from one box or rut to the next, as it were), verbal mix-ups like spoonerisms, dyslexia, and of course stammering. Also asthmatic and other kinds of sudden 'attack' – perpetrated by himself on himself, it always has to be added: another potential root of auto-immune reaction? This sort of attack would notably lack the emotional connection, being partly natural condition, (so maybe genetic) and, in addition, a failure of co-ordination in the widest sense. Perhaps music therapy, establishing an orderly and persistent yet forward-going rhythm, could be particularly useful with all these conditions?

And so one could go on, trying to trace superficial symptoms back to their true underlying malaise, finding many forks in the road, and confluences. To go back, though, to what I said about the Healer pattern as the fundamental prototype of things going physically wrong with us – and none to blame but himself. What does that tell us about disease as such? Falling over your own feet as serious disorder? Sickness as absurdity? But contrast that with our other expert at ailing, the Thinker who, if she doesn't ignore it, punish it for existing and starve it, makes a whole new science of what's wrong with her body. Hypochondria is her middle name. There may be nothing physically the matter with her at all, and still – from inside her mind's perfectionist enclave – she frets ceaselessly and finds a million faults. Illness as an uneasy mixture of expectation and perception, the intellectual and the sensory. Illness as the serious downside of self-consciousness.

So whose fault is it if I come down with some disease tomorrow? Do I blame, for instance, my own given predisposition, my genes (Healer); my naturally always-imperfect body (Thinker); my environment, exclusively (Thinker); my own deliberate if unconscious short-sightedness, or indeed covertly manipulative carelessness (both Healer); or my being purely 'neurotic' about what are no more than 'imaginary', that is mentally generated, afflictions (Thinker)?

The answer has to be: it might be any or several of these. Obviously, I might as well avoid using my motivation patterns badly, so as not to cause or contribute to my own ill-health. Other than that, we are back with the perennial theme of self/other, the inter-relationship between the two. Let me put it like this: at the Healer level, things happen to me just as I happen to them; there is an equality of self and environment. So the most I can hope for is that I will manage to do my bit trying to get it together. Meantime, at the Thinker level, inner idea translates into physical reality *and vice versa*. But if that two-way link is mentally denied, then we ultimately fall victim to nasty things, things that go quite against our best intentions and plans what to be and do. Life, environment, other, will have its input, whether we consciously allow it or not. In fact, the more we fend 'other' off to preserve a pristine self, the sneakier and more shocking that something other will *have* to be. Disease, in this instance, as a balance-restoring agent of life itself!

The bottom line seems to be that we can't expect health any more than we would, sensibly, count on wealth. Life is a give and take, the body an interface between other and self (and it is up to us not to let it become an outright battle ground). Maybe we will have to regard illness not so much as a personal loss but as a reasonable, or at least natural, demand: to keep adapting inner self to physical environment, outlook to events; to keep interacting in new ways, make new connections between an *in effect* imperfect self and an always imperfect world. And following what I said above about disease as a restorer of natural balance, maybe we can even see it as, not at all accidental, but a positive *chance* – a spell of potentially curative isolation, say: less of life's crazy excesses, of society's ills and institutionalised madnesses. Here we come back to the most fundamental message the Healer pattern has for us, namely that all disorders contain the seed of their own cure.

Before we can attempt to find that cure, though, we need to be reasonably clear what is outward symptom and what is primary, possibly 'inner', disturbance. For a start, if we look at it in the round, we find that symptoms ultimately come only as one of two broad types. The first shows up as a *disturbed flow*, whether of emotion, perception, activity or whatever. And the other manifests as *schism*, all those splits within and without or indeed between inner and outward state that we have already observed.

As to what underlies these symptomatic disturbances, we again find two categories. The first is *excessiveness*, and it applies in every case, each time a pattern is misused. Examples are wilfulness, overdoing things (even the theoretically most laudable efforts), wanting to give or take or know too much all in one go. The second is *loss or lack of centre*. As when the Eternal Child projects himself outward to become a 'soul-less man of substance'; or the Priest settles for staying a 'heartless' user of the best others have to offer, or a 'homeless' recipient of the worst. But this issue of centre obviously does not apply across the board to all patterns. In the case of Hunter and Maker not at all; and with Artist and Destroyer only in the limited sense of something impersonal, an instinct if we want to call it that, central to their functioning.

Of course the moment we consider the whole person – our different impulses working together, our motivational strands combined into a single weave – we know that having, and living in, our centre does have to come into it somewhere. We need our inner 'place' of rest, safety, regeneration, automatic well-being and free-of-charge joy, perfection even (if of a rather abstract sort, available as a ready inspiration, if you like).

This personal centre is something to find and fill (Priest, Thinker), but also something to regain if we have lost it (Mother, Eternal Child etc). Because a state of innerness promises healing: if we can only centre ourselves, we immediately touch on an underlying wholeness and health. And from there we can go forward in a renewed effort to stand ourselves in a better relation to everything outward, including our bodies.

Remains the question how do we successfully centre ourselves, given how much we enjoy our excessive worldly appetites – even the ones that manage to put us off our food – which clearly all pull us in the opposite direction. We need to be cautious which of our impulses to follow inward too readily. Both Priest and Thinker, for instance, only too easily have us deceiving ourselves. Pretend-inner emotion is of no help to us; nor is a fanatical puritan's intellectual cocoon. Neither will really help make us better. I would suggest intuition as our safest road inward, via the Eternal Child in us. At least with this impulse there can be no mistaking where we are, inwardly settled... or its thoroughly unsubtle opposite!

A relaxed playfulness, couldn't-care-lessish and bordering on the introspective, ready to giggle at the absurdities of life: this could be our first milestone on the way to better health.

Visions, Insight and Superstition

In the course of these chapters we have seen a lot of what I have variously called falling for the world altogether, prolapsing, losing hold of one's inner anchorage while becoming a slave to compulsive cravings, inextricably bound to the materialistic life. Alternatively, we might speak of 'projection': whether of our inner values, which come exclusively to take on the form of precious possessions, jealously guarded; or of our inner feelings, which become embodied in something or someone other, only to be rejected, cut off, when they are no longer comfortably owned.

Again and again we face this danger of cutting ourselves off. From the world, or certain parts of it; from our inner selves, or parts of them; or from parts of our outward active-selves which we simply no longer recognise as being us in action. Losing touch with the inner self, though, we lose a lot more in the process: we no longer have access to the wider inner world of knowing – what I have here called Inner Reality or the Inner Plane, or Creative Base, and what the established religions variously call Allah, God, Spirit, and so on. It is our connectedness to this non-material 'environment' beyond the personal inner self that truly constitutes re-ligion.

Using the word in that sense, religion allows us knowledge that is in addition to what we may know from using our physical senses and our earthbound reasoning or feelings. The Artist in us, for instance, has an innate appreciation of balance, beauty, harmony, fairness, justice. The Boss in us has, again, what we would call an inborn knowledge of logic and basic rules, whether governing grammar (as such, in any language) or moral behaviour (a 'natural' conscience, if you like). And the Eternal Child in us, our prime access route to intuitive inner-knowing, yields holistic insights: an integrated or overview which tells us how things relate and hang together, now, in the past, in the future – in 'eternal' Truth, rather than in the few 'live' scattered material facts around us.

We are clearly designed to live out this inner perception of how things hang together. We are meant to implement this sense of an overriding oneness of everything. But while some of our motivation patterns have an element of accessing and using insight directly, others ask us to do so only indirectly. For instance: in Truth all things obviously hang together; but via our Healer impulse we are able also *to make them* hang together a bit more *in fact*.

But there of course the trouble starts. Not any relating is right relating, not every connection a logical or helpful one – we have seen the kind of mess the Healer can make of things, cobbling odds and ends together, fabricating tales, jumping to conclusions, and so on. We could add that at the same time the Eternal Child, once he has projected himself wholly outward and lost touch with true insight, will rely entirely on material substitutes to take the place of the transcendent, the spiritual (not to mention his making extravagant claims for himself, setting himself up as a bogus holy man and the like). We could add other examples, but the Healer and the Eternal Child seem especially relevant here. The net effect is clear: we have left the area of the truly religious, acting as your own inner guru; we are now firmly in the world of superstition.

Yes, in the wider view all things are meaningfully connected – but peering at chicken entrails and tea leaves in search of the future? Praying to gilded gods? Trusting in magic words? Lucky numbers, talismans and good or bad omens: we do find it difficult to avoid this kind of thing altogether. But, as the saying goes, there is no smoke without a fire. Even the most ludicrous belief has *some* sort of basis in Truth. The problem is, we take things too literally. Too concretely. Too pinpoint exactly. If we grab hold of the words like the terrier the rat, we are bound to lose sight of the spirit of them. And conversely, if we lose touch with the spirit, then we will of course find ourselves wringing each single word dry in search of meaning... which still won't materialise. And images, representations, symbols become the thing itself to us: Truth pinned down on parchment, insight made concrete in a colourful charm, the future *literally* visible in the steaming guts of a slaughtered sheep, cracks in the pavement, a somehow 'fitting' post code.

It is the Healer impulse, needing to find meaning, true connectedness, via our intelligently used physical senses, that has us developing that great kaleidoscope of superstitions. Now the Healer impulse is a splendid tool for applying unconscious insights to practical work, but it is no use at all for gaining conscious insight; for that we need to turn inward, not surprisingly, rather than out towards facts. The Healer will help us look down microscopes, deftly handle slides, write up notes, disseminate the knowledge gained. And this scientific assemblage of facts is fine as far as it goes. But for the ultimate setting in perspective, if we are to understand what all this really means, we need to apply the inner-intuitive understanding of the Eternal Child in us. Or to put it rather strongly: objective reality in itself is never meaningful, not reliably anyway. We can try and make it so, using our Healer impulse, but to expect to reap guaranteed meaning among files and slides and pie-charted facts is folly. Rank superstition.

In a slightly different take on that, we might say that God *is* in all the titchy physical details, but *not recognisably* so. That meaning is not in the isolated details *as such*, but can only be found in the process of putting them together. To find meaning in the world around us requires work; it is not a matter of passive perception.

In other words, it is no use at all wondering about whether or not some event 'means something'. If we can somehow subjectively make sense of it, derive a lesson in truthful living from it, work with it in whatever positive ways, then if it doesn't already do so, it will certainly come to mean something.

Going from our scientific superstitions to the other end of the scale, though, as it were: what about the so-called paranormal, telepathy et al, crystal ball gazing even? I have already stated clearly that we do have the power of insight, including knowledge of past (retrocognition), future (precognition), of others and their lives. If contemplating the blankness of a crystal ball can help us relax and genuinely withdraw inward, fine. If on the other hand we stare fixedly at the thing, expecting to see something *in it*, then of course no good will come of it. And don't frauds abound? Then again, even the worst of the bogus spirit message merchants appear sometimes to be genuinely insightful. Well, if they are, it should come as no surprise: those of us with the strongest talent also stand in the greatest danger of misusing it. Being truly insightful and being a fraudulent windbag come out of the same pattern, after all; prophet and charlatan are twin brothers.

Why in any case do we bother to invent fancy terms like telepathy, clairvoyance etc, when all we are speaking of is the natural gift of insight? Why describe as somehow *super*natural the perfectly natural inner-seeing the Revolutionary in us can and does do – if at times he is rather more spectacularly inspired than at others, has great flashes of mental illumination, so what? We do so love to draw all sorts of artificial distinctions (the Healer in us at work again). Also, in our present scientistic culture, we still do not give proper recognition to our feeling and intuiting functions, as yet. Neither are we particularly good at exercising them, in the prevailing materialistic climate. The Eternal Child in us, especially, is more often seen ramraiding the world for physical pleasures than making for the more refined joys of insightful living!

All in all, inner-knowing is not much practised. Instead, we *believe*. We believe in the theological dogma of the institutionalised religions; we believe in science as the provider of ultimate answers; we believe in the supernatural or paranormal, taking it to somehow transcend the terribly and terrifyingly mundane.

All these 'outward' beliefs are of course an inappropriate concretisations: the likes of literalism, religious fundamentalism, materialistic reductionism, a pagan muddle of much smoke and very little genuine fire. We may laugh at shamans with their weird incantations, witch doctors slapping filthy dung plasters on wounds – and who knows whether there is not maybe something pretty efficient about those dung bacteria; and the power of suggestion may well dispel some complaints – but really we are no better. We too try to simplify life, willy-nilly drag things down to a purely physical level (Healer: active), while at the same time making a fuss about keeping our beliefs or whatever discipline we practise, pure, unmixed and unadded-to in a box of its own (Healer: passive).

It may be a good idea to distinguish a bit more clearly between faith and belief. Obviously, we stand in danger of putting too much emphasis on words again, so let me just say that there are two very different processes here which we need to tell apart. The one is based on personal *experience*: staying centred, 'plugged in', using our natural inner access to the meaningful, we keep faith with That. The other process, what I would call belief, is based on *teachings* received from others, second-hand wisdom at best, false and deliberately manipulative at worst.

As I have mentioned repeatedly, each pattern needs the help of the others to work to its best potential. Thus the Healer in us needs the Eternal Child to provide the underlying Truth without which he can neither properly work with facts, nor evaluate them in context – not rightly, not to any lasting, overall beneficial effect, at any rate. If we allow the Eternal Child in us to lose his inner place 'near God' in frantic pursuit of a place (position, standing) in the world, then we should maybe at least admit to ourselves that we are bound to exchange re-ligion for crass superstition.

We see the same kind of descent of Meaning into gibberish if we turn to other examples. Take the 'divinely inspired' Artist, or the 'born genius' Revolutionary: both highly visionary patterns. Misused, they only lead to make-believe, corrosive fiction, living in unreality, making no sense, madness. In fact, visions of one unhealthy sort or another abound. From the simple – like the Hunter's unrealistic view of his self, the glorious future one, the chimera that never does replace the rough reality of the present – to the complex spooks the Mother will invent to explain her shocking behaviour. And the Destroyer, much as the Mother, may really *feel* possessed. Both genuinely feel they have been taken over by the invisible and inexplicable, some living agent who performs what are obviously (even to them) their own actions. But the genuineness of the emotional experience as such does not conjure reality out of wilful misinterpretation. We ably create our own demons, out of all the cast-off parts of our selves.

The Creator in us too can come to believe in alien forces. The details of such a notion will depend on the prevailing images of his culture: fairies, goblins, green men from Mars… now turned a fashionable grey, and no longer from so humdrum a planet. Admiring himself in a mirroring world, the Creator finds it especially hard to conceive of others also acting independently of him, having an input into his mirror image, an influence, power. So who does he blame when things go wrong? Not himself; nor those obvious others still not recognised as such by him. No wonder he begins to 'see things': thoroughly alien forces about to steal his essence and identity – be they the crew of a flying saucer violating him in pursuit of samples of his DNA, or the Devil himself after his soul.

And then there is the Priest. Genuine channel? Or false medium? Or just playing along with the expectations one foists on her, allowing herself to be used, possessed, in that sense?

Given all those bits of disowned self, split-off self, mislaid self, unrecognised self – and at the same time our genuine ability to transcend self and touch on inner states beyond our own – the question arises: where are our boundaries, really? In the world of matter the answer is fairly obvious. But in the purely abstract sphere of the mental, intuitional, inner-emotional etc, the answer has surely to be: there are no *set* boundaries. The pattern of the Revolutionary in us probably demonstrates this most clearly, with his instant inner transformations. It tells us that, essentially, we are one another; or we can be. And while some of our motivation patterns may, rightly, work towards keeping us apart, as distinct units, others, like the Priest, can so deeply reconcile us as to fuse us, meld us, make a oneness again of the scattered parts-of we are.

But how, especially via the Creator and the Healer impulses, do we project that inner kinship out? Not just, obviously, in acts of generosity and brotherly kindness. Our welcome and unwelcome apparitions, the spectres of the living, the ghosts of the long dead, may be our true relations made all too palpable – though they are just as likely to make no sense at all.

Myth is what we call the key process of a deep Truth translated into the world of colourful facts. Oneness dissolved and scattered, to be captured again in matter: painted, sculpted, sung, written or recited. Invested in public figures, too, making them stand for something bigger and truer, purer than the 'reality' of what they are. The god-kings of old, or a Princess Diana for our own age; living icons who demonstrate openly what is 'in our hearts'. Both Healer and Creator are involved in this business of trying to find the ultimate reflected in the detail, and the eternal in the passing craze; of voicing a collective unconscious Truth by laying on a chosen few the burden of taking on a 'divine' or supremely meaningful role.

The more we can work with all this in a playful, imaginative way, the better. Truth may become reduced to a poor approximation in the process, but at least it is still roughly recognisable as such. 'It's a myth' ought to be a term of high praise! Likewise, paganism at its best presents its followers with a glimpse of the ultimate one-ness of all: trees, people, soil, streams, dreams and business deals. But the more literal it all becomes, the more we allow ourselves to get carried away with serious outward elaboration, counting angels and fussing over the right form of ceremonial dress, the more ludicrously inaccurate a representation of Truth we end up with. In the end we are left with rituals that have gone stale: in grand palaces, ornate churches, in rationalistically spindoctored interviews with polished public figures meant to be larger than life; in dry formulas for plush performances on stage and TV screen; in various desperate fashions in 'spirituality', undines this year, tree sprites the next; in ossified dogma and, hot on its heals, headlong conversion crises and a sizzling missionary zeal... to offset the deadness at the centre. In short, we are back with superstition, the bottom end of the scale that starts so sensibly with myth.

The true meaning of a myth should lie in the active living of it, working with it (Healer). And in generous co-operation with others, accepting how it may develop in front of your eyes (Creator) rather than insisting on its set 'performance'.

But myths not only go wrong by becoming overly literal. They can also – whether in some way perhaps helpfully, is a matter for discussion – embody not the Truth as best potential, but instead the misuse of a pattern. Let me give an example. This one comes out of the Priest pattern and in Europe is chiefly to be found as a tale of vampires. Consider the Priestly ingredients there: the undead (not having become properly detached from the world), the helpless victim who turns victimiser (the two dark sides of the Priest), lack of resistance and being infected/trying to infect the whole world with a form of living death, feeding on another's blood (borrowing their inner life for one's own), appearances that prove utterly false. In a way, blaming the historical figure of Vlad the Impaler for this weirdly otherworldly tale seems just as concretistically superstitious as literally believing in vampire attacks.

It takes a wooden stake through the heart to drive the undead finally into that other, inner world where life blood is not required. Given that using the Christian cross or bible is the only way to fend the blood-sucking menace off, maybe the stake is but a variant of the cross? The Christian myth is, after all, a positive counterpart of the above: an explicit encapsulation of the highest potential the Priest pattern can offer us (though what superstitious practice has made of all this is another matter). 'I am the way', the Christ says – not: I am captured in historical fact, dates and details, cross-shaped trinkets hung round necks, words found exclusively in one book, unalterable ritual, red liquid drunk etc.

The 'Christ' way is the way to mystical union *followed by* selfless activity in the world out there. And of course it isn't exclusively 'Christian' at all. All the world's religions, at their highest, ie their least superstitious, follow that same Priestly path of deepest insight and highest standards of behaviour towards others. – These patterns, let us be clear, are about universal Life Principles.

What a minefield! Truth becomes fact, many facts, shedding its capital T as it goes, progressively becoming untruer. Somewhere along the line, the crux of the matter, the spirit of the thing, will be lost. But where? And how, with mere word-facts, do we try and communicate the Truth we may well know, each in ourselves, to those around us? We start off with mythical representation, symbol, metaphor, simile, imagery as fertile ground: the dance of the details lightly performed. For a while we may juggle valiantly with broad ideas like synchronicity and correspondence. But soon we sink to the level of literal interpretation, institutationalised beliefs, dogmatic 'explanations': events are automatically taken to be miracles; or part of a solid chain of cause and effect; or mere coincidence.

We can rely on things coming together if we genuinely turn inward. But there is no knowing what out there may or may not be 'true', or significant. Everything around us does ultimately hang together; but that does not mean that the few things and events right here, right now, automatically have some kind of meaningful connection *with each other*, in the absence of all the rest, so to speak. A few stray pieces of a jigsaw: they may be contiguous, or they may not.

Of course, if we unconsciously use our powers of insight, we will not-so-accidentally stumble across many significant facts and figures indeed. But if it was done unconsciously, how do we know it was done at all, or how? We dismiss our own powers, or we misattribute them to unseen forces. We ignore the meaningful and call it random, and elevate the random to a state of immense significance. In the last analysis, we are not only ignorant, we are incapable of knowing for sure what we know. - But then, what do analyses tell us?

Having knowledge, *having* insight is beside the point, after all. One thing our different motivation patterns all clearly show is that nothing can be grasped for good, had for keeps, invested for ever, imposed wholesale, and so on. Instead, if we are to use them wisely, there has got to be endless work, constant in/outflow, give and take, change, development, moving on. This much we can safely take quite literally. Our clever species ever reaching the frontiers of knowledge, on the other hand, that's a bit of a m... misunderstanding.

Part Three

PEOPLE

Being Whole

We are made up of different strands. Not concrete and unchanging parts, but rather a hive of active motivations, each urging us on to go in a different direction: bravely projecting us forward, cautiously holding us back, asking us to shine on the public stage, demanding that we turn inward, away from the material world, and so on. A set of distinct impulses which, while having definite aims, are open to a great many interpretations.

But we are also whole, and this wholeness is clearly reflected in the way these component strands hang together, interdepend: none of them can function in isolation. The Boss can't function without the Mother, the Artist needs the Hunter's co-operation, the Creator is lost without the Revolutionary in us. They may seem to want different things from us, or for us, but if one looks closely (and, more especially, if one considers them in their positive aspects) it becomes clear that they mesh, slot together most satisfactorily. Together, they make a balanced whole capable of a variety of responses: a pliable whole, jointed, articulated. Something that is entire, but which also has the sort of give that is the hallmark of aliveness.

I have spoken of patterns, motivation patterns, our eternal archetypes. I have also called them our root impulses: our given, active urges to behave in certain ways. Innate, universal. And yet in describing the internal nature of each pattern I hope to have demonstrated clearly that, even if we dig right down to the foundations of what shapes our behaviour, we find an inherent flexibility there, a limitless potential for variety. What makes us behave the way we do may be given, is undeniably given, but not tangibly, literally, exactly spell-outably and predictably given. Far from it.

How does all this apply to you and me, the different 'personalities' we are, the various roles we play in each other's lives? It goes without saying that each of us has, uses, the full complement of archetypal impulses: six ways of becoming ourselves, six of being ourselves. And yet, as every parent can vouch for, we differ from the outset, this one much more the impulsive go-getter, that one maybe predominantly the dreamer. Predominantly. We need to be as careful as ever not to rush into typecasting and mentally filing each other away: so-and-so is 'very much the Hunter type', so-and-so's brother 'a typical Eternal Child', or whatever. Being composite as well as whole, we are obviously a lot more complex, colourful, self-contradictory, and problematic, than that.

This, if we want to use it, is where natal (and psychologically oriented) astrology comes into its own. This is where it has its proper function. Anyone with no experience of it will find it hard to believe – and I would hardly advocate such belief, having described the act of believing as the first easy step on the road to superstition! – but those of us who have worked with it have found the natal chart extremely useful in highlighting which patterns are emphasised in an individual's make-up. Like some psychological DNA test, it reveals the hidden and the (as yet) only potential.

To give the reader a general idea: the Hunter pattern, for instance, will be represented by such indicators as Mars, Aries and the first house. Have Mars rising in the first and four other planets in Aries, say, and others may well be tempted to call you a typical Hunter. But have, in addition, Saturn high up in the chart and placed all on its own there, and you have a much strengthened Boss pattern to vie with your Hunter – a rather different story. Substitute Moon for Saturn, or place that Moon in opposition to Mars, and now you have the Mother pattern adding its distinctive flavour, *in a particular way*, to the whole psychological mix.

Our motivation patterns make a kind of interdependent family not just in the theory of it, but also in the practice of precisely how each of us is 'composed'. They are the building blocks of our individual psychological make-up: together they amount to a characteristic structure of a kind that, again, is given but infinitely variable in the way it can be lived out. The beauty of the natal chart is that it shows us a symbolic representation of this 'abstract structure' that is both graphic and succinct, and open to endless interpretation. With the help of such a chart we can do more than just set up a rough league table of motivation patterns, according to how dominant or weakly represented they are; with skill, we can gain a much more precise picture of the nature of our inner cast, our inner family of impulses.

The Mother in you may well be constitutionally at odds with the Revolutionary in you – in which case we could speak of both being problem patterns for you, not comfortable to handle, not easy to make the best of, and yet demanding your (and everyone else's) attention. The stresses, antipathies, competitive jealousies, as well as the easy alliances, within your family of archetypal impulses will clearly show up in the chart, for instance as aspects (spacial connections, relative positions) between planets. This is what makes it such a sterling aid in understanding how you hang together, individually. Without it, we have to rely purely on observing 'symptoms': all those different kinds of greed, ambition, helplessness, etc we aren't after all so terribly good at telling one from the other, just looking from the outside, as it were.

We have seen how our basic impulses, even in themselves, have a job to get it together, schisms and the like for ever threatening. Now we have to add to that the possible internal strife between impulses jockeying for position, virulently contradicting each other, four making common cause against two others, a single one being sidelined altogether, or a host of other possible configurations.

No wonder we tend to make a point of seeing ourselves as unequivocally whole: good and solid chunks of one sort or another (with our faults, personal failings, acquired bad habits etc somehow *attached*; if only we could rid ourselves of those, we think, rub them off like something incidental, superficial). We find it extremely difficult, indeed quite alarming, to view ourselves as something indeterminate and fluid: strands that just about hold together, more or less well intertwined; functions we can employ this way or that, everything variable, everything up in the air. We would much rather take ourselves to be rock-solid. The Mother in us, for one, tends to feel she will be a lot less vulnerable if she can become inflexibly fixed. We are only too ready to mistake solidity for security.

But if we subscribe to the solid-and-whole model, in preference to a composite-and-fluid one, then we will inevitably come a cropper on the question of our obvious shortcomings, our frequent misbehaviour. Each time we catch ourselves doing something horrid, this blatantly contradicts the potential for good we also know we have in us, thus neatly splitting our precious integrity in half. Whatever can we do with the 'bad bits' to stop them spoiling our simplistic, concretitistic view of our personal integrity? Banish them to the periphery, somehow: 'warts', attachments, almost foreign to us. Blame them on others: their behaviour has, temporarily, rubbed off on us. Say we hope to rid ourselves of them, then desperately ignore them. We do anything but own and work with these misused impulses.

The moment we abandon this all-to-solid view of what we are in favour of a more dynamic understanding, the question of good and bad is revealed as having to do, not with wholly or partly, reversibly or irreversibly *being*, but with *actively doing*. Once we can accept that, we no longer have a problem with owning or disowning what we 'are'. Potentially we are it all – the real point is, what are we doing with that potential? Fear of 'contamination', chronic self-doubt, blaming others and endless self-justification, the whole theology of 'evil' people, devils incarnate, all that can be dismissed as a waste of time, while we actively get on with making a better job of our lives.

No, the 'bad bits' aren't irredeemably part of us. Because they aren't 'bits' at all: they are something happening, possibly in an entrenched, too-habitual way, but still insubstantial. They are activities which can be modified, if we so desire, and are prepared to work at it.

This raises an important question: who, in the last analysis, is actually in command? Who is it that chooses how to use or misuse these innate impulses? If my 'personality' can be defined, and shows up in my natal chart, as an abstract structure composed of the various motivation patterns there are – with some at the top and others at the bottom of the pile, the connections between them strong, weak, sympathetic or antagonistic, this lot in close accord, that one making the odd one out, and so forth – then who on earth am 'I'?

The million-dollar question of psychology. If I am reluctant to offer an answer, then this is mainly because to do so involves inventing new words, expressions obviously not yet in use, or else borrowing existing terms like higher self or Self or even

Overself which may speak to some, put others off, and also imply that I subscribe to the theories of those who use such expressions. Not for the first time, it all comes back to the problem with *words*: meaning fixed in sound/writing.

We can't even look to our newly acquired vocabulary of abstract and potentially variable patterns for an answer. Six patterns of being, six patterns of becoming; twelve different answers to what 'self' is about, but a single 'I' never mentioned! So the Hunter pattern tells us that doing can simply equal being, a ceaseless becoming the only 'am' possible. At the same time, the Boss shows us that being can be both more abstract, inner, and a quite concrete acting out of that inner nature – though for practical purposes it needs to be modified, adapted. The Thinker on the other hand demonstrates the reverse process of (more or less freely) chosen activities becoming something deeper, something we newly 'are' inside ourselves; and new doing also leading to revised inner-being. Finally, the Revolutionary in us makes it clear that both being and becoming can take place in a sphere far removed from any substantial doing, at a level of purely inner existence and self-renewal. And all this goes on at the same time: inside me, actively emanating from me, as well as 'happening into' me.

All rather more complex and confusing than me simply maintain 'I am this, or that'. It does rather look as if this 'me' or 'self' in its many guises and functions is no more than an agent of a more potent, and distant (and stable?) 'I' which acts as a sort of centre of gravity around which the whole saga of self goes on revolving.

When I discuss a client's natal chart with them, I first of all ask them to regard the structure they see there on paper as a representation of their 'psychological body' – and then go on to explain that it is a very abstract and insubstantial sort of body, something that can be fleshed out in many ways (including positive and negative ways), something variable, fluid and so on. This is how I have come to view 'personality'. As a set of key data we work with/the world works on, something that we and others between us bring to life, now like this, now some other way. The 'I' that does the deciding how to use its given 'data' is of course as much of a mystery to me as to anyone else. But it is there, for me, for my client, in the centre of the (circular) natal chart, the blank space where the hub of it is, the yet-more-abstract invisible centre.

Others of course may prefer to put a proper name to this blank on the page, Higher Self, soul, or whatever. It is the indefinable constant that links the helpless child you just about remember being, and the cringe-makingly awful youth you would rather forget about, and the fine upstanding adult you'd like to think you have become. That was me then, we say, staring at the photo, or the memory, knowing it to be true, and puzzling at the same time. But pondering this mystery of the ultimate 'I', we may come to find it a lot easier to regard our everyday 'self' in action as something entirely flexible, freely mutable.

You Influence Me, I Influence You

Start a debate about personality, and pretty soon someone raises the question: what shapes it - really? Nature vs nurture has been running for a long a time. Is it the quality of the parenting you receive, with the wider social environment thrown in for good measure? Or is it all laid down in your genes anyway? And just when you thought you could comfortably say, oh a bit of both, someone like me comes along with all this wild talk of natal charts. So then which is it to be, where is the real cause or influence supposed to lie?

Let's start from the given personality pattern, the 'psychological body', as I have called it. Underlying and inalienable, we could rate it as cause; except to our normal way of thinking a cause should have an exactly predictable effect and, as we have seen, our inner scripts do nothing of the sort. Each motivation pattern as such is open to all manner of interpretation, within its unifying parameter of overall meaning. And so is the individual 'pattern of patterns' (as seen in the full configuration of each natal chart): it too is no more than a highly abstract sort of cause - of many possible actual effects. *And* you get to choose.

Our psychological make-up is precise enough to draw a black-on-white picture of. But only in symbols. Symbols, moreover, that hold a multitude of possible expressions each. What is this? Some kind of proto-cause? Supercause? Or would we be best advised to forget about 'cause' altogether?

Making the connection to another contender for the title of cause, it may well be that your physical body reflects the patterns of the psychological body in a pattern of its own: your individual genetic make-up. In effect, what this would mean is that *some* of all those 'possible interpretations' become permanently, unavoidably fixed. The colour of your eyes, your general build, any congenital handicaps you may have etc. At the same time everything about you that is living, changing, happening, obviously retains its indeterminate nature: those after all only abstract causes leave your life in effect open-ended, full of different possibilities. We speak, cautiously, of genetic predisposition.

You may have the genes associated with some disease, but it needs certain favourable environmental conditions - favourable to the disease, that is - before it will develop. Now we wouldn't say that those environmental conditions influence your *genes* and thus get them to start doing things to your ongoing health, or your behaviour. But then what are we saying? Predisposition remains something of a mystery. And in the last resort 'influence', like 'cause', fails to explain anything.

Maybe both concepts are simply to one-directional - doing things to, rather than interacting with - too fixed in themselves, too. What I am saying is, we may have to consider that what we call cause can be influenced by its recipient, modified by its own effect; and that what we call influence can be caused to swing into action, provoked, or at least attracted.

It seems that causes, and causes behind causes, influences, free choices (and compulsive ones), all meet in a dynamic inter-play.

Using the word cautiously then, what are the different influences that determine how we handle our innate impulses? It may well be that some or even all of our motivation patterns are genetically encoded, as fixed bodily facts, or as instincts we cannot avoid having, but equally inescapable will be the early influence of parents, educators, society at large. The way they treat us, and each other, will condition us in the use and misuse of the Revolutionary in us, the Creator, the Mother. Our 'inner family' and the biological/social family out there interact. And it is the latter who, initially, has very much the upper hand.

It is under their guidance that we begin to interpret our (predominant) impulses and lay down the groundwork for our future handling of them. All sorts of words spring to mind here: prompting, promoting, provoking, quelling, stifling, misleading, seducing, perverting, priming, initiating into, sparking off.

Suppose for a moment that you have the Destroyer pattern not only strongly emphasised in your individual make-up, but stressed: in an awkward relationship to the rest of your inner family. We could say that you have a predisposition for gratuitous violence. We might equally say that you are predisposed to become a crack psycho-analyst. Or a first-rate surgeon. Head of the crime squad. A wood or stone carver: creativity-by-getting-rid-of. A respected family butcher (rather than the wholesale butcher of families, that is). Much will depend on the supporting cast within you; whether the Maker in you can provide an effective counterweight, for instance, or whether the Eternal Child in you is well placed to allow you to rise above the perceived imperfections of your environment, rather than reacting angrily to them.

But the greatest influence will inevitably be the kind of upbringing you have. Father thumps mother, mother leathers the kids, uncle in jail for assault, a neighbourhood whose preferred form of communication is yelling and swearing, all set in a landscape of broken windows and rubbish blowing in the streets: outlook bleak.

The worst out there can only activate the always-possible worst inside you. A better environment would teach you early on to draw on your better potential, even supposing your personal make-up is inherently fraught with internal stresses and imbalances. Yes, some of us are born more 'difficult' – which means just that and neither bad nor hopeless. It means more of a struggle, having to work at it all the harder, but then work can pay off: 'difficult' could just come to signify brilliant.

Now suppose instead that the Destroyer pattern comes bottom of the list in your psychological profile. What effect will a desensitising, brutalising, bad-Destroyer-like environment have on you then? (To pluck the Destroyer strand out of the whole picture like this is of course to simplify terribly: there is no way the depths of our living complexity can be presented flatly on paper. These are 'dead' sentences, paragraphs, which only the active imagination of the reader can piece together again into a vital whole.) On the one hand, it clearly depends: with Priest and Healer dominant, for instance, you could easily be mislead, used, end up imitating the bad boys. If the Artist is more to the fore, though, you might find yourself developing a persistent habit of make-believe: pretend your scamster dad is really a hero, contrive to see cheap trash as desirable, learn the art of the resigned shrug: just the way, innit?

On the other hand, what we must not forget is that each of us has to live out the Destroyer pattern in some measure. In each of

us the Destroyer will be expecting a perfect world, and be disappointed, want to prod, chuck out, complain... next step, maybe
seek revenge for all those 'broken promises'. The more deprived
our environment, the more there will be rightly to complain
about. The Destroyer in us gets more to do, so to speak; and is
subject to a range of poor examples as well. What we end up with
is a vision of perfectly 'normal' people who all trash things
routinely, see nothing unusual in the inflicting and bearing of
pain, delight in the shoddy and the cruel as much as in glittering
superlatives – and really only a few individuals among them who
could be counted as being truly destructive (ie negative
Destroyer-like). Did I say vision?

The question whether a man is a 'born criminal' or whether
society or his childhood experiences 'made him into one'
demands a more complex answer, obviously. We are all disposed
to do wrong, period; but we are also individually disposed to do
quite specific wrongs. Add to that the specific conditions we
encounter as we grow up, and the chemical reaction starts there.
It is simple enough: if parents and society were perfect, there
would be no criminals – and if we were all born perfect, there
would never arise any of this bad parenting, no bad examples, no
'evil society' to pervert the 'innocents', no man-made deprivation
to set the tone for shabby behaviour.

Our parents however aren't the only ones to set the tone, to
condition us, or more subtly influence the way we behave.
Relationships in general will draw a response from us. At the
extreme ends of the spectrum they can prod either the devilish
devious or else the saintly in us into life. In any case, they will be
asking for some response, some echo at the least.

There is more to it, though. We have all come across people
who act out another's aspirations for them, or somehow take on
a role that actually 'belongs' to the other: it may be plain to see,
or we may just suspect it. Working with the birthcharts of couples
and whole families, I see this on a regular basis.

The girl who takes ballet or piano lessons on her mother's
behalf – because mother never got the chance to realise that part
of her potential, in that particular way. The wife who can 'legiti-

mately' express her husband's strongly Motherly attributes for him – it being unacceptable for *him* to do so in the kind of community they live in. The son who finds himself virtually pushed into open rebellion, provoked to deviant attitudes and a wilfully weird life style – because in his father the Revolutionary impulse is much put upon and needs to find a cure, a chance, an opportunity to be openly expressed and dealt with *somewhere* in his life.

Manoeuvring others into doing our living for us, at least in part, is nothing out of the ordinary at all. The Creator in us, remember, does it all the time, depending on it for his self-realisation. Naturally, if none of these proxy performers had the 'talent' for it, they would not be in a position to oblige. Which brings us back to the idea of mutual influences and the mysterious interaction of cause/effect.

What we oh-so-abstractly are, our given personality pattern, seems to play a large part in whom we meet, the kind of people we attract into our lives. Like meets like, in no superficial manner of speaking. But opposites too attract: *my* powerful innovative urge may boost the poor neglected, afflicted Revolutionary in you, and prod and nurse him into healthy action... or else you may just let me do the being bolshie for you (confessing yourself shocked perhaps, but with a certain twinkle of satisfaction). Conversely, *your* thoughtful acceptance and quiet working with the material at hand may help the Boss in me develop... or else I may just lean on you, fall back on your reassuring normality and established position as a solid bedrock from which to launch my revolutionary agenda.

We constantly work not only with our own material, our own complex 'pattern of patterns', but with other people's, from partners to passing acquaintances. We reflect things to each other, lend and borrow strengths, dump and take on weaknesses, highlight, arouse or soothe each other's unintegrated, unlived impulses, awake, evoke, heal or aggravate, compound.

We are for ever (unconsciously) inviting others to help us, somehow, cope with the job of being us. And this process, puzzlingly, does start with our parents. To stay with the example of the Revolutionary for the moment: there is no way a child could live out much of this impulse herself. Needing safety, protection and a dependable environment, how can she possibly throw established tradition to the wind, have better ideas, go against the grain, rebel? Should this pattern be prominent in her make-up, it will be *her family* who have the job of living it, for the time being, in one shape or another.

Her mother is a red-hot Marxist then. Her father aloof, disdainful of what he calls mediocrity, normality, more especially the predictability of little children. Both parents work as research scientists, in the field of genetic modification. Big brother is the archetypal self-appointed outlaw, never out of trouble. Her favourite uncle, somewhat unusually, thinks he personally invented the light bulb. Grandmother, the prime carer, takes a fiendish delight in controversy and foxing everyone's justified expectations...

Well, alright: maybe not all of it at the same time. But if you were to compare the daughter's birthchart with those of the people who most 'influenced' her during her early life, you would find a very prominent Revolutionary there somewhere, to match her own. Such themes can run strongly in families, over several generations. You could of course say that we inherit something of our parents' character, and leave it at that; it really does not matter. The important thing to recognise is the level of dynamic interchange that takes place between what seem to us to be isolated lives, exclusively owned. Such 'privacy of being' is an illusion.

(In another twist on the tale, the stressed impulse may lie latent, repressed, in both parent and child, till the youngster is ready to assume responsibility for living it out herself – for both of them. This is the classic tale of the black sheep in the family: 'Who would have thought it of Janet, such a good girl she always used to be, must have been that friend of hers, bad influence *she* was and anyway, she didn't get that from *our* side of the family!' Well, who knows.)

One last thing we may note in this context, even if it is stating the obvious: as long as we (have to) allow others to live out our own inner scripts for us, we will not be in a position to decide on their good or bad interpretation. We just have to put up with whatever we get.

If relationships – at least of the mature kind – look like the sort of influence we might 'influence back' and so have *some* control over, there are plenty of others that have us inescapably in their grip at some point: life phases, group belonging, jobs.

The development phases of childhood, for one thing, will take us on a conducted tour through the highs and lows associated with each motivation pattern in turn. There is a time when we have to concentrate on 'learning': ie learn how to make connections both mental and physical (Healer); there is a phase when we deal with our inner-emotional footing, and learn to express our deepest feelings in a sufficiently controlled way (Mother); there is puberty, when we deliberately retreat into ourselves, become 'separate' beings, tend to view even our own body with endless criticism (Thinker).

But it does not stop there. During our married years, for instance, we are all being Artists and Destroyers: standing ourselves in relationship, deeply sharing the essentials, to the exclusion of all else. At the height of our professional lives we are all being Bosses of sorts; and that does include the office drudge who automatically follows orders.

Some patterns have a decidedly youthful feel to them. Hunter and Healer, for instance. Others, like the Boss, have more of a flavour of maturity. Some can be visualised in more than one way: the Eternal Child as raw beginner, endearingly clueless; or the Eternal Child as wise old prophet and philosopher. But we will live all the patterns, not just those like the Eternal Child, differently depending on what age we are. Thus the Boss may materialise in our youth as a bookworm with no gumption to speak of, develop into a respected administrator in our middle years – or a bureaucrat from hell, if we don't watch it – maybe to end as a rather depressed old man who thinks no one ever listens to him anyway.

What I am saying is that every one of us goes along a trajectory a bit like that, some version of the Boss's path, and the Healer's journey, the Mother's, and so forth. And always one or some of them will be more emphasised than others, throughout the different times of our life, imposed on us as 'typical' young men, old men, middle-aged men-with-kids-and-careers *as such*. All this over and above, in addition to, our individual living out of our own complex personal scripts.

Belonging to a family group, to an age group – we can go on from there. The behaviour of gender groups we have already met with: Man and Woman as such, in their various guises, roles which we can also call group-characteristic.

Another thing that has had a mention in passing is the cartoon figure of the loudly braying upper-class ass perched on his high horse: one particular interpretation of the Eternal Child, making something rather ghastly of inherent good fortune and privilege. If you are born into any kind of position of relative wealth and leisure, you find yourself with this pattern's option of lording it over others. The better option, also yours if you want it, is to give of yourself freely: do voluntary work, or make some philanthropic use of your 'higher understanding' (possibly derived from extensive studies that others were not able to afford – though you better be aware that, where the Eternal Child is concerned, pretentious garbage is quite apt to masquerade as wisdom!). Either way, as the rich man's kid, all your life will in a way be under the special auspices of the Eternal Child, a pattern you will have to engage with whether or not it figures in your personal make-up. Just as, as a woman, you *will* have to engage with the Feminine triumvirate of Artist, Mother, Priest.

These are some of the things we have to live our way through, a sort of impersonal substrate, before we ever get to the top of the pyramid, the individual self. At base, we are mere objects. (Not? Try falling 'humanly' from any height.) After that, we are animal. Then we are our gender. Then ethnic group, social class, neighbourhood, family. The 'I', or Self, gets all that to deal with, before there is ever scope for being oneself. In some societies such individualisation is barely given room. And in extreme conditions (eg life-threatening situations) those personal flourishes, like mere icing on the cake, are liable to go by the board first.

This is not a view of self we relish, in our egocentric culture. We inflate our personal importance, usually to the detriment of our collective living. The result is that individual 'social awareness' has to work overtime in the face of such general aggrandisement of the self. As a culture, we can be said to be sidelining the Priest pattern (conducive to humility, selflessness, service as an agent of something larger than and beyond the individual). But just as in the case of persons, families and whole sections of society, the neglected impulse will have to find its place in our collective cultural experience somehow: failing all else, it will be brought to us by outsiders, others we unwittingly provoke into playing the relevant, missing, part in our life. As our self-worshipping culture gets ever more imbalanced, we may yet 'invite' invasions and take-over bids from cultures less fixated on the importance of 'ego'.

Some groups, rather than inherently or automatically belonging to them, we join voluntarily at some stage in our lives. Professional groups are one example. Personal interaction with colleagues is one part of it, bringing with it all the usual mirroring, borrowing, filling in of each other's 'gaps', and so on – let's maybe call them pattern transactions – found in relationships. But then there is also the nature, the demands, of the job itself.

If one wanted, one could draw up a list for each motivation pattern: all the various kinds of job that go with the territory. Conversely, one could list against different jobs the pattern or patterns most likely involved. Some occupations have numerous aspects to them – take a businessman: he may be working out of the Healer pattern (forging business links, distributing goods, trading, wheeler-dealer type activities); or the Maker (the manufacturing side of things); the Hunter (the entrepreneur aspect); or for that matter the Mother (with the accent on supply, support services, 'hatching and rearing' new things to feed into others' manufacturing process etc). If you are an artist, your work could be motivated along the lines of the Creator, the Maker or indeed the Artist, to name only the more obvious ones. If a sportsman, the Hunter is really the most likely motivation: the Thinker may be into physical jerks, the Eternal Child into playing games, but for the seriously professional sportsman or woman we have to look to the Hunter pattern. 'Performance' is what matters here – there's no substantial end result or product in this job – and activity, its onward-developing characteristic nature, is of course precisely what the Hunter at his best is about.

If you were to be a journalist, the list of possible contenders would be even shorter: the Healer pattern springs exclusively to mind. Other patterns might be *involved*, a dose of the Revolutionary (trying to undermine the Establishment), or the Artist (giving the unfair no rest) for instance. But the chances still are that in your own 'league table' of patterns the Healer will feature especially strongly, with the likes of Artist or Revolutionary maybe providing the additional personal nuances you bring to this most Healer-like of jobs, with its inquisitive nosing around, spreading the word, putting in touch – and its lies, and calculated slander.

These are jobs we choose, following our inclination. We join the business world, a fraternity of thieves, the local mechanic's workshop or the newsdesk, on account of the Healer strand in our make-up being somehow emphasised, awkwardly or straight-forwardly, whichever.

Meantime anyone coming into more fleeting contact with the characteristic work environment we set up will be subject, for the time being, to the influence of the pattern or patterns involved. And no matter how good you are at your job, you will still be faced with the downside of the impulses that feed into it: the job itself opens doors, offers temptations, is spun around with its own ambience, demanding a reaction from you just as a rela-tionship with another person would.

Can we be forced into a job 'against our inclination' at all? Well, we could be forced to become thieves rather than (relatively) honest newshounds, or pressured to take over dad's business when we would rather do seriously satirical sketches on national radio. Conditioned, coerced, we may stick it out, or not. And if we do suddenly change jobs, it may not be the big change it super-ficially appears to be: we are only re-interpreting what we are about – pick-pocket into actor; actor into sales manager; manager into travel writer, dumping suit and donning T-shirt. It's still the same old Healer in us. But we can of course also choose to express different strands of a thoroughly mixed potential at different times of our lives.

And then, on top of all this more or less free self-expression through work, there are always those 'jobs' (not usually referred to as such) we find ourselves propelled into, individual inclina-tion or no. Caring for an elderly relative, or a suddenly handicapped wife. Or motherhood, to take an obvious example.

It does not matter in the least whether you are a Motherly sort of person or not: as a mother you find yourself forced to act out of your Mother pattern, supposing it is weak, peripheral or badly stressed. You might leave it all to nanny, you might even give up your son for adoption at birth, but doing anything, even doing nothing at all, you are still acting your part. Fatherhood, while rather less of a 'job', is no less of a role to fulfil, drawing on the Creator pattern. Parenting as such will also involve the Boss impulse; while caring and nurturing in general will activate both the Mother in us and the Priest, for selfless service.

These are the sort of life demands that work on us as influences, that condition us in ways not all that different from what happened to us during childhood: locked in a relationship, going through a life phase, in the grip of an inescapable situation. Even if some of these situations can be optional life phases, like parenthood – it still 'transforms' us.

Situations are not always as gripping and demanding as that, pulling new active roles out of us (or at least brand-new interpretations of old ones). Nevertheless, situations in general will be experienced as influences.

Of course you can say that, after all, everything is a 'situation'. A relationship, the job, your current life phase. What I want to point to here in particular though is, first of all, the whole idea of *resonance*. What we are inside ourselves actively looks for the right life partner, occupation, congenial environment etc. But it is also there to be played on by the passing stranger, the rare moment, the stray opportunity. We get caught up in accidents and incidents, ensnarled in situations someone else might easily walk out of – because something in our whole personality pattern, maybe something hitherto neglected, resonates to what is going on.

We become transfixed, momentarily obsessed, even. We turn out 'suggestible' to a degree no one, least of all ourselves, would have foreseen. An off-beat remark, an unimportant little incident in a restaurant, and something in us is jolted awake. Suddenly we are acting totally 'out of character'. We laugh it off nervously, afterwards. Put it down to a momentary aberration, blame it on that rather 'daft situation' we happened to find ourselves in.

Situations work on us: prime us, draw us out, educate us, provoke us, never let us forget that we have to live with the *whole* of our complex self. Refuse to acknowledge any of what you are, and sure as anything something will come along to prod you in exactly that spot. But the less often you exercise a psychological muscle, the less impressive your performance will be when it is called on to bestir itself. A neglected pattern tends to surface as a misused one. An incensed Hunter, torn from his customary inactivity, blundering about in a frightened rage: what's going on, somebody's trying to get the better of him! A Destroyer who can do nothing but, just very occasionally, go completely berserk.

Life asks us to be whole; to wholly be what we are, whichever way we want to go about it. There can be no better demonstration of our dynamic nature, than these constant reminders to actively-be all we 'are'.

Another thing about situations: influencing us and being influenced back, drawing us in or being voluntarily sought out – in addition to all this they can also make us experience familiar patterns in ways we would not normally handle them. This is another instance of being passively in the grip of something: a situation that would condition our responses, that virtually dictates to us how we should use a particular pattern.

Illness is the obvious example here. Your body plays up, suddenly becomes a problem, makes itself felt none too gently as something in its own right, separate from 'you': those violent aches automatically alienate you from your body. You draw back from it, into yourself, and a mental distance springs up. Straight away, you become absurdly 'self-conscious' about your physical functioning, body-conscious. Alarmed, suspicious, neurotically symptom-watching, divided, at odds with everything out there: body, doctors, hospitals, pills... and could it have been something in the water? Is the air safe to breathe?

Leaving aside for the moment the possibility that you have actually precipitated the problem yourself, just being ill in itself has foisted on you some of the downside of the Thinker pattern (and no doubt some of the Healer's as well), dragged you willy-nilly into living it out. It is as if the pattern were capable also of working in reverse: the symptom or outward effect preceding what would normally be the underlying cause.

This goes way beyond the sort of situation where you find your-self in a deprived area and have to make frequent use of the Destroyer impulse, one way or the other; or live through a period of civil unrest that spurs the Revolutionary in you to more promi-nent action, one way or the other. Here, there is no one way or other way to it: sickness as a situation automatically brings out the 'sick' Thinker in you.

Anything that has a go at us in such a relentlessly physical way can have this reverse effect. Drug-induced hallucinations plunge us deep into the Priest's shadow land, supposing we only fell victim to a party prank. But once a particular negative expression of that pattern has been established in us, who knows what other neighbouring 'sins' it might not trigger too? Dependence. Compulsive craving of illusory joys. Or overwhelming fear and a sense of everything, self included, being worthless. The fatalism of the lost. Or the easy criminality of the self-loathing. Extricating ourselves from this psychological mess we have been landed in (the idea of 'influence' surely at its most crudely literal) will be more uphill than the average struggle – depending of course, in this example, on how Priest-literate we are, personally: we might just turn the story round with the greatest of inward-based resilience. Either way, it is no use our thinking a chemically caused brain event is just that and no more. It does not sit in a physical-world vacuum, this side of an effective divide between psyche and soma.

What situations like that, where 'matter over mind' clearly starts the ball rolling, demonstrate most clearly is that 'our' moti-vation patterns are not exclusively ours at all. They are also life patterns as such, capital L, capital P, if you like. This should not come as a surprise. No woman is an island; no man can really stand alone. Internal and external intermesh, just as the personal and the collective do. And causes and influences are for ever criss-crossing busily in all directions.

The Dance of the Details

By now pattern has been added to pattern to make the unique personality pattern we think of as self, only to find – the moment it swings into action – that it is intertwined with and overlaid by the more generic patterns of various group identities and, as if all this weren't complicated enough, engaged in endless interaction with other people's patterns as well.

The imagination has to work overtime trying to picture such complexity. It doesn't help either that we tend to visualise static representations, rather than moving ones. Self as a composite thing is just manageable; self as open-ended, indeterminate, a great hoard of possibilities, a long stream of different ideas, a whole tribe of people to be, that's a lot more tricky. The living, active self as a dynamic dance of factors personal and borrowed, chosen, mirrored, suffered, shared, imposed and heaven knows what: at that point we need to sit still a moment, make a serious effort to picture all that. Yourself: the movie.

It must be clear by now that what it needs above all is flexibility of interpretation. This applies most importantly to the motivation (or life) patterns themselves. I have already pointed out that the names I have given them are not to be treated as perfect summaries of all the many things they can stand for. Also that the activities of these archetypal figures do in places overlap. And lastly, that the language we use for our psychological reality is anything but precise: words have to be taken with a pinch of salt. So it should not cause too much logical upset to acknowledge that the Priest can act as healer, especially where emotional hurts are concerned, and that the Healer, as we have seen, can make us quite ill.

It may be useful to view each pattern as a spectrum; or rather several, stretching from one extreme to the other: from best to worst, from active to totally passive, from the most 'human' expression to the automatic or even inanimate. One could also follow particular themes. Thus one can take any number of trips along the length of a spectrum, each time seeing a range of figures that gently transform one into the other, a sliding scale of manifestation. Let's have a go at the Priest pattern by way of example.

Aware channel or medium between inner and outer worlds; genuine seeker; credulous believer; escapist, fraud, cult follower; meek or rabid adherent of dogma; fanatic given to self-flagellation or to torturing misfits and heretics. Take two: securely centred; your own person but in touch with the transpersonal; inspired performer of given works (music, dance etc); unquestioningly obedient; anonymous particle in the larger mass; helplessly enslaved; zombie, automaton; one who can only blindly follow instinct – or: deliberately giving up on yourself; 'selling', prostituting what you are; an avid voyeur; blood-sucker. Take three: emotionally stable; capable of empathy and selfless acts; identifying only too easily with other's feelings and problems; emotionally all over the place; living on borrowed emotion, mimic, personally hollow – or: deliberately withholding own feelings. As can be seen, there are no really sharp divisions anywhere. Somewhere in the middle range there is the proverbial fine dividing line between iffily right and getting-to-be-rather wrong. But who will be the arbiter who defines where the cut-off point is going to be, exactly?

Likewise, if one contemplated a sliding scale from sanity to madness, who would decide where 'mad' turns into really mad? There are cultures where a vigorous self-flagellant is openly admired and applauded. No one would dream of questioning the sanity of his actions. But then what about some of our Western social institutions and mores, or even just publicly sanctioned habits: is it entirely sane for a man to drive two hundred yards to buy a paper? Or for a woman to be 'properly' enough dressed for polite society when virtually bare-breasted... while all hell is let loose should she 'indecently' expose a nipple? Others may think us quite mad for that sort of thing, collectively neurotic, and probably bad to boot.

These things are debatable because it is not just the personal habits we establish for ourselves that tend to make us stick to a certain range within each spectrum, but also the institutions of our society, those publicly favoured and maybe long-established interpretations our country or wider culture subscribes to.

One comes away with the impression that different countries too, and cultures or ethnic groups, have their own personality patterns, as it were. France, or the French people, to take a random example, appears to have much of the Thinker about it. There is the pervasive accent on style and a certain body-consciousness: fashionable or at least fastidious dressing, stylish accessories, perfumes and so on. The un-naturalness of clipped poodles and the thought-out formal gardens first introduced by the French, all hen-shaped shrubs and trees obliged to be globes or pyramids: these smack of the Thinker having a field day. And when we perpetuate the notion of the French as sexy, it's not rampant basic lust we have in mind so much as novel sexual *techniques*. On the other hand, French scientists have contributed more than their share to European scientific advancement, experimenting, analysing and peering down microscopes with a Thinker's passion for examining details and then doing things with them. Which in turn reminds one of the wonders of haute cuisine: elevating the beast-ly habit of eating to something resembling a well-ordered science. Then there is the French Revolution, with its falling from one extreme into the opposite, and the distinct overtones of moral inquisition – a clear indication that this one was not purely a Revolutionary-led event. And 'I think, therefore I am' would take some beating as an unequivocally Thinkerly statement. Lastly, during the Second World War, with both a collaborator government and an active resistance, we see a typical Thinker-pattern split: each side or part of the once integral whole quite refusing to acknowledge what the other stands for or is doing.

But whether French, Scots or Chinese, collectives or individuals, we should all be aware that there is an infinitely larger range of behaviour at our disposal, in addition to what we have personally chosen to live out, or received as a living tradition: alternatives that are nevertheless essentially 'in the same vein', being more or less neighbouring options within one spectrum. And while suddenly dumping the habits of a lifetime in favour of brand-new ones is hardly wise, there is always scope for sliding along a particular scale to get away from poor towards better usage, saner expression. Drastic conversion, in that sense, is never what's required. Only re-interpretation. A gradual shifting in the right direction.

It might be thought that if we look at the whole story each pattern presents, the length and breadth of every spectrum we might envisage for it, then that would assure flexibility of interpretation enough. Paradoxically, if we really want to understand all a pattern can throw at us, we need to be able to forget the whole for a moment and instead ponder the fragments and close-up details of it in isolation. True, it only makes sense in the round; the meaning of it attaches to the complete 'story': the Maker in us endlessly repeats himself *because* first of all he has a problem with loss, *but* also needs to make new gains at the same time... *and so* he hits on this device of starting afresh, yet making sure he always ends on the same note – a solution of sorts. It may be stupid, but at least it hangs together if we put it like that, in context.

What one has to bear in mind, though, is that this is an abstract context, an abstract pattern (even if I have personified them all here) and there is no guarantee it will be lived out like that: whole and complete and hence meaningful. Meaning does not simply translate itself intact into practice. The theory may be tidy enough, but real life tends to come at us more often like a series of painful puzzles.

This may be especially so where we experience the underlying meaning of a situation only second-hand, at one remove, so to speak. We get saddled with a role from out of a visitor's script, we resonate to some event in passing, or ever so sketchily take part in a friend's all-important Maker scenario, or whatever. Suddenly our lives are touched by that short snatch or that solitary word from out of a whole long archetypal storyline – to remain meaningless for us. Or maybe to take on significance as we actively make something of it. Or just possibly to prove itself the missing link that at last makes all sorts of other things fall into place for us.

What I am getting at is this: we need to be prepared to look at 'short sequences' and even 'stills' from a pattern as if they could manifest all on their own; because they do, whether it makes sense to us or not.

Take for example the Priest, who internalises emotional experiences, and finding them painful, voids or releases them again. This may 'pull apart' into separate bits that no longer necessarily chime with the overall meaning of the story at all. Internalising painful feelings, period. Emotional catharsis, by itself. Internalisation *and* voiding, but with the 'emotional' bit cut out: eating followed by vomiting, as has already been mentioned. Or more broadly still: failure as such. An experience of loss. Poverty.

Looking at the separate facets of a pattern, we must consider all the possibilities. The sense of it, and the non-sense of it. The most narrowed-down earthily literal, and the broadest imaginable interpretation. The material, the psychological, the logical, the philosophical. This puts us in the weird position of sometimes having to say 'both are true' when discovering two (or more) divergent aspects to the same pattern. The Creator can gives us one example of that.

On the one hand, the Creator 'is all'. Essentially, he stands for a limitless inner potential which has to be realised bit by bit, in a zillion permutations, endlessly. As such he shows us that we are all capable of anything. But at the same time, in the applied practice if you like, the Creator 'is unique'. Here he stands for the separate inner being of each of us, your and my unique core potential, to be expressed generously and responsively (and fully 'owned' only in the process of sharing it like that). But as such he obviously shows us that we are limited: each of us quite 'differently able' to fulfil another's needs.

Now how can both be true? We are capable of anything. Our potential is limited. It'll have to be either/or, surely. That it doesn't should become obvious if we give it a little thought: like two sides of a coin, the ultimate and the circumstantial exist side by side, concurrently. It is a bit like the question 'Do things hang together, make sense, or not?' to which the answer can only be that, at the subjective level, meaningful connections are all too probable, so we better be alert to them at all times; but objectively speaking, we simply have to acknowledge that there's no knowing – bits and pieces *might* be no more than that, random, coincidental.

For a rather more concrete example of the both-is-true sort we can turn to the Boss pattern; the Boss's background, specifically. Here not only two but quite a number of aspects can be found.

From a psychological viewpoint, we can see endless intelligent introspection there. A long history of subjective knowing, maybe the wisdom that can come with old age. And a firm personal basis of inner standards of truth, of right and wrong, a conscience.

Looking at it more from a metaphysical angle, we might even speak of an intelligent attunement to Inner-Plane truths (and hence absolutes of right and wrong, pure and purely in an abstract dimension).

If, on the other hand, we adopt a more scientific outlook, we might interpret the 'given inner-knowing' in the light of instinct: the innate moral code or 'conscience' that says dog should never eat dog; an intrinsic capacity for logic; our apparently inherent ability to understand grammatical rules, even.

However, a 'background of given knowledge' from which to proceed could also be interpreted differently: it could be taken to mean what our parents din into us. Their accumulated flawed wisdom which is supposed to serve us as gospel, and of course the moral code they impose on us, twisted as it may be.

This is the kind of latitude in interpretation we need to allow ourselves. Consequently our full spectrum stretches from the further reaches of sublime subjective insight, to the very best that parental brainwashing has to offer. And both these extremes can be accounted 'true', both are valid expressions of what the Boss is about.

Obviously, there is all the world of difference between inspiration and indoctrination. How then can the Boss pattern as a whole be said to make any sense, if its separate facets are all plainly at odds, in terms of meaning? The key words there are whole and separate. The moment we pull isolated aspects out of their context, we will find that they no longer automatically subscribe to the parent pattern's ideas, to put it like that. Standing on their own, bereft of all becauses, they are like little laws unto themselves.

So we are left trying to mentally round up all these strays – in addition to trying to capture the essence of each pattern as a whole in the first place – but in the end it is still not enough. Having successfully pulled one pattern apart, we now also need to see how we can stick several of them together. In the last analysis we have to study them all within their own greater 'family' context. We have to examine what they are, do, in relation to each other.

If for instance one looks at the Boss pattern alone, it could signify inherent or intrinsic knowledge here; knowledge that is acquired via culture and parents there. In terms of conscience, this is the difference between either naturally knowing inside yourself that fairness is a good thing and murder wrong, or having the moral certitudes you do only because you were taught them and have stuck to them ever since. Holding your inner counsel vs obeying orders. The still small voice vs mother eternally scolding.

If on the other hand one brings the Boss's equally intellectual pattern into the picture, then the difference between Boss-type and Thinker-type inner knowing immediately helps clarify what each is 'really' about. Boss stands for fundamentally given, Thinker stands for newly acquired; Boss is about inner moral absolutes, Thinker about flexibility of outlook, learning new things; Boss is basically theory, to be applied, Thinker is basically about practical detail and the ever shifting mechanics of things. In that context, it becomes clear that *essentially* the Boss pattern stands for underlying absolutes – instinct and inspiration, not worldly indoctrination – while in practice, in the disconnected details as they occur, it may well also materialise as an instance of father wagging the admonitory finger.

There is a surprise insight in all this, by the way. On the one hand, courtesy of the Boss in us, we have an innate grasp of fundamental rights and wrongs; and on the other, we have that DIY construct of a conscience the Thinker in us makes up as she goes along. We have two consciences, *in effect*. One permanent and unshakable – even if we don't always have the guts or stamina to apply it, in practice. The other a malleable thing, subject to frequent review as we allow our mind to be changed in this or that respect, in response to new experience – though that one too is liable to be ignored in practice, while we go off and do the complete opposite of what we think we ought! So we have a conscience of the highest standards, inevitably part of what we are, 'deep down'. And we have a more 'superficial' workaday conscience that tends to take its cue from what goes on around us. Needless to say, there are many situations when both Boss and Thinker would claim the job as rightfully theirs, each thinking to be better equipped or able.

The Thinker, for all her careful choosing, does depend for what she is on what's available: what others offer her by way of raw material. So when one looks at the two patterns together, it turns out to be the Thinker, not the Boss, who is essentially amenable to indoctrination, brainwashing, mind control techniques. She need not be ashamed of herself for that. It is the Boss in us who needs to hang her head if she ever succumbs to witless obedience when she could, should – does – know better.

Clearly, it is not enough for us to draw up separate lists of words, attributes to be pinned on individual motivation patterns, this one belonging here, that there. We need the whole integrated picture if we are to figure out the complete theory of our behaviour, the hidden meaning behind what we do. And then, if we want to grasp the practice of it as well, we need to make a further mental effort: dismantle it all, help the theory come apart. Parts large and small, to dance through life the way they do, confusing every issue, scrambling every plot.

If we are going to be really flexible in our interpretation of all this, one other thing we have to learn is to be *optimistic.*

So far we have worked mainly outwards from the gist and meaning of a pattern, pulled it apart, seen how it becomes ever more relative and uncertain, seen the fragments ultimately end up as random and making no apparent sense at all. But we can also work from the scattered outward 'symptoms' inward, observing, drawing conclusions (as I have done with the example of the French nation above). And our conclusions, however much we may try to avoid it, will tend to be judgmental: we identify examples of Bad Mother, instances of Heroic Hunter, a piece of pure Priestly fanaticism, or a moment of Healerish adaptability at its best. We may think we have got it all worked out now, reckon we know where a situation is headed if, say, there seem to be a lot of negative symptoms on the go. What's the world coming to! we cry.

But for all we know it may, collectively, be coming to its senses. We may be wasting our time agonising. Just for a change, we might try looking for the wisdom in the nonsense. Experiment with a positive spin and see whether there could be something in that.

A good example, already touched on in passing, is the way public figures, the rich and the famous and those suddenly catapulted to their own fifteen minutes of fame, are used on the stage of the collective imagination to play out hidden, taboo, half-forgotten or deeply significant but currently unfashionable themes. Archetypal scenes of jealousy and rivalry, sex, power, death, revenge, remorse, transgression and forgiveness, loss and regeneration. Powerful stuff. Often rendered in an absurdly over-done way: melodrama, bathos, the seeds of mass hysteria. The wrong sort of 'actors', pretending badly. A heap of lies, minced further by the media. Complete humbug, when you look at it closely.

But is it? The details may be all 'wrong', the participants' behav-iour egregious, but is it not really rather wise of us, collectively, to be playing around with these ideas at all? A garish public 'performance' may not give us the concrete answers to deep and troublesome questions that we might like, but at least it stirs up the imagination and offers a chance of sharing and comparing our common human problems. It allows us to release pent-up feel-ings and maybe even openly display something of us we normally sit on – those unintegrated strands, aspects, of self that more than anything are in need of frequent exercise, no matter how ungainly.

What at first may seem no better than a mindless mass infec-tion with mawkish sentiment over the death of a princess, a heart-rending screen divorce, or whatever, may well be sanity in disguise. Feeling, still relegated to an inferior role vis-à-vis ratio-nality, hits back: claims its proper proportional share of life at last. However awkwardly. However 'badly'. The better use of it may come after. This is what I mean by optimistic interpretation.

The trick is of course again to see the wider picture, the collec-tive effect, the future trend, the deeper hanging together behind the frantic random wing beats of a thousand insects: step back and you see a column, a symmetrical wave, indifference or annoy-ance swept aside as we catch an inkling of purpose.

The fight for acknowledgement of the Feminine in our culture is probably as good an example as any of 'something' trying to right itself and in the process 'using' a lot of haphazard bits and pieces, like people's fleeting sentiments, momentary fashions, a spate of accidents, chance remarks that make the headlines on a dull day.

Spirituality (as the modern take on religion likes to call itself), caring, environmental pressure groups, recycling, renewable energy, ethical investment, Gaia and Goddess and Neo-Pagan rituals: what the New Age is about is the holistic and the Feminine, both neglected for far too long in our culture. Critics interpret this is as a veritable tide of silliness and superstition. A lot of it *is* silliness and superstition, what with juvenile different-ness-for-the-sake-of-it, cynically manipulated movements for the gullible, self-indulgent trendiness, shallow lip-service, fake spirituality and cultic brainwashing. But who would claim to know – objectively, reliably – wisdom from humbug, the definitely false from the guaranteed real?

If Norse legend saw the night sky as a broken speckled egg, is that too daft for words? Or could it perhaps have been an expression of a deeper understanding: all of life as a whole, its parts interconnected, often interchangeable, a fluidly variable world. It has to be said that critics of that kind of 'nonsense' are often more literal-minded than the faithful, past or present. The poetry of it quite escapes them. They may study the musical score of it with their heads, but never catch the true flavour of it in the singing and drumming and dancing.

Mulling all this over, the kind of question that arises is: do what look like truly meaningless details ever add up to something that makes sense; and, to put it bluntly, can a million wrongs somehow combine to make a relative right – as when one extreme calls forth its opposite number and a balance restores itself. It looks like it. Except, who is this chap called 'balance'; who can we realistically point to as the active agent in this perceived event?

Much of the landscape of modern life has become a maze of busy city streets, a confusion of computerised information, tech-nobabble, speed, media-spin... all Healer- related. At which point, enter the craze for getting back in touch with nature, worship trees, save the whale and contemplate bird song, hear the inner voice too, in the quiet beyond the reach of traffic and everyday business, forget about the bottom line in favour of something more transcendental... very much the Eternal Child's province. A pendulum swings in the other direction. A counter-craze establishes itself. Or, something having gone too far, something else comes to the rescue. But rather than go on about faceless 'somethings', we might as well name them, know them, relate to them as what they are: see the life patterns as *live* patterns.

I offer this with some trepidation, for fear of being misunderstood by the too literal-minded, but the Healer in you or me, the Eternal Child in us all etc, are not just 'in us'. As individuals, we can direct them within us, use them (or of course allow ourselves to be used by them). But beyond the level of individual psychology, these 'things' would appear to have a life of their own. I will illustrate this with a true account of something that happened to me a few years ago, and would ask the reader to receive it with understanding rather than credulity.

I was just finishing a chapter of my last book, and getting rather fed up after a whole day's writing. It was past midnight by then. Hell-bent on getting to the last paragraph, I decided I would drop that scheduled passage about the Creator (or 'Leo') principle. Leo be dammed – I wanted my bed!

I was about to brush my teeth when I heard a loud scrabbling at the window. When I looked out – it was a moonless, foggy night in March, in the middle of darkest rural nowhere – I saw a blackbird there, systematically belabouring the window pane with wings, claws and beak, as if intent on making his way in. I stood a good while watching this puzzling, un-birdlike behaviour, and when he showed no sign of stopping at all, I went outside.

I put on the yard light, opened the door, said 'Hey, don't be silly, off you go now', even went over to stand directly behind him: none of it made that bird miss a beat. He simply carried on with his weird moth-like act. So I gently took hold of him. But he was all slippery feathers and immediately wrenched himself free, went back to bothering the window. I grabbed him more firmly and threw him straight up in the air – only to feel him swoop past my face, plop back against the window, not to be deflected from his mysterious purpose. He seemed as in a trance.

Losing patience with having to endure the, if not impossible, then at least unnatural, I finally took that bird and carried him to the other side of the porch and hurled him skyward there. And then he did another un-blackbirdlike thing: he hovered, hawk-like, or the nearest thing. He must have had his eye on the outside light now, because he flapped up and down ten feet above it, in a fast columnar movement that made him appear suspended – while I, below, shouted and shooed and generally jumped around.

And suddenly he snapped out of it, 'peeled off' like an airplane, and flew away like a normal bird (except that normally blackbirds don't fly around at all in the middle of a pitchblack night, when you think about it). End of spook: good!

I didn't know what to make of all that – till I got back inside and the bright glare of the desk lamp hit me. Moths at windows drawn to the light... light-sun-Sun: the symbol of the Sun is associated with the Leo principle, the Creator pattern. The Creator not-just-in-us. Crumbs. I sat down there and then and wrote that passage I should have but didn't earlier. I penned some really fulsome praise and due acknowledgement of Leo/Creator, with many muttered apologies besides. Alright, message received. Sorry.

I wouldn't attempt to explain what 'caused' this event. I experienced it; I can still feel that determinedly struggling bird in my hands, blindly on course to go about its imposed task, oblivious of me, and much of its own nature set aside for the moment: a selfless agent. A Priestly medium. But an agent of what or whom? A totally awkward question, this, inviting nothing but ultimately futile intellectual speculation. One might just take the message, of course, and dismiss the 'sender' as irrelevant. This is probably what most people do when faced with weird stuff that nevertheless holds obvious meaning for them. Don't talk about it, don't think about it more widely than you have to.

But rather than either fruitlessly theorise or fearfully ignore, why don't we take the imaginative approach? *Personified* archetypes, springing to life for us, making sense of our own actions: they can be just as usefully employed to 'flesh out' collective trends in society, reversals in history, and so forth. Plus all the things that happen which apparently have both meaning and meaningees, so to speak, but no discernible meaners.

These archetypal figures are aspects of both our inward and outward lives; they are aspects of life itself; aspects of divinity, ultimately. To be handled carefully, exuberantly, respectfully, and always with a pinch of salt to hand – in case we begin to take our imaginings too concretely-seriously.

The Good, the Bad – And Whose Fault is It Anyway?

Some people seem to have it all. 'He is always offering to help.' 'She's ever so generous.' How very nice for them. They will be popular.

But what of those whose personal make-up has its strongest emphasis on changing the existing order, rather than underpinning it? On ridding the world of undesirable elements, rather than adding something to it in the usual sense? They may not be obvious givers, but they aren't any less 'good' for it, contributing something in their own way. People with one motivation pattern particularly dominant can find themselves cast almost in the role of a walking archetype, called on to mother, heal, destroy or boss at every turn – and pity those who haven't landed one of the nicer of these life jobs! No matter how well they play their role, they will be perceived as being dodgy, disruptive, too forceful, presumptuous or whatever. We favour those who give unmistakably, uncontroversially.

Mother and Boss certainly need to give; and in a different way so does the Creator. Turning to the 'takers', we find the Hunter having to take *on*, make something *his* business. The Maker needs to take *and make something of*, as does the Thinker, in her fashion. And then there is the Destroyer, who needs to take *away* and destroy what clearly must be… popularity is definitely fading fast here. And yet all these life jobs are obviously equally valuable, equally part of the whole scheme of things.

This basic unfairness – condemning the tough, controversial, demanding in favour of the forgiving, glib or persuasively smiling – is deeply ingrained in our culture. And yet, if we give it some thought, we would agree that the thing that matters is not so much what a person does, as how they do it. Everything depends on the way we handle our life impulses. But it needs more than just trying to avoid the wicked end of the scale. It also needs picking out the more appropriate options, by way of aware response. Above all, it needs gentle handling, subtle interpretation. Our Mother impulse may tell us that Woman, in one of her several aspects, requires a sheltered environment for the kind of job she does in the world. This has been, and still is, (unconsciously) used to serve as an excuse to force women into purdah, or to chain her kind to the kitchen sink. And conversely, it becomes the basis for demanding kid-glove treatment and special privileges at every turn. Gross interpretation is not much better than misinterpretation.

As I mentioned in the last chapter, often the rather negative use of an impulse will bring something of the positive in its wake, come time. Seriously fanatical protesters hurling bricks today; men in suits putting together a business plan to save the planet tomorrow – or the year after. Optimism rarely does any harm, especially when looking at collective trends. At the same time it has to be said that a lot of mistaken behaviour can be exquisitely habit-forming. The chances of anything good coming out of it do rather diminish with time then. 'Getting high' will never take off into the realms of genuine transcendence, so rarely achieved anyway.

Then there are the things we count as blessings in disguise. The evil that counteracts the other evil. Regrettable behaviour that actually, also, does some good. The journalist from hell who drags down his victims one by one with cold efficiency: no one would condone his behaviour, and yet if we are honest we are grateful for the investigative clout, the cut-throat vigilance on our behalf, the insurance against secretive wrong-doing in high places that his abusive practices also provide. We could picture a situation where the extremes he goes to might pit themselves just nicely against opposing if closely related extremes – also from the Healer stable – not so much restoring a proper balance as holding an unfortunate one: the sleazy businessman (dubious morals, deceptive fronts, can't stay out of any deal) versus the unscrupulous journalist (ethically illiterate, lies and pretence, can't keep his nose out of other people's business). Dog eats dog and we stand by, glad enough to benefit.

Another thing to ponder, once we start watching out specifically for 'good' and 'bad' use of motivation patterns, is just how mixed up together they invariably are. The upright citizen lightly tells a 'necessary' lie. The fraud tenders a truth by way of simple explanation. These are the always shifting sands of self we are looking at. We slip across the non-existent border between right and wrong umpteen times in the course of a day, in the course of a single action or response even. And we slide upwards as well as downwards on the moral scale, often as inadvertently in the one direction as the other. The wise become bombastic; the censorious show themselves to be truly knowledgeable; gentle nurturers turn emotionally tyrannical; the relentlessly imperious take us unawares with their genuine generosity. All of which should give us pause for thought: not just whom to judge, but how, by what standards.

We start out by considering the theory – and there the down-side of each pattern is perfectly clear, as in the first part of this book, with goodies and baddies neatly segregated. But as we go on to include the imperfect practice, we find it full of 'unhinged' details and the loose, flexible view of things: our cartoon blood-sucking vampire Priest shades into a homeless, hapless victim for ever needing our change; and then, in the wider view again, she becomes a milk-sucking infant; or, prior to that, an even more 'parasitical' foetus! Are babies *bad*, being relentlessly dependent, amoral, incontinent in all respects and too emotionally touchy by half – all those negative interpretations of the Priest pattern? Bad can hardly be a sensible verdict here, though maybe we can call it a primitive expression, rather than the highest, of the Priest in us. Trying to pass judgement on anything bar our own behaviour, we are always on shaky ground.

And it gets more confusing still. That the highest, subtlest, most civilised expression of a pattern may be the best, and yet the most primitive not automatically reprehensible, we can just about accept. But what about the evident *need* for failure, defects, 'badness' in the world?

Quite simply, it would be folly to expect the world to be totally good. If it obeyed the laws of the Perfect in all respects, it would grind to a halt in no time at all. Think about it: how, in practice, can perfection be envisaged to be alive? Maximum attainment means nothing more to do, supreme achievement spells *finis*. From the summit every possible onward road goes down, and the perfect balance (picture a pair of scales) obviously just sits there, unmoved and unmoving. If all of life were suddenly truly successful, it would only be rushing to meet its end, in effect: perfection reached, curtains, death. Life itself depends on the missing bits, the uneven, the crooked, the mercifully deficient.

And the deeply shocking? The unspeakable disasters? The utterly, insanely 'evil'? The criminally perverse? What starts as a tame argument acknowledging that life can not be expected to be perfect, soon becomes an uncomfortable demand to accept the unacceptable (while obviously not condoning it), because who, again, would decree the cut-off point?

We have to come to the strange conclusion that our failures and even our wilful mistakes are part of the very fuel that keeps the world going, madness, obsessions, disgusting habits and all. We fall down and someone has to pick us up; someone, that is, gets the chance to 'do good' by us. Interaction, at its best, is all about fulfilling each other's needs - strictly speaking: deficiencies, imperfections - as well as one's own at the same time. And all action is interaction. So at the end of the line we find the 'bad' fuelling the 'good', by creating the need for it. We find, if you like, perfection *moved to action*. In a necessarily imperfect sort of way.

Of course, instead of helping us in our needful state, our neighbour may choose to give us a kick in the teeth instead. But the point here is that at least some of the fine theory always finds its way into practice. Evil begets not only more evil but positively invites some good. And good, while begetting some good, equally tends to go off the rails and land in an unlovely heap. As it must, if it is to be active, become alive, become a life, *become...* other than itself.

We can go further and say this: from the perspective of the Perfect Good all *other* states can only be worse, ie *relatively* bad. So while there exists an Absolute Good, in the realms of the abstract or transcendent, the bad as such never makes it beyond the ranks of the relative: a strictly lower-case evil, with no reality beyond that of the fleetingly happening. In other words, nothing that change couldn't cure.

Flawless theory coming alive to make a so-so practice is something that has cropped up in many of the stories I have told here: whether it is the Artist with her sublime inner visions or the Boss knowing exactly what's right and what's best, none of them escape a measure of compromise, settling for second-best or simply letting something go, even at their most exemplary.

The Creator pattern may be the most pertinent in this respect, being the story of self and other at its clearest. There is the uniqueness of self, and the always so faulty-looking, needy otherness of others. There is the limitless potential of self, and how it can be realised only piecemeal, in relatively shabby, fractured bits: constantly becoming 'other'. There is the theme of creativity, a giving out of oneself, giving oneself over, broken, into states of relative imperfection – a self-sacrifice which leads to both life and self-awareness. It is the archetypal story of the One and the demanding/refusing many. The story of the over-riding Meaning in its dry-dock world of theory, and the 'disobedient' details of it in the world of living practice. Creator and creation, or self and other: the story is the same, telling of inseparability, inter-dependence, even a sort of mutual life-giving. And an inbuilt need for mistakes.

All this talk of 'relativism' and the positive role of wickedness will not, however, stop the Boss in us thinking about the fundamental rights and wrongs of things, or the Mother in us feeling for the helpless, or the Eternal Child in us intuitively keeping the razzmatazz of modern life in some kind of perspective. If keeping the downside of each motivation pattern in check is bound to be difficult, it would be equally impossible to stifle their positive expression altogether. Life, every moment, presents another chance to choose from where on a pattern's spectrum to operate, which bit of it to fire into action. Never mind relativism, lax ideas and bad example. The real enemy to watch out for is *habit*.

Another approach to the question of good and bad is to consider the usefulness to us of negative experiences. The broken leg that enforces much-needed rest, disengagement from work pressures, a deeper-going review of what one's life is about even. But also the more serious calamities that open up whole new areas of activity, like first-hand insight into other people's problems, informed empathy, the first inklings of social protest, the will and the courage to 'do something about it'. On the other hand, we may simply learn from our mistakes.

Some would say all of our life is a series of lessons, laid on for us by our karma, God, the evolutionary designs of the Self, or whatever; and while freedom of choice may have become the mantra for our times, still the notion of fate hasn't died entirely either – at least the idea that there is a measure of fatefulness to the bigger events in our lives. There is of course no knowing any of this, objectively. What we do know, though, is that for every objective happening there is a subjective one that precedes it, accompanies it, or follows it: life as we know it is not complete without them.

What I mean is, quite simply, that every event in my life automatically has the subjective element I bring to it added on. My feelings about what happens count, they really count: they have to be factored in if one wants to arrive at the sum total, an accurate description, of the whole experience. Or to put it another way: no experience in my life is a pure it-event, some 'thing' happening out there. It is always *my* experience, 'it' is partly 'me'. Fate, for the sake of the argument, throws something at me and I react, courageously or fatalistically, complaining bitterly or else taking it up as a challenge – either way, even a faceless fate at its most crunchingly imposing could not be held solely responsible for the *experience* I am having.

We are back with the issue of cause and countercause/effect, the interplay between the two. Objective fact is only ever half the story. It's how I see it, react to it, my subjective experience, that completes it. And if one looks at it closely, then even my most passively-receptive reaction is an action, part of the whole drama as it unfolds. (If we are wondering where in all this 'reality' lies, maybe we could usefully borrow some computer-speak and refer to hard and soft reality respectively.)

So where does that leave you, the outside observer of the drama? Certainly (yet again) in the position of needing to be careful not to judge rashly. No matter how competent a spy and how astute a thinker, you can never claim to have gauged the situation completely, because part of it is always in my head – where the most unpredictable things might be going on, for all you know.

Uncertainties abound: all part of life waiting for us to make the next move. One useful image might be of an intricate fretwork, firm, set, and yet loose in a sense, with an abundance of empty spaces between: this to symbolise our freedom of choice (if nothing else, at least at the subjective level) within any given framework – whether we take that framework to be a predetermined fate, or simply our native personality pattern in all its 'incomplete abstractness'.

Another good picture to hold in our minds at all times is that of the literally half-situation: if you mentally, roughly and raggedly, tear off and discard half of anything you observe, half of every situation you witness, half of each bit of reliable information that comes your way, then you may be just about playing safe enough. You will never objectively know what's going on, in all. Better not to judge.

'She's been beaten up by her man? Only herself to blame, probably been asking for it!' 'He's terribly henpecked, isn't he. Well, must be his own fault. Obviously deserves no better.' Maybe so, maybe they really are making a mess of letting the Priest in them tap their partner's boundless contempt or all-surpassing rage: the abusive Destroyer in the other supplying them with the emotional life they no longer know how to lead themselves. If you were faced with a routinely battered wife or long-term abused husband, you would need to give some thought to that.

A single incident or a short episode is a different matter, though. There may not be a coherent and meaningful story in it at all. It *may* be only one of those 'floating details' that happen to people, a passing influence that sparks off emotional or volitional paralysis, hypnotises them into momentary compliance. We must not imagine we always have the explanation; sometimes there simply isn't one to speak of.

On the other hand, that same incident could be part of a story not only coherent and meaningful, but meaningful in a way that necessarily escapes us, going way beyond the parameter of the 'psychological body', the personality. A Self in search of the worst, immersing itself in pain and distress for some good future purpose? A 'life lesson' about to pay dividends? One wouldn't know.

So it's karma – or it isn't. It is all someone's own fault – or not a bit of it. We better make sure we tread warily in this minefield.

Having a vision of a just society, better treatment of all, better behaviour *by* all, is one thing. But where the individual is concerned, only tender patience will be an adequate response. Above all, we must resist the temptation to rush in and judge, condemn.

We could try doing without the word bad altogether, in this context. We could speak of the 'healthiness' of behaviour instead. Ask diagnostic questions about it: what effect does it have on others? Is it in any way habit-forming? And if the answer is a complete thumbs down, one last thing to bear in mind, before we puff ourselves up with self-righteous rectitude again, is that the entrenched smile is essentially no more healthy than the suddenly clenched fist, ersatz tolerance no less sick than destructiveness enjoyed for its own sake. Once we get going, we are all as 'bad' as one another.

Living It

I started with the theory of motivation patterns and then went on to the theory of the practice, so to speak. In this chapter, at last, I come to the nitty-gritty of living it all.

The first thing to note is that, if we are to handle ourselves well, we need to gain a reasonable idea of what it is we are handling. In other words, we must try and find out which of our impulses are particularly prominent in us. This to be followed by a closer study of them, allowing them more thought, intuitive getting-in-touch, emotional mulling over, or whatever forms of inner experimenting we may come up with. The question whether they are strong as such – well represented in us, as it were – or perhaps highlighted by virtue of being the butt of every internal-composition stress going, is secondary, really. More relevant at this point is to note the kind of mixture they make, taken together: a large slice of Mother and a good helping of Artist, with just a smattering of Priest? A fairly easy mix. A very different story would be to have a lot of Mother and a fair bit of Hunter, plus some Revolutionary... and a loose strand of Priest, not easily woven into what is already a potentially fraught combination.

But to start at the beginning: the detective work. Honest self-observation will only get us so far (one's honesty with oneself not usually going all that far). And while collaboration with a close friend is an interesting possibility, it obviously has its own dangers. Our behaviour is only one diagnostic pointer, though; plenty of other clues are to be found in our childhood experiences, recurrent episodes in our past life, the kind of relationships and situations we have a funny knack of always ending up in.

Our 'fate', as we have experienced it, is just as indicative of what we are about, inside ourselves, as the things we have actively done. By and large, we tend to be more comfortable looking at what we have passively suffered, rather than the crimes we have also committed, so making an inventory of the abuses, disasters and challenges life has thrown at us over the years can make a helpful lead-up to the more demanding question: how am *I* treating *life?*

To get a really full and accurate picture of one's personality pattern, the obvious thing to do (for those who can ascertain the time of their birth) is to work with one's natal chart. The advantage of this is that trouble areas would be hard to miss: the chart holds nothing back; it reveals every internal stress, each inbuilt 'self-contradiction'. And the graphic nature of symbols placed in a circle – some plainly opposing each other, others at sharp right angles, others again bunched chummily together, 'bowl' shapes with nothing but empty space in the other half, 'buckets' with oddly sticking out 'handles', and so forth – seeing all this black on white certainly helps to bring the nature of that abstract pattern of patterns, the composition of our psychological body, to life a bit.

But there are potential disadvantages too. How professional is the professional one has gone to for a chart interpretation? How good can *any* one-off interpretation be when each symbol can be seen, and lived, in a multitude of ways? The chart's very precision can tempt the obstinate or self-deluded to get pleasantly exercised about minutiae. And the wealth of detail it contains can in itself be quite bewildering, ultimately more hindrance than help. Anyone wanting to take the DIY approach of buying a computer-generated chart I would advise to work with it only *after* having made a good effort at self-observation, maybe consulting with trusted friends, certainly trawling their past life for as many clues as they can find. (For those who do want to use this diagnostic tool, there is a table in the Appendix giving the correspondences between motivation patterns and astrology's symbols.)

An explanation what on earth this whole 'astrology' business is about anyway may be in order at this point. How is it supposed to work? What does it do? The first thing I would point out is that no one is suggesting a literal cause and effect link. Synchronicity is the word in favour these days – not that that explains much! The unvarnished truth is we don't know why, we don't know how, we only observe *that*, quite as puzzled as everybody else.

The nearest I can personally get to an explanation is to envisage the whole cosmos as one integral being that evolves through time, its every moment having a slightly different character, disposition or 'mood'. Everything has its starting moment: a business contract signed, marriage vows taken, a newborn drawing its first independent breath. The general character of the moment and that of the business, marriage, animal or person starting there coincide, are in synch – though not because the moment itself or something about it does something to you, influences you, seals your fate: as a matter of fact, you happen to it just as much as it happens to you.

And why should a map of the solar system as viewed from Earth tell us something about the nature of a moment and the things that partake of that nature by virtue of being 'born' in it? Search me. It doesn't sound like a sensible thing to assert. Except that, for one thing, I know from long experience that it works, and for another, if I can put it in the more general terms of 'All things hang together', then it looks a rather more reasonable proposition. 'As above, so below', past practitioners and scholars of astrology (of whom Newton, incidentally, was one) would say. A modern buzz-word like 'synchronicity' may sound a bit snappier, but essentially says the same thing.

Experience, a thoroughly grounded working experience, must be the deciding factor whether we 'believe in' this strange phenomenon or not. And given that we bring our own subjective spin to even quite concretely demonstrable facts, more caution than ever is needed when handling these abstracts. We might suspect meaning where there is none; then again, we are free and able to *create* meaning... and comforting pseudo-meaning, of course. This is not a toy for the idle; nor a handy tool for those out to enrich themselves. It is for the wealth of its endlessly adaptable, timeless symbolism that we should value the zodiac, above all.

But to get back to the practice of living it: the weird mixture, the impossible combinations, the too-different strands, personas, public and private faces that all vie with each other for the privilege of being you, and ask to be handled somehow. What if, for the sake of the argument, the Hunter in you would have you swagger with bravado, while his main rival for prominence, the Priest in you, just wants you to be utterly self-effacing. No prizes for guessing who wins that one. 'Of course he's got this massive chip on his shoulder, that's why he's such a loud-mouth. Typical, isn't it.' Is it?

Let's straighten that one out a bit. You might have enough chips on your shoulder to disable a dozen of you (a Priest become fearful, a Thinker chronically suspicious, an abnormally hesitant Maker, an undeveloped Boss still full of self-doubt etc) and you might have a surplus of 'go' about you (Hunter conditioned to be over-eager, Creator irrepressible, a Mother who won't stand for no's or maybe's, your Eternal Child brought up to be a model of unstoppable bombast); but unless you actually have *both* strong in you, there can be no because this, because that.

No doubt we all tend to push the stronger members of our inner cast to the front of the stage. But it is simply not the case that each and every bossy-boots is only trying to make up for some weakness, and every grandiose show-off only doing it to hide an unacknowledged insecurity – they may be singularly lacking in the basic wherewithal for weakness and uncertainty, for all we know. Though if they do have plenty of those too, then they will naturally be especially keen to hide them and compensate for them.

In short, the kind of mixtures we are, in terms of impulse emphasis, can differ tremendously. Whatever our personal composition, though, there is one thing we all need to constantly work at: self-integration.

For a start, we need to retrieve what has become sidelined. We need to repossess and transform the awkward and troublesome, and then go on to nurture the less developed impulses in us, the ultimate aim always being that we should be comfortable with living out all of them.

Using pen and paper and a quiet moment may be all it needs to get us going. A 'psycho-diary' perhaps, to make sure we notice ourselves more. Relaxed, no-holds-barred doodle sessions that might put us in touch with the otherwise indescribable. Or neat tabulations, followed by close analyses. Whatever comes naturally. Even a change in preferred reading matter could allow us to catch facets of self that have previously escaped us. From there, we could progress to visualising (even drawing portraits of) and speaking at length to the members of our inner family, even introducing them to each other – maybe letting them have that over-due row openly at last: all perfectly legitimate tricks and tools to help us make contact with the whole of what we are being, and the whole of what we potentially could be, negatively as well as positively.

With practice, we will inevitably acquire a rather wider repertoire of being ourselves. The problem we then face, though, is that we may no longer be 'safely' homogenous or set in our ways. With our inner family as it were expanding, growing up and getting lively, we may begin to vary widely in our responses, swither and change and at times blatantly contradict ourselves, all bendy and bitsy and psychologically untidy – not at all what our rules-ridden society wants us to be like.

But then consider the kind of Jekyll and Hyde existence we were leading before: our neglected impulses were for ever butting in uncontrolled, 'provoked' by this or that situation, like embittered outcasts seeking revenge, and frequently a shocking nuisance. 'Honestly, I didn't mean that. I really don't know what took me.' Yes, well. Better, surely, to express your different 'faces' in a controlled and positive manner, than to live with a repressed, mutinous rabble inside you that will poke out your tongue for you when you least expect it!

Discovering new aspects of self. Examining suspicious blanks on the personal map. Re-admitting the banished to see what can be made of it, after all. Growing in areas formerly shunned, maybe even despised. All these are necessary to self-integration. Living it all, being whole, is the aim – a kind of aim that is all process. Above all, we need to remember that our twelve life impulses do constitute and operate as a whole, co-operate, help each other. Thus, if the Mother in me is not fully functional, how can the Creator, or Boss, or Hunter be expected to work properly?

Self-integration is necessary if we are to make the best use of each motivation pattern, but conversely it is true to say that making the best possible use of those we can means they will be able to help us with integrating the wilder ones among them, or supporting and guiding the weaker ones.

The interesting thing to note is that it doesn't really matter how much at odds say your Hunter and your Revolutionary inherently are. At the perfect end of the scale – in theory – they all co-operate beautifully, no conceivable quarrel amongst them. It is only when they (ie you) are behaving really badly that they manage to do each other an outright injury instead of favours. So making a better job of handling each of your motivation patterns in itself will help you be more whole and together. As well as allowing any constitutional potential disharmony between them to be expressed instead as noticeably strenuous 'work': more a case of endlessly, harmlessly, wrangling to get it right. This is the sure road to success, paved with inner disputes repeatedly resolved, personal cussedness constantly made good.

Having to make renewed efforts – flexible, varying efforts – is very much what it is all about. Continuing to newly-become right into old age; but also being ourselves in a myriad ways along the way. We might as well be clear that there aren't any goals to be reached, just as there is no one 'thing' for a person to statically, permanently be. Our various motivation patterns demonstrate this beautifully: none of them ever 'get there' or find rest. The Healer has to go on healing... what he himself keeps damaging. The Creator has to constantly create more, unable to give it all in one go and be done with it. Even the Priest isn't allowed to rest in hard-won transcendent bliss but is propelled, by her nature, to actively return to the world and work selflessly among misery and affliction.

These stories can serve us as inspiration, reminding us that, literally, the best aims are never reached. Perfection is fine, as long as we only pursue it, do not try to possess it. Status is futile. Habit is a very bad idea. If we conduct ourselves truly livingly, there never comes an end of the line: even the most genuine 'I can't do any better than that' does not prevent us doing things *differently*, newly, setting out on an as yet untravelled road. If we could subscribe to the idea of being (actively busy) agents of Life, rather than seeing ourselves as units of life supposed to be (as in: statically be) complete in ourselves, we would ultimately be doing ourselves a favour.

Self-integration, as I have said, goes hand in hand with self-transformation: making a more positive use of our inherent impulses. Does the leopard change his spots? we ask, choosing an unhelpful comparison. There is nothing *wrong* with our spots, stripes and assorted individual markings, though some of them may be easier on the eye (and the owner) than others. We can't rid ourselves of any of it and even thinking in such terms is counter-productive. But a smiling leopard rather than a snarling one, to compound the horribly inappropriate metaphor, is a transformed beast, though of course exactly the same in terms of his given number of spots.

But pitfalls to stop us 'smiling' abound, as the stories of our inner cast have shown: ruts to get into, boxes to shut ourselves in, extreme swings and repeated inside-out flips, strict exclusivity, multiple splits, bits of our (inner) self lost to us, unaccountably mislaid, or permanently hovering on the horizon, stagnation grinding ever closer to stasis, followed by involuntary dashes to take hold of life once more... Pen and paper could come in handy again here, this time to draw a graphic picture of what's up with us. My Unglorious Misdeeds, the strip cartoon.

But the next pictures to attempt could be those of the cure, the antidote, the deed well done instead of badly: our stickman self develops wonderfully wiggly flexi-joints, 'flows with it' on a lilo mid-river, has three smiling heads firmly attached to one neck and a variety of arms and legs to draw on as well, juggles a great stream of parcelled gifts given/received, and so forth. If we can prevail on the Eternal Child in us to playfully produce intuitive insights, so much the better; or else the Revolutionary in us, master at visualising the hitherto unthinkable, invisible, unfelt and undone.

Those two free spirits, the loosest strands in the weave of our psychological make-up, are generally better able to escape the effects of any negative conditioning. They tend to wriggle out from under prohibitions or prescriptions with a minimum of encouragement, in a way that say the Mother or the Maker or even the Creator can't as readily. Revolutionary and Eternal Child are potentially extremely good at, respectively, breaking with adverse tradition and finding the best way forward. From that point of view they ought to be our closest allies in this 'putting a smile on the face of the leopard' job.

But that is generalising again. There can be no stock diagnosis, no stock cartoon depiction of *you*, no stock prescription how you can transform the way you act, react, reflect and reverberate and attract events from out of your environment. You have to find your own way, with the help of your inner cast, all of them. And finding out your strengths is just as important as cataloguing your motivational Achilles heels: a healthy Thinker, for instance, can steer the Hunter out of confrontations, or stop the Priest dreaming a worthless dream too far. But it may take repeated detours and much experimental toing and froing before you find an effective way of handling yourself.

It is of course not just specifically your self you are dealing with at any point, but the situation you find yourself in. Grasping the underlying principle of some personal problem is one thing. You still have to fish around each time for the meaningful response appropriate to the context, the situation. To give an example, if the Destroyer in you is in the habit of being a bit heavy-handed, you may well by now have understood the theory behind the 'destructive' face of this impulse: you cling where you should let go; you come to enjoy the unenjoyable; you become a vengeful cynic bent on putting the boot in. But in your current situation what does 'letting go' mean? Leaving it, quietly walking away, simply doing without? Or getting rid of it, determinedly and maybe with a certain amount of unavoidable upset throwing it out of your life? Or even altogether, and rightly, destroying it, finishing it off, stopping it dead? Only you can know how best to handle the Destroyer in you at each new point in your life.

That is the whole idea of this book: to make you familiar with the motivation patterns we all inherit, and to give at least some indication of the many *individual* interpretations, choices (good, bad, and simply choices, as in: different) to be found in them. It is intended primarily as a guide to understanding your own behaviour, a tool to help you with those two continuous processes: self-integration and self-transformation.

It should also give you at least some insight into why others behave towards you the way they do – from two different angles: yours, in the sense that you recognise that your psychological constitution invites certain categories of experience, to put it like that; and theirs, in the very general sense only of having a broad idea why people might act like that.

(Here I would remind the reader that when I say that things are done to us on account of what we are, this 'we are' is entirely in the realm of the abstract; and inescapably given only as such. If people treat us in certain ways because of what we 'are being', the actual behaviour choices we are making, that is obviously a different matter. In other words, we do have some measure of control over what *exactly* is done to us, once we understand how best to handle ourselves in a particular situation.)

The temptation to try and analyse others with our new-found insight is naturally great. But I hope to have spoken sufficiently long and often about flexibility, complexity, uncertainty and an ultimately elusive wider meaning to deter the reader from rushing round to her neighbour demanding he get a proper grip on his Eternal Child, right now and like so.

Still, with the proviso that we proceed with the greatest caution – and bearing in mind that we can't self-integrate and self-transform others for them – we can at least apply some of the general insights we have gained to other people's lives. Maybe more especially at the social level: looking at the circumstances people have to live and grow up in, and how that conditions the use of their inherently 'neutral' impulses to take all manner of undesirable directions. If we want to draw out the best in people, we have to first offer them the best; the best in terms of raw material, choices, example. So there the ball is back in your own court.

At a more personal level, and hopefully with more sensitivity than aplomb, one can use the same technique for 'diagnosing' others as for oneself: consider their history, both passive and active (and remember that these two aren't just connected in a linear cause and effect train of events, but more deeply and reciprocally), and maybe where suitable and possible work with the natal chart.

Obviously, if people are caught up in mega-manias and obsessions, way-out unhealthy appetites, self-denials, sicknesses, asocial activities etc, they will not be in a condition to get to work on themselves, with or without the aid of some fine words on paper that set out a new and dynamic view of self! What this book can offer is really no more than the equivalent of a packet of mixed seed, dry as the dust. Where the soil is unreceptive, and any kind of self-help patently not an option, therapies or treatment of some sort will be needed to steer people in a more positive direction. These would ideally be person-based, not theory-as-I-your-helper-interprets-it-based. But the person as a whole, living fact as well as innate potential, is unknowable to us as outsiders – so how do we devise this therapy that will suit him or her as an individual?

We can't. The best we can do is try and identify the key problem patterns and then offer as many *positive* aspects of these as feasible: to become a person's new natural and social environment, job, new activities, skills to acquire, creative hobbies and mental pursuits, all in the hope that something may 'take', that a healthier use of these patterns may be induced, at least momentarily, or hopefully established through prolonged exposure.

We are speaking about re-conditioning here, no less. And to be justifiable at all, it needs to be respectfully done, offered. Demonstrating the more lasting satisfaction of 'rightdoing' over wrongdoing, let's say, rather than forcing and forbidding, which at any rate tends to have an uncertain and short-lived effect.

Then again, nothing as serious as doing the right thing may be required at all. Something as simple as learning to have the right kind of fun may do the trick. Let me explain. Suppose we are looking at a high-flying executive for ever getting depressed at the slightest professional set-back and spending it compulsively as fast as she can earn it, plus some. We rather think she is not handling the Eternal Child in her too well. We might want to help her get off the treadmill of purely consumerist pleasures, beyond that sort of thing, ready to turn inward... How about learning to dive, entering 'another world' as a total beginner again, rediscovering childlike wonder? Swim with dolphins? Get involved with animals in general, laugh at their antics, fumble for totally new lines of communication? Being struck dumb, lost for response, having to draw on that neglected inner intuition: it can be as simple as that. No need for a solemn retreat at some unworldly monastery. Learning to make the best of an impulse *can* be fun.

One thing we need to become aware of is that 'good like' doesn't just cure 'bad like', but will be helpful for other conditions as well. This brings us back to the idea of all our impulses being related, interdependent. Give someone's stronger points maximum opportunity, and you may well find that he cures himself in respect of his problem areas, the healthier among his inner cast pulling the sick ones along, educating them, strengthening them. Encourage someone's Maker to make satisfyingly beautiful and durable things, on a regular basis, till she knows she can do it for sure, and suddenly her Destroyer may quit chucking things about and hurting other people's feelings, able for the first time to 'let things go'.

We all need positive experiences; not just good feedback, but the opportunity to flex every one of our psychological muscles, and in a life-affirming sort of way: do a proper bit of 'healing' or 'creating' or 'mothering' at least every now and again, aptly 'revolutionise' something just occasionally. This has nothing to do with self-fulfilment in the facile and individualistic sense. Psychological well-being is nothing to do with what we *want* to have or do or be, but with what we *can most positively do*, for others as much as ourselves. But for that we need to be at home inside ourselves, on better than bare speaking terms with every member of our inner family. Odd as it may sound, but to be happy and helpfully effective in the world, we need to practice the different ways of being and becoming ourselves constantly.

And obviously we need to allow others the chance to do the same, or else our best therapies will be in vain. The dynamics of what a person 'is being' has to be uppermost in our minds at all times. The multi-faceted nature of what a person 'is', the scope and flexibility inherent in that, demands it. And if nothing else, being varied, variously being, ensures we always stand a chance, we really do get one new try after the other – forget about the past as determining factor, forgive yourself the eighty-seventh lapse this month (and your neighbour his eighty-eighth) and try living it *differently*. Innovatively, imaginatively, creatively.

Psyche

People have always tried to make sense of their own and each other's behaviour according to the prevailing philosophy of life. Where once we may have seen the influence of gods and daimons, spells at work, souls in thrall to elemental beings, at this point in our collective journey we pride ourselves on a 'realistic' and rational outlook. We look for that cause/effect chain of events. We look for an account of what happened, what was done, that makes some kind of sense: there should be a neat line-up of logical links to lead us seamlessly from 'He was an unwanted child' to 'And he disposed of the body in a pond'. Anything (negative) not explicable in these terms stands in danger of being branded, mysteriously, 'evil'. Reason has failed to cope with it – it must be bad!

There is of course nothing wrong with applying logic to behaviour. The mistake we make is to take behaviour to be something that always emanates whole from the person as a whole, the complete human being, personal history and all. But behaviour as such actually starts at the lowest biological level: as soon as there is an integral organisms that is mobile enough to act as well as being acted upon. Even plants don't just stand there; trees may not look particularly lively to us, but when it comes to the likes of a Venus' fly-trap we can hardly deny that it does things, however 'soul-lessly' pre-programmed its actions may be.

Personally, I would go so far as to say that the roots of human behaviour lie even 'further back' than that, in the abstract realm of an underlying reality that is the common source of both mechanics and meaning in the world.

The twelve motivation patterns as I have described them show us the basic mechanisms whereby action and reaction can take place. In the wider view we might even discount the involvement of thought, feeling etc, and just observe the procedures, steps, manoeuvres, the manner in which things are striven for in different ways, acquired, retained, applied, changed. The rude mechanics of behaviour; but the raw material of meaningful conduct as well.

We are composed of these building blocks. That is to say our different personal dispositions can be understood as different emphases on, arrangements of and relationships between these universal impulses. But it is the I or Self behind the composite self that can choose to make meaningful use of them, employ them as tools – the Self as it were treating its self as a handy tool box to tackle its life tasks with. More often, unfortunately, we live purely at the level of self, scattered, riven, pulled about, unsure how to hang together, divided against ourselves, unable to handle it all and, ultimately, ordered about by our own impulses as if *they* were the masters, we the tools. (Or, in the wider view, used by universal Life Impulses as faceless raw material, agents with no say and no awareness of the import of our actions.)

At our worst, we clank along in a horribly predictable way, blow automatically following blow. But, as I hope to have shown, even the crude psycho-mechanics of enmity and wilful destruction are only one expression of something both 'neutrally' abstract and superbly varied, in itself. Re-interpretation, living the same impulse pattern a better way, is always an option. It is at this level of deliberation and interpretation of our fundamental givens that our true humanity lies, rather than with our 'personality'.

In short, if we really want to make sense of our behaviour we must begin to look closely, on the one hand, at something much more basic and *less* 'human', and on the other at something rather *more* exalted, than the middle ground of everyday self-awareness we tend to focus on.

I said at the beginning of this book that the psyche has no parts to it, no concrete areas, no hard and fast divisions, upper and lower storeys etc. And promptly went on at length about 'the building blocks of our psychological bodies'!

It is difficult indeed to maintain an inner vision of something given yet fluidly variable, never mind verbally pinning it down: it can't be done without momentarily doing violence to it, forcing it to stand unnaturally still, as it were. To describe something dynamic requires a ceaseless stream of words or images, and ever new angles from which to assess what is happening. Which is why, to understand this text, the reader has to carry on the writing of it, the exploring, updating, extending and transforming. Knowledge about the dynamic self can't be *had*, deposited in the memory bank like some precious mental possession.

Is there much point at all in adopting such a slippery view of what psyche is about? Would it not be more useful to divide it up, for instance, and describe it in terms of our various functions, our rational faculties, the emotional side of self, etc? One could try.

Starting with thought, one would have to speak of two kinds of thought, relating to the two thinkers among our inner cast: the Boss, with her innate or otherwise 'inherited' knowledge that asks to be applied to life; and the Thinker, with her need to enquire into, choose, acquire a constantly updated understanding of world and self, in response to outside stimuli. One could work with that, building up a theory of the two aspects of rational mind.

What about the Healer in us, though? He may not be primarily a thinker as such, but he does make connections, including logical ones. He puts two and two together (almost automatically, in fact), as well as communicating. He does his sums, reads, writes. This isn't maybe the stuff of deep thoughtfulness – more a basic monkey cleverness, applying itself to simple Lego jobs, yet easily stretching to high-tech computer work. Three aspects of rational mind then.

But what of the Revolutionary in us, with his new inventions, his 'brilliant ideas'? And where does the Artist's 'imagination' slot in? And does the Hunter impulse not also involve thought, to work out what is worth aiming for?

Looking at our emotional faculty, we fare no better. We start off with two main areas of emotional functioning, represented by Mother and Priest, with the Destroyer allowed an additional (partly emotional) role, but soon have to admit that feeling is at least marginally involved in all we do. This is because our motivation patterns are in themselves composite, in a sense: each makes at least some, if only unconscious, use of every available function. Really, it is *they* that could best be regarded as our basic 'functions'. We may speak of say thought as such, but when it comes to *our* thought processes, we find them scattered and distributed, if in different measure, among our twelve root impulses, each of which makes a distinct use of them.

Add to that that most of the time we don't seem to reliably know thinking from feeling, and certainly not intuiting (not even a verb in common use) from inner-sensing (Western vocabulary goes silent at that point), and there seems no good reason to pursue that particular avenue.

Language on its own lets us down all the time. Also, it can only too easily come to determine both direction and extent of our understanding. What, after all, can a word like imagination tell us? Using the imagery and symbolism of our twelve motivation patterns, playfully working with it, variously interpreting it, we can find 'imagination' at work in the Artist, the Destroyer, the Revolutionary, the Creator, the Priest... it depends how far you want to stretch the word. (Words are Healerish things, after all: inclined, one moment, to be too limited, the next too all-engulfingly stretchy).

Let's dispense with the supremacy of words. They make poor guides. We speak of fear, anxiety, hesitancy as if they belonged in a box labelled emotional state, ignoring the fact that emotion is not something in and for itself, but rather an active part of any of a number of *motivational* states: a Hunter, Maker, Boss or Priest-type situation, each a very different kettle of fish. Ultimately fear, anger, trust or whatever aren't something, period– they are something happening. As all the patterns have shown us, we aren't in that sense designed to *have* thoughts, or feelings, but to apply them, flexibly or partially, or else gain them and relinquish them again, in part, changing, responding. Maybe we should just forget about the functions we might be said to have. It will do us a lot more good to become fully aware of our richly varied potential for functio*ning*.

If dividing psyche into four categorically separate functions does not yield a useful model after all, are there any other angles we might adopt – how about a two-fold system of the introvert/extravert sides to our nature? We might for instance say that the introvert (in the sense I have used the word throughout) side of us asks to be accepted for what it is; unlike the extravert, which asks to be shaped by its environment. This is all very well, but doesn't really get us anywhere, being pure theory with no correspondence in what actually informs or drives our behaviour.

Far better, if we are looking for something simpler than the full twelve-fold system of patterns, to bear in mind that they come as pairs of 'introverting extraverts' and the like: there is plenty of scope for working, productively playing around, with that. For instance, we could assign questions, statements or demands to the various pairs, giving us a set of six basic attitudes, or fundamental requirements, or whatever spin you would want to put on it. Here is one such model, offered as no more than a suggestion:

1 extraverting extraverts . . . . .Hunter, Maker
   'I need you to provide me with a (new) identity.'
2 extraverting introverts . . . . .Creator, Healer
   'I need you to confirm who I am, inside myself.'
3 introverting extraverts . . . . .Artist, Destroyer
   'I need you to conform to my (innate) expectations.'
4 extra-/introverting extraverts . . .Thinker, Priest
   'I need you as a stepping stone towards inner independence.'
5 intro-/extraverting introverts . . . .Mother, Boss
   'I need you to accept and validate my subjective self.'
6 introverting introverts . . . . .Eternal Child, Revolutionary
   'I am whole inside myself and have things to give you.'

We can of course go on from there again, state how each pattern within a pair deals in its own way, well or badly, with the situation. More complex, but still a simplification (ie something to be handled with care). Here is my suggestion, leading on from the above:

1 Hunter
positive: 'I promise that whatever I take (on) will also be turned to your advantage.'
negative:'Give me that! I need it all for my own self-ish purposes. More!'
1 Maker
positive: 'The variety I produce from out of our common raw materials will be for the sharing.'
negative:'Mangle your things? I'm only busy building my very own model – again.'

2 Creator

positive: 'Giving to you, out of myself, I glimpse myself in the effect I have on you.'

negative:'Tell me how splendid I am!'

2 Healer

positive: 'I recognise you all as (my) equals, each an aspect of the varied whole I am.'

negative:'I refuse to recognise more than one of you. Go away and stop confusing me.'

negative:'I want you all to be identical: so stop annoying me with your differences.'

3 Artist

positive: 'I will help you improve till you do.'

negative:'You don't? Well, I can always pretend to myself that you do.'

3 Destroyer

positive: 'I can persuade you to let go of your most negative traits.'

negative:'You don't? Let me tell you then: you are rubbish!'

4 Thinker

positive: 'I choose my company carefully; then from inside myself I adapt and respond.'

negative:'I'm now perfect inside myself. You disgust me. (No, really?! Tell me more…)'

4 Priest

positive: 'Any help you give me now will be repaid with unflinching, selfless devotion.'

negative:'I'll just let you run my life for me, borrow *your* inner strengths… good enough.'

negative:'I want you all to live in perfect harmony: how else can I find inner peace?'

5 Mother

positive: 'Please know that my love and support are there for the asking.'

negative:'You can't do without me, can you – good!'

5 Boss

positive: 'Please accept my informed help, if it's going to be of any use to you.'

negative: 'Believe me: I know best. So do as I tell you and you'll succeed (for me).'

6 Eternal Child
positive: 'And you can have my gifts free of charge.'
negative: 'My gifts are *so* superior, you better reward me *extremely* well for them!'
6 Revolutionary
positive: 'We are all potentially one another: I could help you loose the shackles of self.'
negative: 'You're all wrong, all except me. I'll soon see to it that you change!'

This, obviously, is only one playful attempt at summarising our twelve attitudes to other, showing their various angelic and satanic faces. The motivated reader may like to experiment with other kinds of pronouncements, existential questions, needs, talents; or to draw piecharts with symbols liberally strewn across the slices... Feel free - always remembering, though, the risks when reducing a magnificently rich but flighty reality to no more than a set of squiggles on paper, condemned to un-lifelike immobility.

One more angle I would like to offer, this one based not on pairs of patterns according to their intro/extraverting, but on the so-called Elements involved. The table below will speak for itself, though I would point out that the word 'active' does of course apply across the board, not just under the heading Fire (even if that is a particularly 'happening' Element) and using 'purely active' is admittedly a case of grasping the best bad expression I could find! Still, I trust the reader will get the idea. One could headline this:

Aspects of Self

FIRE: the purely active self - explorative
Hunter:	where 'self' is defined as the assumed character of our actions as they take place
Creator:	where our activities lead to the gradual realisation of the inner self
Et. Child:	where a consciously known inner self serves us as guide to future action

EARTH: the structured and structuring self – productive
> Maker: where we build up a range of new identities from
> the basic givens in our environment
>
> Thinker: where we style and re-style a developing (inner)
> self in response to a changing world
>
> Boss: where we introduce some of our conscious inner
> order into the working and structure of our
> current environment

AIR: the actively and passively transforming self – relational
> Healer: where we combine secure inner selfhood with
> much outward flexibility and a multi-faceted
> approach to all we contact
>
> Artist: where we effect changes in our environment that
> allow us to relate to it meaningfully and thus 'find
> ourselves'
>
> Rev'tionary: where our conscious inner transformations are
> conducive to outward changes and a new inner
> kinship with others

WATER: the actively and passively integrating self – contributive
> Mother: where giving in self-controlled ways from out of
> the conscious inner self gains us acceptance
>
> Destroyer: where, sharing in all essentials, we enter into
> symbiotic closeness with others
>
> Priest: where the achievement of conscious inner
> harmony impels us to selfless service to *all*

Can this be at all helpful? Or is it entirely counter-productive,
a sterile boxing-in, like a freeze-frame view of running water? If I
offer it here then only as an example of the different kinds of angle
on behaviour one can discover, just playfully investigating this
new territory of a 'motivational psychology'. I hope it will stimulate the reader to experiment for themselves.

As people, so-called individuals, we don't seem to make sense.

As personalities, we are anything but literally 'individual': we
are composite, often in ways that won't slot smoothly together.

Opportunities for misunderstanding are legion: 'So what happened to the great iconoclast I thought you were? Turns out you're just another social climber after all! Well, make up your mind where you stand.' Or: cuddly earth mother type one moment, acting seriously competitive the next, my view of you upended, my expectations broken. 'Make up your mind!' No, we can't make up our minds. Short of perfection, we can't be totally consistent, of a piece. If living it all takes the form of a rather hopscotch serial affair, this may be the best we can manage by way of self-integration. Add to that all sorts of 'influences', the way one person will 'bring out something' in another, and we have to ask ourselves how we ever manage to make any kind of sense to each other. Possibly by dint of much fond and faulty conjecture!

As easily, instantly, recognisable 'characters', though, entirely predictable and unmistakable for 'what we are', we are really no more than incompletely living: maybe voluntary amputees in some area of our active being – or perhaps split into compartments: hidden faces, secret lives.

What we 'are' can't be pinned down concretely, predictably. Not even by ourselves, never mind others. We can't be grasped, in any sense of the word. And yet when it comes to the things we *do*, we find a noticeable logic there, even supposing it is totally crazy. People as such may be a mystery, but at least behaviour as such should be amenable to something better than rank guesswork.

The problem is, while people's behaviour can be objectively observed, effects assessed, statistics compiled, and so forth, what kind of conclusions do we draw at the end of it all? The subjective element will always be missing from the equation, and simply asking 'How do you feel about this then?' won't provide it either. If, on the other hand, we take as our starting point an abstract theory of behaviour – not based on the Smiths' and the Blogs's here-and-now doings, but on some notion we have conceived that we reckon might explain the doings of people in general – then do we not stand in danger of letting such preconceptions get between us and subsequent perception (when it comes to checking out our theory, that is)?

Maybe the advantage of motivational psychology, as I have presented it here, is that it is based on *both* theory and observation: Jung's theory of abstract types, and the symbolism of the zodiac which is ultimately derived from a mixture of objective observation and subjective insight, and has been honed and confirmed in practice for not just hundreds but thousands of years.

What I am offering is nothing as fixed as even the most general theory. But unlike a set of purely practical observations it does apply to human beings anywhere, any century, any culture, subject to any conditions. It is something that can grow into the future: adapt, expand, translate and transform itself, yielding up new abstract understanding and application in practice. It is a tool, more than anything else.

A living tool, because it relates to something complex and alive, both in us, and outside, 'beyond' us. These are animated Life Principles. These are Archetypes that really do jump off the page. Considered purely as *patterns*, they tell us about the abstract nature of the composite selves we are, generally, and in particular. Understood as *impulses*, they show us the dynamic nature of self: we happen, and we can access new ways of happening all the time – because what is abstract has many living interpretations. As *living tools* they serve the Self (the true 'individual'?) in its life aims and tasks. And, we have to add, as *forces* beyond our capacity to steer, handle or deflect, they will use and abuse the self as they see fit: caught up among them, failing to rise above them, we can easily find ourselves at the receiving end of every trick and delusion they can throw at us – the stage direction of our inner scripts taken out of our hands, every word dictated to us.

It is up to us what we make of them.

Appendix

It would be true to say that, within the context of a living person, all our root impulses work together. But at the same time there is a special affinity between certain motivation patterns as such that makes them not just especially supportive of each other, but has them contributing to each other's internal nature or composition. The interested reader can refer to my earlier book *A Psychological Zodiac* where these relationships are shown in detail, and where the patterns themselves are also described in much more depth. If you want to know the ins and outs of why the Hunter in you, when looking for his emotional support system, will rope in the Priest rather than the Mother, that is where to find out.

Below, for anyone interested in beginning to work with the natal chart, is a table of correspondences between motivation patterns, zodiacal signs, planets, and the 'houses' and main 'points' found in charts.

1st Principle	Hunter	Aries	Mars	1st house and Ascendant
2nd Principle	Maker	Taurus	Venus	2nd house
3rd Principle	Healer	Gemini	Mercury	3rd house
4th Principle	Mother	Cancer	Moon	4th house
5th Principle	Creator	Leo	Sun	5th house
6th Principle	Thinker	Virgo	Mercury	6th house
7th Principle	Artist	Libra	Venus	7th house
8th Principle	Destroyer	Scorpio	Pluto	8th house
9th Principle	Eternal Child	Sagittarius	Jupiter	9th house
10th Principle	Boss	Capricorn	Saturn	10th house and Midheaven
11th Principle	Revolutionary	Aquarius	Uranus	11th house
12th Principle	Priest	Pisces	Neptune	12th house